D1478548

Conversations with John Fowles

Literary Conversations Series

Peggy Whitman Prenshaw
General Editor

Conversations with John Fowles

Edited by
Dianne L. Vipond

University Press of Mississippi
Jackson

http://www.upress.state.ms.us

07   06   05   04   03   02   01   00   99   4   3   2   1

⊗

Library of Congress Cataloging-in-Publication Data

Conversations with John Fowles / edited by Dianne L. Vipond.
     p. cm.—(Literary conversations series)
   "Books by John Fowles": p.
   Includes index.
   ISBN 1-57806-190-3 (alk. paper).—ISBN 1-57806-191-1 (pbk. :
alk. paper)
    1. Fowles, John, 1926–   —Interviews.   2. Novelists,
English—20th century—Interviews.   3. Fiction—Authorship.
I. Vipond, Dianne L.   II. Series.
PR6056.085Z6315   1999
823'.914—dc21
   [B]   99-21452
                                                               CIP

British Library Cataloging-in-Publication Data available

Books by John Fowles

The Collector. London: Jonathan Cape, 1963; Boston: Little, Brown, 1963.

The Aristos: A Self-Portrait in Ideas. London: Jonathan Cape, 1964; Boston: Little, Brown, 1964.

The Magus. Boston: Little, Brown, 1965; London: Jonathan Cape, 1966.

The Aristos. 2nd ed. London: Jonathan Cape, 1968; Boston: Little, Brown, 1970.

The French Lieutenant's Woman. London: Jonathan Cape, 1969; Boston: Little, Brown, 1969.

Poems. New York: Ecco Press, 1973.

The Ebony Tower. London: Jonathan Cape, 1974; Boston: Little, Brown, 1974.

Shipwreck. Photographs by the Gibsons of Scilly. London: Jonathan Cape, 1974; Boston: Little, Brown, 1978.

Daniel Martin. London: Jonathan Cape, 1977; Boston: Little, Brown, 1977.

The Magus: A Revised Version. London: Jonathan Cape, 1977; Boston: Little, Brown, 1978.

Islands. Photographs by Fay Godwin. London: Jonathan Cape, 1978; Boston: Little, Brown, 1978.

The Tree. Preface and photographs by Frank Horvat. London: Arum Press, 1979.

The Enigma of Stonehenge. Co-author Barry Brukoff. London: Jonathan Cape, 1980.

Mantissa. London: Jonathan Cape, 1982; Boston: Little, Brown, 1982.

A Short History of Lyme Regis. Wimborne, U.K.: Dovecote Press, 1982; Boston: Little, Brown, 1982.

Of Memoirs and Magpies. Austin, TX: W. Thomas Taylor, 1983.

Lyme Regis: Three Town Walks. Lyme Regis, U.K.: Friends of the Lyme Regis Museum, 1983.

Medieval Lyme Regis. Lyme Regis: Lyme Regis (Philpot) Museum, 1984.

A Maggot. London: Jonathan Cape, 1985; Boston: Little, Brown, 1985.

Land. Photographs by Fay Godwin. Boston: Little, Brown, 1985.

A Brief History of Lyme. Lyme Regis, U.K.: Friends of the Museum, 1985.

Lyme Regis Camera. Wimborne, U.K.: Dovecote Press, 1990.

Wormholes. London: Jonathan Cape, 1998; New York: Henry Holt, 1998.

Contents

Introduction

"What is irreplaceable in any object of art is never, in the final analysis, its technique or craft, but the personality of the artist, the expression of his or her unique and individual feeling," writes John Fowles in his autobiographical essay *The Tree*. Complex and multifaceted, John Fowles, the man and the artist, speaks openly with journalists, scholars, and academics in the interviews that follow, producing something on the order of an intellectual/artistic autobiography which might well be called "Fowles on Fowles," as Susana Onega so aptly titles her interview. Fowles has been described as "the only writer in English who has the power, range, knowledge, and wisdom of a Tolstoi or James." The accuracy of this description is borne out by each of the interviews collected in this volume.

The literary interview has become something of a hybrid critical genre which blurs the boundaries of everyday conversation, journalism, literary criticism, and scholarship, its multiple nature providing a unique prism through which to view the artist. The facets of the prism—artistic process and conviction, philosophy, political orientation, biography, as well as personal interests—serve as useful reference points in any reading or rereading of the writer's work and expand the context in which it may be considered, yielding perspectives that may lead to new critical insights. A collaboration between writer and journalist or critic, the literary interview provides an additional resource for scholarly research and raises interesting questions about a writer's multiple personae, his or her public, private, and fictive selves. In the case of a subject as honest and forthright as John Fowles, it further acquaints his readers with the genius of the man behind the work.

Although the body of a writer's work undoubtedly is the vehicle most revealing of his or her world view—ideas, allegiances, and sensibilities—a different kind of revelation characterized by immediacy or intimacy, perhaps a more literal version of the "I-Thou" relationship that Fowles strives for in his novels, is achieved through direct dialogue. Largely a result of his candid and direct responses to interviewers' questions, readers are left with a sense of "being there," as if they were overhearing or eavesdropping on the conversation.

The interviews provide glimpses of Fowles in a variety of conversational contexts, from casual chats to free-ranging debate. Whether he is engaged in rather informal conversations about his work in general, discussing a specific novel immediately following its publication, or responding to specialized questions about a particular subject such as history, he navigates each conversation with grace, patience, and aplomb. His quick wit, sharp intellect, and subtle sense of humor often laced with irony are evident throughout. No matter what the circumstances of the interview, casual or more formal, stylistically, all provide some inkling of his polymathic knowledge, the agile play of his mind, and the sound of his personal voice.

John Fowles is a man of letters—a writer of short stories, poetry, novels, essays, and screenplays, as well as a highly respected translator—who prefers not to be imprisoned in the cage labeled "novelist." Although he is best known for his ground-breaking novels, above all he wants to remain free to set himself artistic challenges, which he does by writing both fiction and nonfiction in a variety of genres. The themes of personal, social, political, and artistic freedom are central to his world view, and he conscientiously exercises them to whatever extent he can in his life and work. As he tells Raman K. Singh, "All my novels are about how you achieve that possible—possibly nonexistent—freedom."

The remarkable consistency of Fowles's thought as revealed in the interviews and the persistence of major themes in his fiction might best be described as a recursive spiral not too far removed from the Heraclitean concept represented by the following fragment cited by Fowles in *The Aristos,* his "self-portrait in ideas": "Potters use a wheel that goes neither forwards nor backwards, yet goes both ways at once. So it is like the cosmos. On this wheel is made pottery of every shape and yet no two pieces are identical, though all are made of the same materials and with the same tools." The language of Heraclitus captures the concept of paradox that Fowles says "has always fascinated me." Such a metaphor also illuminates the manner in which he employs a variety of genres to revisit the same themes as he continues to experiment with literary form. It seems particularly fitting when applied to a long-time collector of New Hall pottery, as Melissa Denes observes in her interview.

An internationally acclaimed novelist whose work has been translated into many different languages, Fowles is quick to point out that he identifies with England, not Britain, but confesses to Daniel Halpern that he sometimes feels as if he were an exile in his own land, a condition of marginalization not uncommon among those who have committed themselves to writing as a vocation. In broader terms, he sees himself as European. He deliberately expunges any details from his narratives that would limit understanding based on national boundaries. France and Greece are his two adopted countries; he finds the internationalism and refreshing lack of Puritanism of the French and the natural beauty of Greece with the truth-telling quality of its light most compatible with his spirit. Fowles tells interviewers that he venerates language and speaks of the endless possibilities that the English language affords the writer. He feels that it is important to live where the language is spoken and is an intrinsic part of the culture but eschews the "literary life" of London and the lionization it entails.

There are so many references to books and writers throughout the interviews that if one were so inclined, it would not be difficult to draw up an extensive and eclectic reading list. Fowles is an avid reader whose catholic taste in fiction and nonfiction spans all centuries and national borders. The Monaghan interview centers around his reading and collection of old books. Although generally loath to discuss influences, in the interview with Aaron Latham, Fowles reveals the names of his English and American literary fathers: Hardy, Lawrence, James, and Melville. While often generous in his praise of other writers, he prefers to think of them "in a natural history way, like the plants out there in the garden. Some interest me more than others, but I wouldn't use the 'best/worst' notion of them." He does, however, single out William Golding as a kindred spirit in conversation with Jan Relf. When responding to the perennial question of influence during the McNamara interview, he remarks, "At my age, the major influence on a writer is always his own past work." No facile quip, such a statement reasserts the uniqueness of the individual artist without discounting the impact of literary predecessors.

Discussion of the reading and writing process recurs throughout the interviews, areas that Fowles faults the academy with having neglected to some extent, while he remains very much aware of the inherent mystery and indeterminacy of both processes. The prescience of the artist is reconfirmed; since the time of the interview where he makes this comment, much has been written about the role of the reader and the reading process. Fowles credits the importance of the reader's response to his work, and in his conversation with Katherine Tarbox emphasizes the significance of gaps in the text, what the writer deliberately leaves out in recognition of the collaborative roles of both reader and writer in the making of meaning. He favors ambiguity partly for this very reason; it leaves the reader more freedom to choose from among

a variety of possible interpretations. Although literary theory tends to dismiss
a writer's intentions, there is no question that information provided by an
author about the meaning of his or her work is of interest. Unhesitating in his
response to such questions about his novels, Fowles provides his readers with
valuable insights as they pursue the heuristic journey that is reading.

A writer who half-seriously admits to his belief in the power of the Muse,
Fowles follows no set writing routine. He describes the thrill and obsession
that accompanies the inspired composition of a first draft, while acknowledg-
ing how necessary and demanding the blue pencil must be during the revision
stage. In the Baker interview for *The Paris Review,* he discusses the "image-
constituted kernels of a story," as he recounts the catalytic power of the
haunting images that sparked the genesis of *The French Lieutenant's Woman*
and *A Maggot* but refrains from delving too deeply into the wellspring of his
creativity. He does, however, share his speculations on the psychological
origins of the novelist. One of the aspects of writing that he finds most fascinating and mentions more than once is contained in the concept of the fork
in the road—the endless choices that fiction presents the writer, each of
which could change the direction of the narratively greatly. He attributes
some of the results of these choices, at least partially, to hazard.

No believer in creative writing programs, Fowles advises neophyte writers
to read, think, travel, and learn from their experiences because "all good
books are distilled experience." During the Campbell interview, he tells
young writers to take risks and avoid imitation. He charges them with the
task of learning, exploring, and respecting the language in the service of their
craft. A consummate wordsmith, Fowles acknowledges his "conservationist
view of language" in dialogue with Carlin Romano, a desire to preserve the
richness of the English language. The point is understood in another interview: "The book starts with love of each separate word."

Only too often accused of being a didactic writer, Fowles sees the novel as
a vehicle for expressing his view of life, as he tells Roy Newquist in the
earliest interview. It is difficult to conceive of any writer who is not implicitly
didactic, and as Fowles suggests, it might well be better to regard the term as
purely descriptive rather than condemnatory. His novels certainly depict his
view of life, but it is presented nowhere as completely and succinctly as in
The Aristos. An invaluable book in the Fowles oeuvre, it affords something
of a blueprint of the concerns that continue to resurface in his fiction and
unequivocally defines his position on a variety of issues. *The Aristos* appeared
against the advice of his publisher, a strategic effort on Fowles's part to avoid

generic categorization. It is a philosophical treatise in the epigrammatic pensée style of Montaigne, as he notes in conversation with James R. Baker, not
meant to be read at one sitting but rather savored and argued with over time.
Years after its original publication, Fowles asserts that he would stand by
much of what he said in that book although he might have expressed it differently. *The Aristos* covers topics ranging from the existence of God to educational reform and is definitive verification of Fowles the philosopher as well
as the novelist of ideas.

As Fowles reveals in several interviews, in descending order he would
have preferred to have been known as a poet, philosopher, and novelist. Nevertheless, he readily admits to his special gift for narrative. Arguably the
greatest novelist writing in English, he weds traditional narrative with metafiction to create an open-ended labyrinthine fictional universe that challenges
his readers to re-examine and reconstruct their perceptions, assumptions, and
beliefs. Self-reflexive, intertextual, and historiographic, the Fowlesian fictional landscape is composed in equal parts of fabulation and realism, a narrative combination that exemplifies the postmodern novel by interrogating
the premises upon which its antecedents rest. Characters are engaged in the
never-ending quest for self-discovery. With each subsequent novel, the protagonists make incremental progress as their mettle is tested against an ever-
changing historical backdrop, and the constant battle of the individual against
the social pressures of conformity is dramatized in existentialist and humanist
terms. As the selfish passions of a Nicholas Urfe evolve into the other-di-
rected compassion of a Rebecca Lee, this protean novelist tells and retells the
story of what it means to be human and live authentically in a postmodern
world.

With the gift of storytelling comes a singular power, a power to effect
social and political change. Cognizant of the responsibility of this power,
Fowles has modified his position on the efficacy of the novel in this regard
over the years. As he tells Christopher Bigsby: "I think [the novel's] main
power . . . is in enlarging or focusing sensibility—changing climates, a little,
not inspiring action directly."

With the publication and subsequent success of *The Collector* in 1963,
Fowles achieved the economic freedom to leave teaching, which he refers to
as "a noble profession," and devote himself fully to the art of writing. Ironically, he seems never to have left teaching at all, only to have expanded his
"class" through the vast reach of his international reading audience. Mistak-
enly too often reviewed as a thriller, *The Collector* is much more a fable

about the responsibilities of the Few to the Many, categories designated by Heraclitus, and an implicit critique of a society which compounds inequity. Fowles describes himself as a democratic socialist and tells the Socialist Review that his politics have been shaped as much by the myth of Robin Hood, one of England's original "green" men, as by the political writings of Karl Marx or Antonio Gramsci. Every one of his novels lays bare the prison of social class and reveals its devastating effects on the lives of his characters.

The Magus, Fowles's second novel according to its publication date, is for all intents and purposes his first novel. He first heard the sound of his own voice during its more than decade-long composition and with its publication won himself a loyal international audience. A novel of education for both author and protagonist, The Magus maintains "favored child" status with him in spite of, or perhaps because of, what he considers its faults. Revised for republication in 1977, its continuing hold on its author is evident. An admirably ambitious novel, it enchants the reader with irresistible fantasy firmly grounded in a psychological reality that continues to ring true as it faithfully echoes and surpasses its inspiration: the concept of loss as depicted by Henri Alain-Fournier's Le Grand Meaulnes. Throughout the writing of The Magus, Fowles kept a quotation from Alain-Fournier close at hand: "I like the marvelous only when it is strictly enveloped in reality." He credits Alain-Fournier with the origination of magic realism, a term which in its literal rather than its literary meaning is a good description of much of Fowles's own work. During many of his conversations, he calls for greater realism in fiction and sees it as beneficial for the future of the novel. Indisputably a master of form, for him, content always drives narrative. Existentialism, which Fowles sees as "the great individualist philosophy," provides the philosophical infrastructure for this novel that he has characterized as "a fable about the relationship between man and his conception of God." The motifs of creator and creativity often take center stage in his work. Although Fowles is a self-described atheist who regards nature as sacrosanct, he uses religious imagery liberally and based A Maggot around a religious sect, the Shakers.

With the publication of The French Lieutenant's Woman, Fowles achieved unmitigated critical and popular success and secured his place in literary history. This postmodern novel is a tour de force of literary technique in which Fowles explodes preconceptions of the historical novel by using Victorian narrative in innovative ways to speak to the twentieth century in existential terms; it simultaneously looks backward and forward. At once an indictment and exoneration of nineteenth century mores and social convention, *The French Lieutenant's Woman* exploits the discoveries of Darwin and the theories of Marx in anticipation of the dawning of a new age, and the "New Woman."

Much critical debate has surrounded this novel as to whether or not it is a feminist text. And although Fowles sometimes hesitates to call himself a feminist, he has energetically defended Sarah Woodruff against "the universal male crime—exploitation of women." He describes himself as being an intuitive as opposed to a rational, linear thinker, a product of the well-developed "feminine" aspect of his psyche, his anima. According to Fowles, women possess "right feeling" and are more adept at living in "the now," a quality he champions. He believes "right feeling" is the major civilizing influence of the novel in general. Fowles likes, admires, and possesses a special affinity with women. The Streitfeld interview-based article elaborates on this relationship. He often speaks of his feminist sympathies and reveals how his first wife Elizabeth is the ghost behind most of his female characters. In the Denes interview, we learn of his happiness in his recent marriage to Sarah, "she of the ravishing auburn tresses" and resident of Lyme Regis. An echo of life imitating art, or simply a demonstration of the verity of the happy ending?

A writer who is interested in historical interregna, points in history where an age is poised on the brink of socio-cultural change, Fowles is a serious amateur historian who has written two novels set in such periods, *The French Lieutenant's Woman* and *A Maggot*. Because, as he relates during his conversation with Rowland Molony, he believes the novel should treat the present or the future and not become mired in the past, he doesn't consider these two works of fiction as belonging to the genre of the historical novel—their purposes are different. His reading of old trial transcripts, historical documents, and literature from the past are all preparation for his writing. Fowles does the research after the narrative has been written and is more concerned with rendering the mood of a particular period through such devices as dialogue than with the accuracy of every detail.

The Ebony Tower, Fowles's only collection of short stories, is a good demonstration of the recursive spiral of his themes and technique. Almost titled "Variations," it is in some ways a microcosm of his earlier work. From the title novella through "Poor Koko" to the final story "The Cloud," echoes of *The Magus, The Collector,* and *The French Lieutenant's Woman* reverberate. This collection of short stories demonstrates the value of what a writer may leave out in fiction, i.e., the gaps that Fowles discusses with several different interviewers and compares to the image suggested by the Rorschach test. These are metaphorically writ large in "The Enigma," where the sounds of silence resonate right into the story that follows it, "The Cloud." A masterful exercise in intertextuality, both among the texts of *The Ebony Tower* and within the larger Fowlesian fictional world, this volume unequivocally establishes Fowles as a virtuoso writer of short as well as longer fiction.

With the appearance of *Daniel Martin,* once again Fowles proves himself to be a master chronicler of the second half of the twentieth century. This panoramic, almost cinematic novel, in which Fowles explores the subjectivity of time, foregrounds politics, and examines what it means to be English, signals his movement from existentialism to humanism, to greater realism, and perhaps somewhat paradoxically, to incorporation of the "happy" ending. *Daniel Martin* is another quest novel in the form of circular narrative, where Daniel might be thought of as Nicholas twenty years later. It turns on the opening line of the novel: "Whole sight; or all the rest is desolation," which best summarizes the centrality of the quest in the search for personal identity that runs through all of Fowles's fiction. As he reveals in the North interview, "You always write for yourself first, to discover yourself first." One of the discoveries in *Daniel Martin* is humanism, an approach to life which emphasizes tolerance and denounces violence. For Fowles, writing *is* self-discovery. Originally conceived as a "homage to Lukacs," as the Graham interview reveals, *Daniel Martin* overtly engages in social critique. As Fowles says in one of the interviews, "true humanism must be feminist." Further, in another conversation about the structure of *Daniel Martin* he says, "I wanted to treat the various incidents in Daniel's past much more emotionally than rationally or chronologically." These two statements illustrate the seamlessness of Fowles's thought and his superlative command of literary technique—his ability to interweave disparate but related concepts and deploy them unobtrusively, almost invisibly, into his fiction.

Fowles's interest in both human and natural history have led him to volunteer his time and expertise as curator of the Lyme Regis (Philpot) Museum; his knowledge of these fields suffuses all his writing. He says that his dominant outside interest is natural history and writes extensively about it in *The Tree* and "The Nature of Nature." In his autobiographical essay, *The Tree,* he writes: "The key to my fiction . . . lies in my relationship with nature. . . ." For Fowles this relationship is ineffable; it lies in "the now" of the present experience which tends to reduce him to feeling that is virtually impossible to articulate, as he discloses to Carol Barnum. Perhaps more importantly,

Fowles's experience of nature nourishes his spirit, and by extrapolation, his art, where creativity is a recurring motif. The interviews reveal his propensity for using natural images as metaphors to explain his own writing process. His essay "Behind *The Magus*" relates the extent to which the natural beauty of the Greek landscape was the haunting impetus that fueled the writing of the novel. The motifs of relationship and interdependence that permeate Fowles's fiction are evident on a more microcosmic level in his detailed descriptions of landscape, flora, and fauna which are such a subtle but intrinsic aspect of his writing style. His concern with the relationship between nature and culture also surfaces in much of his writing. A not unexpected consequence of Fowles's interest in nature is his staunch, serious, and generous support of environmental causes. He sees the interrelationships among all aspects of the universe and has worked unflaggingly for the preservation of the planet. Much of his nonfiction, *Steep Holm—A Case History in the Study of Evolution* and *Land* for example, speaks to these issues with urgency and eloquence.

Fowles does not believe that writers must continually produce major work. He explains how *Mantissa,* a word meaning "of little importance," was originally intended to be privately printed with limited distribution, but his publishers insisted on treating it otherwise. A hyper-postmodern narrative that takes self-reflexivity to the nth degree (the novel is set entirely in the head of the writer Miles Green), *Mantissa* is a pun-filled comic parody of contemporary literary theory, a playful satire, whose target is as often Fowles himself as it is the literary establishment or academia. It is also a boisterous meditation on creativity and the role of the Muse as personified by Erato, as well as an arena for feminist debate. This "secondary" narrative, fairly bursting with jouissance, comes up often as a topic for discussion during the interviews.

Utilizing an unusual blend of history, fantasy, and science fiction in *A Maggot,* Fowles once again extends the boundaries of contemporary fiction. With characteristic good humor, during the Romano interview Fowles describes the novel as "Mr. Fowles's magic-guided tour of a curious period in English history, the early 18th century." This is a narrative focused historically on the rise of a movement of dissent as the harbinger of a better world, one based on the feminine principle as the Shaker doctrine professes it and a social organization certainly closer to socialism than capitalism. Structurally and thematically, it seems to call the very notion of individual perception into question and raise the issue of whether there is any such thing as verifiable truth. Einsteinian relativity comes into play as Fowles continues to probe the cosmology, not only of his own time, but that of the past and of the future, for how else can any sense be made of the present, "the now"?

This brief discussion of Fowles's novels very sketchily attempts to trace his development as an increasingly influential force in the world of letters, but more importantly it may suggest the intoxicating power of his books to set the reader free. This magical, shape-changing Prospero figure of contemporary literature defies capture in any summary terms, personal, literary, or otherwise, which is as it should be for someone whose watchword is freedom.

The idea of this book came into being during the spring of 1996 when John Fowles was on a lecture tour of the West Coast. One day as we were browsing in a local bookstore, I pointed out a volume of interviews with Saul Bellow, a writer whom Fowles admires; he promptly added it to the already large pile of books that he was about to purchase. I asked how he would feel if a collection of his own interviews were to be published. His response: "Would you do it?" And a nod of assent.

Despite the fact that Fowles has been described repeatedly as somewhat reclusive, the interviews have been culled from among the more than one hundred that he has granted over the last four decades. They have been arranged chronologically for easy reference, and are deliberately unedited (although spelling has been Americanized) to be of maximum value to scholars. In some cases, the interviewer's introductory comments have been omitted because the information appears elsewhere in the collection. Interviews were selected in an effort to best reflect Fowles's concerns over the years, to provide the widest discussion of his fiction, and to represent a variety of venues including critical works, academic journals, and the popular press. Every effort has been made to secure permission to reprint interviews. Although the Question and Answer format has been favored because it seems to present a less-filtered view of the writer, a few key interview-based articles by journalists have been included, which add another dimension to the portrait of the artist. The range of subjects covered in the conversations extends from religion to politics and touches upon almost everything in between, but the focus tends to be upon Fowles's writing process and his fiction. His responses to questions and the manner in which he sometimes subtly redirects them are indicative of the issues that are preoccupying him at any particular time. Naturally there is a certain amount of repetition, so that with each additional interview another aspect of a topic which may have been mentioned in an earlier one is elaborated, extended, and clarified.

The title of an early essay, "I Write Therefore I Am" (1964), which almost became the title of Fowles's most recent work of nonfiction, *Wormholes* (1998), clearly illuminates his identity as a writer. And, as he states in a relatively recent interview: "Deep down, I write today because I shall die tomorrow." There is no question that over the course of his life as a writer, John Fowles has continued to leave a lasting mark on literary history.

This book would not have taken shape were it not for the help and encouragement of many individuals, first and foremost John Fowles, whose work has brought so much pleasure and insight to readers all over the world, and who graciously agreed to submit to *yet another* interview for this collection. I also wish to thank Earl Ingersoll for his encouragement, generous help, unstinting advice, and for editing the many volumes of interviews which were an inspiration for this one; James R. Aubrey for writing *John Fowles: A Reference Companion,* which has proved such a rich resource; James R. Baker for his helpful suggestions; Sarah Smith for always kindly and efficiently facilitating communication about this book with John Fowles; California State University, Long Beach for providing me with assigned time during the spring 1997 semester to begin work on this project; the many librarians for their assistance in locating interviews and tracking down publishers, especially those at California State University, Long Beach Library, Honnold Library of The Claremont Colleges, and Joan Sibley and Cathy Henderson of the Harry Ransom Humanities Research Center at the University of Texas at Austin; the many interviewers and publishers who granted their permission to reprint the selected interviews; Eileen Warburton for her "Texas time" spent verifying a biographical point; Eiman Yacoub for acquiring copies of interviews; Anne Stascavage at the University Press of Mississippi for seeing the manuscript through to publication; and last, but certainly not least, Greg Dickson for his never-ending support, superb editorial advice, astute criticism, expert technological assistance, and so much more.

DV
January 1999

Chronology

1926   Born on March 31 in Leigh-on-Sea, Essex, England to Robert J. and Gladys (Richards) Fowles

1934–39   Attends Alleyn Court School

1939–41   Attends Bedford School

1941–42   Lives in Devon; develops lifelong sympathy with nature

1942–44   Returns to Bedford School; appointed head boy during final year

1944–45   Attends University of Edinburgh

1945–47   Serves as a lieutenant in the Royal Marines

1947–50   Reads French at New College, Oxford University; earns honors B.A.

1950–51   Teaches English at University of Poitiers, France

1951–53   Teaches English at the Anargyrios and Korgialenios School of Spetses, a private boys' school in Spetsai, Greece; meets Elizabeth Whitton

1953–54   Teaches English at Ashridge College

1954   Marries Elizabeth Whitton on April 2

1954–63   Teaches English at St. Godric's College, a private school for girls, in Hampstead, London

1963   Publishes *The Collector*

1964   Publishes *The Aristos: A Self-Portrait in Ideas*

1965   Publishes *The Magus*

1966   Moves to Underhill Farm, Dorset; film of *The Collector* released by Columbia Pictures

1968   Revised edition of *The Aristos* appears; film of *The Magus* released by Twentieth-Century Fox; moves to Belmont House, Lyme Regis, Dorset

1969   Publishes *The French Lieutenant's Woman;* wins Silver Pen
        Award from the English Center of the International Association
        of Poets, Playwrights, Editors, Essayists, and Novelists for *The
        French Lieutenant's Woman*

1970   Awarded the W. H. Smith and Son Literary Award for *The French
        Lieutenant's Woman*

1973   Publishes *Poems*

1974   Publishes *The Ebony Tower*

1977   Revised edition of *The Magus* appears; publishes *Daniel Martin*

1978   Appointed joint honorary curator of the Lyme Regis (Philpot)
        Museum; serves as sole honorary curator from 1979–88

1979   Publishes *The Tree*

1981   Film of *The French Lieutenant's Woman* released by United Art-
        ists

1982   Publishes *Mantissa*

1985   Publishes *A Maggot*

1990   Death of wife, Elizabeth

1997   Elected to honorary fellowship in the Modern Language Associa-
        tion; receives honorary doctorates from University of East Anglia
        and Oxford University

1998   Publishes *Wormholes;* receives honorary doctorate from Chap-
        man University; marries Sarah Smith on September 3

Conversations with John Fowles

John Fowles

Roy Newquist / 1963

From *Counterpoint* (Chicago: Rand Mcnally, 1964), 217–25.

N: *The Collector* was one of the most successful novels published in the United States in 1963. Virtually flawless in form—in the bold yet subtle handling of a unique plot—it was also distinguished by a polished and mature style. The suspense involved in a basic, horrifying predicament became all the more gripping as the perversities of time, place, and person maintained a relentless reality. The success of *The Collector,* both in the critical and popular sense, is all the more astonishing in view of the fact that it is a first novel by a young British writer we might call "unheralded." In speaking with John Fowles, I would like to begin by asking him how *The Collector* came into being—how he originated the macabre situation upon which it is based?

Fowles: It's a complicated story, but basically I think of *The Collector* as a parable. You see, I have always wanted to illustrate the opposition of the Few and the Many *(hoi polloi).* I take these terms from the pre-Socratic Greek philosopher Heracleitus, who's been a major influence on my life. For him the Few were the good, the intelligent, the independent; the Many were the stupid, the ignorant, and the easily molded. Of course he implied that one could choose to belong to the Few or to the Many. We know better. I mean these things are hazard, conditioning, according to one's genes, one's environment, and all the rest. Because of this element of hazard, the proper attitude of the Few to the Many is pity, not arrogance. I wanted to explore this inevitable but very complex tension in the human condition.

I also wanted to attack—this is saying the same thing, really—the contemporary idea that there is something noble about the inarticulate hero. About James Dean and all his literary children and grandchildren, like Salinger's Holden Caulfield, and Sillitoe's Arthur Seaton (in *Saturday Night and Sunday Morning*). I don't admire beats, bums, junkies, psychopaths, and inarticulates. I feel sorry for them. I think "adjusted" adolescents are better and more significant than "maladjusted" ones. I'm against the glamorization of the Many. I think the common man is the curse of civilization, not its crowning glory. And he needs education, not adulation. The boy in *The Collector* stands for the Many; the girl for the Few. I tried to make them individual, so

1

they both have individual faults. But behind them are the faults and complexities of the greater situation.

But to get back to the girl-in-the-cellar situation. How did I come on it? Well, some time during the 1950's, I went to see the first performance in London of Bartok's opera, *Bluebeard's Castle*. It wasn't a very good performance, but the thing that struck me was the symbolism of the man imprisoning women underground. It so happened that about a year later there was an extraordinary case (again in London) of a boy who captured a girl and imprisoned her in an air-raid shelter at the end of his garden. She could have gotten away earlier than she did, but she was—if not mentally deficient—not very bright. In the end she did escape, but there were many peculiar features about this case that fascinated me. And eventually, it led me to the book.

N: I'd like to go into your own rough autobiography—the life that actually preceded *The Collector.*

Fowles: I went to an English private school. Then I went to Oxford. Before that I did some service in the Marines. I was a lieutenant—and hated it. Perhaps this was because I had been head boy at my school, and head boys at English public schools have a lot of power. You run the school's discipline. At the age of eighteen I had had power to judge and punish 600 to 800 other boys, and this gave me a distaste for power that has grown and grown and grown. (Incidentally, if I have any criticism of America, it would be that everything there tends to be judged in terms of power and potency.)

After I left Oxford, I taught at a French university for a year. I studied French at Oxford and came deeply under the influence of French existentialist writers. I've never shaken this off. From France I went to Greece to teach at a boys' school. Then I returned to England and taught for a year or so in an adult education center. Since then I've been teaching English to foreigners in a large London college.

N: Are you still teaching?

Fowles: No. I gave up my job in April of this year. I've always taught in order to be able to have time for writing. It's one of the great advantages of teaching. I think teaching is a noble profession. I have nothing against it, but I've wanted to write, and teaching is the best means to the end. In any case, for me, writing is a kind of teaching.

Well, I've been writing, off and on, for twelve or fifteen years. I haven't written with method, that's my trouble. I started seven or eight novels, wrote twenty stray chapters of each, put them by—and they never got finished. But with *The Collector,* I knew I had the story I wanted. I felt sure of the novel from the start. The few friends who were told about it didn't share my enthusiasm, but I felt intuitively that it could be made into something.

N: If you were advising the young writer on a course of action—training and development, more or less—what would this advice be?

Fowles: First of all, read and think. All good books are distilled experience. Stay away from creative writing courses. Perhaps these courses are useful for people who just want to make a profession of writing: journalism, literary journalism, script-writing or stories for the mass magazines. These people can learn something from creative writing courses. For me, writing is part of my existentialist view of life. It's an attempt to make myself wholly authentic. I think the serious writer has to have his view of the purpose of literature absolutely clear. I don't see that you can write seriously without having a philosophy of both life and literature to back you. Some philosophy of life is a property of all better writers. It may be an anarchistic one, but it's there, part of the writer, part of his work. Ultimately he writes for his view of life—not for money.

N: What do you think of the state of British writing at present?

Fowles: I would say, not too healthy. I think a viable blanket criticism is that we're too insular, too privately embroiled. This may be bound up with the fact that at the moment most of the British Left—the intelligentsia—are anti-European. And there's certainly far too much satirical writing. When everyone "does" satire, it loses its point. Some of our best younger writers belong to the so-called "provincial" school, which is sympathetic. We also have an even worse flock of heavily symbolic novelists. Some of their work makes one fall on one's knees and pray for a Zhdanov. Of course, we also have a literary Establishment to deal with—all the usual incestuous and nepotal features. We need a return to the great tradition of the English novel—realism. English is a naturally empirical language; I suppose that's why realism haunts all our arts.

I think the publishers in London are partly to blame. Far too many novels are published—everyone agrees on that. And the publishers too often seem incapable of seeing beyond their noses—or rather, beyond whatever was successful last year. I mean they're too influenced by vogue. Some of them are very amateurish at their jobs by American standards, incapable both of launching a book properly and of giving a writer the kind of editorial sympathy most of us need. I'd better add that my own English publisher is generally recognized to be an exception to all this.

N: What do you think of allied fields in England, of the theater, for example?

Fowles: If I were to name the field that is healthiest, it would be the theater. We have some good dramatists—Osborne, Harold Pinter, John Arden, Arnold Wesker. They may not always have much to say, but they say it interestingly and well.

N: What about criticism?

Fowles: I think that serious academic criticism is quite good in England, but many of us are unhappy about the state of journalistic criticism. There's too much subjectivity and maliciousness in it; too many of the weekly reviewers are more concerned with showing off than with criticizing. The thing I hate especially in England is the way novelists so often review other novelists. What I would like to see grow in England is a body of independent novel reviewers who are not practicing novelists themselves. We don't find painters criticizing other painters, or pianists reviewing other pianists, so why should one novelist be allowed to review another?

N: How do you feel about American criticism?

Fowles: I think your criticism is healthier, more open. I've gathered, since I've been in New York, that you feel British criticism is more sophisticated and attains a more serious level. But I smell a whiff of fresh air in your criticism. It's franker, more open, possibly more naïvely expressed, but actually, more serious.

In England my novel was reviewed as a crime novel by three of our most "intellectual" newspapers. They gave me good crime-novel reviews, but I was shocked that this could happen. It hasn't occurred in America. Some reviewers have criticized the book, but at least they've taken it for something more serious than a mere suspense story.

N: I wanted to ask you about the reception of *The Collector* in England.

Fowles: I can't complain. It might be interesting to mention that the novel sold eight thousand copies (as of September 1963), and these days that's a lot for a first novel in England.

N: It's far ahead of that in the United States, isn't it?

Fowles: It's over forty thousand copies now. And it was published later, of course. It was very skillfully launched by my publishers, Little, Brown. That undoubtedly helped a lot.

N: What work do you have in progress?

Fowles: I'd better say first of all that I'm more interested in poetry and philosophy than I am in the novel. If I were to specify my aims in life I'd first of all like to be a good poet, then a sound philosopher, then a good novelist. The novel is simply, for me, a way of expressing my view of life.

However, I am writing another novel, set in Greece. It won't be the same as *The Collector,* but I hope it will also contain a very strange kind of situation. I'm certain that I must write in terms of strict realism. I'm a great admirer of Daniel Defoe—what I admire most is his creation of the extremely unusual situation, such as we find in *Robinson Crusoe* treated scrupulously in terms of his talent and honestly in terms of life. I hope this sort of approach will underlie my next novel, the Greek one. I also hope to have some philosophical ideas, mainly existentialist ideas, published in 1964, under the title *The Aristos.*

N: Then you are deeply interested in philosophy?

Fowles: Yes, indeed. This is what I admire about the French school of novelists. Sartre and de Beauvoir and the others. Although I don't necessarily share their points of view, I absolutely share their serious view of the writer's function. I feel I must be committed, that I must use literature as a method of propagating my view of life.

N: To turn to a basic question—what do you feel the obligation of the novelist is to the public as a whole?

Fowles: I'm afraid I'm going to give you an unsatisfactory answer. I don't feel that's a fair question. You can't generalize like that. I think we need novels that provide pure entertainment—novels to read, to enjoy, to put down, to forget. I happen to write novels for more serious reasons, but personal reasons that I have no right to impose on literature as a whole. If any writer says novels should be written *only* for entertainment, parroting the worst of our reviewers who say, "If it's fun it's good," or *only* for didactic reasons, I'd say to hell with him.

N: Conversely—and this may strike closer to your approach—what obligation do you think the writer has to the characters he creates or borrows?

Fowles: Once again, I don't think I can answer that because it depends upon whatever is the case. For *me* the obligation is to present my characters realistically. They must be credible human beings even if the circumstances they are in are "incredible," as they are in *The Collector.* But even the story, no matter how bizarre, no matter what symbolisms are involved, has to be possible.

N: You accomplished this in *The Collector.* The horror grew as the story progressed, but no matter how nightmarish it became, it was still believable.

Fowles: For me, that's a great compliment. William Golding, an English writer who, for other reasons, I admire very much, has to my mind one consistent fault: he doesn't treat his characters realistically enough in the extreme situations he invents. There are times when the credibility begins to wear thin. The same thing mars Kafka. I'm only stating this criticism because it helps explain my own view of life and of the function of the writer. Believability must dominate even the most outlandish situation.

N: In the world of writing, British, American, even the product from the Continent, what do you most admire, and what do you most deplore?

Fowles: Here, I think, I most deplore the stress on purely clever writing— the mere manipulation of words that American writers seem to practice more than writers in England. The danger of this, I think, is that you breed a sort of rococo cleverness which may be interesting to literary cliques and other stratospheric elements of the literary world, but which basically says nothing about the human condition, which teaches nothing, which does not touch people's hearts. I believe in the heart. In other words, I think that writing tends to be too cerebral, both here and, by imitation of you, in England.

In other ways, of course, your characteristic preoccupation with technique pays off. Young American writers often have all sorts of professional virtues young British ones haven't—cleaner descriptions, neater dialogue, a sharper eye for inessentials. But these virtues may be spoilt by the admixture of what seem to us artificial made-to-recipe symbolisms and deeper significances. I mean, I think we retain certain amateur virtues. Your writers have better eyes; ours have sincerer minds. You are, in general, pragmatists, believers in the sales figure. We're in general romantics; we believe in the muses, in writing as a vocation rather than writing as a career. Of course there are exceptions galore. But I think this explains *characteristic* faults and virtues on both sides. After all, it's a good polarity to have in the house of our common language. What's finally important is that it is the same house, not that we're all different in it.

N: How do you feel about Salinger, and the cult he's attracted?

Fowles: *The Catcher in the Rye* is a master book, but after that I feel he fell into an over-cerebral way of writing. We always have to have some cerebral writers. Salinger is a brilliant writer, and it's ridiculous to say he shouldn't have gone his route. He's still writing so far above the level of lesser novelists that I can't include him in my general complaint about the trend. He's not responsible for his imitators.

N: What English writers do you most admire at the present time?

Fowles: I admire William Golding very much. I admire Evelyn Waugh and Graham Greene. Their philosophies of life horrify or bore me, but I think that, technically, they are both masters, especially in narration, which is the key to good novel-writing.

N: Is there any trend in writing you anticipate? I mean, speaking generally and on a world basis, do you feel that any particular school of writers, or type of writer, is going to become dominant?

Fowles: I think the existentialist trend will increase. We're going to get more extreme-situation novels. (Of course, extreme situations go back to Defoe and even before him.) Books like Golding's *Lord Of The Flies,* and my own, will come more frequently. We'll have more of the key existentialist notion of authenticity in life. One is unauthentic largely because of the pressures of modern society, pressures that change from year to year. We'll have, I hope, more penetrating analyses of characters under pressure from society. I would like to see more of this serious and didactic approach. We've had enough escapism and satire.

N: How would you define existentialism as an influence on the novel? What do you think existentialism as a philosophical force *should* bring to the novel?

Fowles: One interesting field is the problem of free will. This is the question of whether you can discover enough about yourself, whether you can accept enough about your own past, to become what we call an authentic character: someone who is in control of his own life, able to withstand all its anxieties.

To me, any novel which doesn't have something to say on the subject of whether and why the characters are authentic or unauthentic is difficult to take seriously. It is merely an entertainment. A very existentialist novelist, in this sense of defining authenticity, is Jane Austen. Most of the time she was writing about a moral tradition, attempting to establish what authenticity was in her particular world and circumstances. This, of course, is Lionel Trilling's approach to Jane Austen, and I am sure he is right.

But I can best answer your question by saying that I think existentialism is going to infiltrate all our arts because its ideas are slowly affecting society as a whole. You know, you become an existentialist by temperament as much as by reasoning. You *feel* it as much as think it. Your life is harried by constant anxieties, fear of things, nauseas, hatreds of things. Life is a battle to keep balance on a tightrope. To live authentically is not giving in to the anxieties, not running away from the nauseas, but solving them in some way. This giving of a solution is the wonderful thing about existentialism, and why I believe it will take the place of the old, dogmatic religions. It allows you to face reality and act creatively in terms of your own powers and your own situation. It's the great individualist philosophy, the twentieth century individual's answer to the evil pressures of both capitalism and communism.

The girl in *The Collector* is an existentialist heroine although she doesn't know it. She's groping for her own authenticity. Her tragedy is that she will never live to achieve it. Her triumph is that one day she would have done so. What I tried to say in the book was this: we must create a society in which the Many will allow the Few to live authentically, *and* to teach and help the Many themselves to begin to do so as well. In societies dominated by the Many, the Few are in grave danger of being suffocated. This is why the Many often seem to me like a terrible tyranny. *The Collector* is a sort of putting of the question. *The Aristos,* I hope, will be a direct existentialist answer. My answer, anyway.

Portrait of a Man Reading

Charles Monaghan / 1970

From *The Washington Post Book World* (January 4, 1970), 2. Reprinted by permission of Charles Monaghan.

What's the first book you remember reading?

Bevis by Richard Jefferies. It's a kind of English *Huckelberry Finn.* About a boy on a farm 100 years ago. It's a very fine book and still a children's classic. You can almost smell the grass—and apples. If I see stored apples, I always think back to *Bevis*. I should think I was eight or nine when I first read it, but I've reread it every two or three years since.

How about adolescent reading?

I remember a terribly sentimental novel called *Lorna Doone.* Hit me very hard. I would have been about twelve or fourteen when I read that. I remember the American college humor, semi-pornographic magazines that everybody in my school used to read. Cartoons of unclothed women. It was the kind of thing which, if you were caught with it, you would have been beaten. That was at a school called Bedford, outside London.

And more serious reading?

Madame Bovary was probably the first serious book I remember reading. I read it in French—I was specializing in French and German at school. For me, it's still the perfect novel.

And in college?

I was at New College, Oxford, from 1947 to 1949, doing French. American ladies sometimes say to me it must have been nice to go to a new college rather than one of those old ones, but New College was new in 1380.

What period in French literature do you like best?

There's no period I don't like. I guess my major interest is in Montaigne and the drama. But existentialism hit the world when I was at Oxford, and

9

we all read Sartre and Camus and completely misunderstood them. My tutor for Symbolist poetry was Enid Starkie, the biographer of Rimbaud and Baudelaire. She was a great character, and we all thought she'd really "lived"—swept floors in French cafés and all that. She'd sit there listening to essays I was reading, with a chalk-white face and a cigarette dangling out of the side of her mouth. She was very impressive.

What did you do after leaving Oxford?

I worked in France for a year, teaching English at the University of Poitiers. That's when I read Giraudoux and went through my Gide phase.

What do you think of Gide today?

To be frank, I haven't read him since then, but if I did I suspect I wouldn't like him. It was at that time that I belatedly taught myself Latin and started reading the Latin poets.

Who is your favorite among the Latin poets?

Martial. He attacked the foibles of Rome, the excess, the hypocrisy. He was merciless on inflated and pompous writing. And I'm a great admirer of Horace, which is very unfashionable at the moment. Robert Graves says anybody who likes Horace is beyond consideration. I once went to visit Horace's farm outside Rome. It was the most touching literary experience I've ever had. It was about an hour's drive from Rome, and the place had the most extraordinary feeling of remoteness from the life of the corrupt city. But normally I don't like Roman civilization or Italy. I'm definitely a Greek.

What do you like about Greece?

The land is the most beautiful I know of in the world. The light there is extraordinary. I like the modern Greeks themselves, even though they have lots of faults. I find classical Greek art visually very attractive.

What do you see as the characteristics that distinguish Greek civilization from Roman?

The things that mark Greek civilization are simplicity, closeness to nature, lack of artifice. I would categorize America as Roman at the moment. Much

of my dissatisfaction with my own writing is because I think it is Roman in
the bad sense. Too complicated, too artificial. Flaubert's "A Simple Heart"—
along with Joyce's "The Dead," which I think is the greatest long short
story—is what I mean by Greek. Simple but perfect. Hemingway is Greek,
Fitzgerald is Greek, but Dos Passos is not. The early Joyce of *Dubliners* is
Greek, but *Finnegans Wake* is Roman.

What about English literature?

I've never read English literature systematically, as I have French. When I
was about thirty, I had a George Eliot phase, and I've read Jane Austen. I
think the most neglected English writer is Thomas Love Peacock. I keep
nagging at people to read Peacock. *Nightmare Abbey* I think is the funniest
satirical novel in English. I guess the reason he isn't read is that to appreciate
him you have to know something about the kind of background he makes fun
of—Shelley and the Romantic poets, for instance. Peacock writes such culti-
vated yet natural English prose. You have to go to somebody like Gibbon for
a comparison. And he has such delicious women characters. He's one of the
three or four English novelists who can create great women characters. Another writer who I think is greatly neglected is the poet John Clare, who
comes slightly after Keats and Shelley. He came of peasant stock and had an
astonishing folk relationship with nature. He went mad and wrote some
astounding apocalyptic poems. He's just beginning to be rediscovered. It's
taken 150 years. For me, he's much more important than Shelley.

What do you read nowadays?

I read a fantastic quantity of books that no one else has ever heard of. I am
an omnivorous reader and collector of old books. I don't want to seem im-
modest but, in fact, I've got a library full of curious old books that would be
worth reprinting. The things I like are those that get you back into a past
period and allow you to travel in it. I have been reading a little book I picked
up in a shop by two English Baptist ministers, written in the 1830s. It's the
story of a tour they make of Baptist churches in America. Of course, they are
very anti-slavery, and they get into trouble down South. The Southern ministers advise them not to bring up the subject of slavery at assemblies. And I
collect Mormon books. I have a sort of dotty interest in the Mormons. There's
one book I particularly like, by a Mormon wife, though I don't recall the

title. There's a marvelous passage where she describes what it feels like when your husband comes home one day and says there's going to be a wife No. 2 around the house.

What books do you recommend for getting back into the Victorian past and traveling around in it?

Of course, there's one marvelous book, which I acknowledge in my introduction to *The French Lieutenant's Woman*—E. Royston Pike's *Golden Times: Human Documents of the Victorian Age,* which Praeger publishes over here. Then, of course, there's *Mayhew's London,* especially the sections on street sellers and prostitution. And I find old copies of *Punch* magazine very enlightening about Victorian times. I have practically all of them—I have all the 1860s, for instance.

You are also interested in philosophy, aren't you?

Yes, I have written a book about it, called *The Aristos: A Self-Portrait in Ideas.* "Aristos" doesn't mean the upper classes. It means the best way to act in a given context. The book leans heavily on Heraclitus, the pre-Socratic philosopher. He believes humanity is divided into the few and the many. Some people argue that he is the father of fascist political theories, but I think that's Plato's fault. Plato interpreted him like that. I don't think there's any master race stuff in Heraclitus. He's simply being biological. Some people are going to be intelligent and some aren't. I am also fairly well read in the existentialists and in Zen Buddhism.

Have you done any reading in American literature?

My favorite American is Henry James. He's your one novelist of the very top flight. I'd rank him with Flaubert, Tolstoy and Joyce. I've recently read William Dean Howells's *New Leaf Mills.* A very funny book. He's a great naturalist. The reader is expecting a happy ending, then wham—it all ends unhappily.

Whom do you admire among your English contemporaries?

William Golding I admire very much. I think *The Inheritors* is his best book. It's a historical novel about Neolithic man. An incredible feat of literary imagination. And I like *Lord of the Flies.* Most English novels are absolutely predictable, but Golding is always his own man. A novel by Kingsley Amis, for instance. You know it's going to be funny, but he'll always do the Little England thing and be predictable. Another novelist whom I like is David Storey, who wrote *This Sporting Life,* about professional rugby playing. It became a movie with Richard Harris. It was the best English movie since the war, I think.

A Sort of Exile in Lyme Regis

Daniel Halpern / 1971

From *London Magazine* (March 1971), 34–46. Reprinted by permission of *London Magazine*.

Halpern: On the way down to Lyme Regis I stopped at a station to check directions. The man at the ticket office looked up and said: "Lyme Regis? You mean the holiday place?" How do you like living in a *holiday place,* somewhere so far from a large city?

Fowles: I think of living here as a kind of exile. I have very little social contact with anybody; they mainly hold right-wing political views that have nothing to do with my own. The old idea of exile for an English writer was to go to the Mediterranean. To do what Durrell has done, or Lawrence did. For me, the best place to be in exile, in a strange kind of way, is in a town like this, in England. That's because novelists have to live in some sort of exile. I also believe that—more than other kinds of writer—they have to keep in touch with their native culture . . . linguistically, psychologically and in many other ways. If it sounds paradoxical, it feels paradoxical. I've opted out of the one country I mustn't leave. I live in England, but partly in a way one might live abroad.

Halpern: When did you first come here?

Fowles: About five years ago. We lived on a farm down the coast that was totally isolated. I realized that was rather bad; you couldn't hear the sound of traffic, nobody came . . . you could go a week, two weeks, and you wouldn't see another human being. Now I like a certain amount of traffic noise and people's voices around me.

Halpern: You started writing *The French Lieutenant's Woman* on this farm?

Fowles: Yes. But I think we'd been there a year before I started that. I had had a year to get to know this area. I'd been about ten years ago for a weekend, but that was my only previous knowledge of Lyme.

Halpern: What did you do after you left Oxford?

Fowles: I went to teach in France, then in Greece, and that took up about

three years. I taught in a variety of schools in England, ending up in London.
I lived ten, twelve years in London.

Halpern: When did you start writing?

Fowles: I think I was writing in France, or trying to write in France. In
Greece I was certainly writing. The first draft of *The Magus,* which actually
came along before *The Collector,* I was beginning to write when I left Greece.
I was writing it when I was back in London and missing Greece terribly. It
was agony; I thought I'd never get over having left. But I'm very glad I did
leave now.

Halpern: Why?

Fowles: Because endless sunshine and cheap wine are usually bad for one,
and too much has been written about them. There's a thing we used to call
"The Aegean Blues." It would come after a month of splendid, flawless days,
say in early summer. You'd wake up every morning and plunge in the sea,
and life was perfect. Then suddenly you got so bloody depressed by sunshine
everyday, and getting mildly drunk at lunch and having to sleep it off all
afternoon, and talking and drinking until two o'clock . . .

Halpern: How old were you then?

Fowles: I was twenty-three.

Halpern: I thought *The Collector* was written before *The Magus.*

Fowles: No, I wrote a number of novels before *The Collector. The Collector* was merely published first. I wrote the first draft of *The Magus* in 1953
or so, and then I dropped it for about ten years.

Halpern: It didn't work out the way you wanted?

Fowles: I still think *The Magus* doesn't really work. In the first draft, it
just didn't work at all; I didn't know what frame, what context to put it in or
what style to adopt. I didn't show it to anybody, nobody read it. I only knew
the basic idea of a secret world, whose penetration involved ordeal and whose
final reward was self-knowledge, obsessed me. In a way the book was a
metaphor of my own personal experience of Greece. An allegory, if you like.
At least, that's how it started.

Halpern: What happened to the other early novels?

Fowles: One of two I have worked over, and I may publish them one day.
They're much more autobiographical than anything else I've written.

Halpern: Were you in contact with other writers while you lived in Greece?

Fowles: No, because this was just after the Civil War had ended in 1950, and there were very few foreigners in Greece then. I travelled on foot quite a lot in the Pelaponnesus, and in many villages one would be the first Englishman they'd seen since before the war. There was virtually no tourism then. This is one reason I can't face Greece at the moment, because I can still remember what it was like when you could wander from village to village in the mountains. It was a kind of nineteenth-century tourism, which has completely disappeared.

Halpern: In reading your preface to *The Aristos,* I had the impression you have ambivalent feelings about being a writer of best sellers. Guilt feelings perhaps?

Fowles: Well, I suppose I partly share the assumption that anything that sells well must be rather bad, that it must be a prostitution of some kind. I mean, I know I have one gift, which is for narrative. I can tell stories and make people listen, and I sometimes think that I abuse that talent. I suppose a parallel in sex would be a skilled seducer knowing his skill. Laying women right, left and centre, just as an exercise of skill.

Halpern: What would you do instead?

Fowles: Perhaps I ought to write more realistically. *The Collector* was a kind of fable, *The Magus* was a kind of fable, and *The French Lieutenant's Woman* was really an exercise in technique. That's how I regarded it as I wrote it—a complex bit of literary gymnastics.

Halpern: All three of your books are very different stylistically. For you does the content suggest the style?

Fowles: Yes. On the whole, I'm getting more and more hostile to people who are over-preoccupied with style and technique . . . I think we—and this goes for painting and all sorts of other things—return to content. Of course style is *an* essential preoccupation for any artist. But not to my mind *the* essential thing. I don't like artists who are high on craft and low on humanity. That's one reason I am getting tired of fables. There's something confected about them. I don't really see my need to be more realistic in theme and treatment as a problem of style, but much more a need to be less artificial.

Halpern: What made you decide to attempt a Victorian pastiche?

Fowles: It's very difficult to be rational and analytical about why you start writing a novel. It is largely a fortuitous, instinctive process: the way the first idea comes into your mind, and gradually begins to take shape as a novel. Personally I am against analyzing it too closely. Certain ideas and feelings and moods, moods especially, begin to haunt you, and it so happens that in this case they had to be expressed in Victorian pastiche style. I dislike the word pastiche, though I realize that that must be the category in which this book is put. At least I dislike the pejorative quality of the word.

Halpern: With your preoccupation with butterflies in *The Collector* and your interest in fossils in *The French Lieutenant's Woman,* I presume you have a great interest in natural history.

Fowles: Yes, all my life it has been the dominant outside interest. I suppose I'm a good field naturalist. I haven't specialized, but I've studied a little of many branches in natural history.

Halpern: You say in *The Aristos* that you think everybody should have a general knowledge of the natural sciences.

Fowles: Well, I do tend to take an ornithologist's view of human beings. I like watching people's behaviorisms as I watch the behaviorisms of certain birds in my garden. I'm not a good person, I'm afraid, with people. They're always slightly alien to me. If I were given the choice between leaving birds or people in the world, I think I'd be in favor of birds. One day I would like to try a science fiction novel. One image in it is a world populated solely by birds. I love the idea of a pure, primeval world of bird song and wings and birdshapes, and nothing else.

Halpern: I've noticed you often use "we" when referring to English writers. Do you think of yourself in terms of being an "English writer"?

Fowles: Very much as an English writer and very much *not* a British writer.

Halpern: A product of English literature?
Fowles: I have very special views on Britain and England. Britain for me is completely hollow, a meaningless concept. It's just a kind of geographical convenience word. And all its political and emotional associations I loathe— the British Empire, the Union Jack, the Queen. But the English are something different. England for me is landscape, and a certain kind of smell, and a certain kind of language, and a certain kind of behavior in life. This last ten years in Britain it's the Scots, the Welsh and the Irish who have constantly been saying, "We're under-rated, we're the people nobody ever notices". It's

the reverse that's true. So I'm an English nationalist, and Britain I have nothing to do with. I'm an English writer in that sense. But do I feel associated with other English writers? Very little. I certainly feel myself an outsider with regard to the English literary establishment.

Halpern: What are your feelings about the English critics?

Fowles: Fiction criticism in England is in an appalling state at the moment. We have grown far more anti-novel than any other country in the West.

Halpern: In favor of what?

Fowles: Mostly television. But the whole swing toward the visual arts has been stronger over here than in the States or anywhere else. The result is the novel is now a completely despised medium. Review space is cut down and the tone is always dismissive, even when it is superficially praise. That's why I feel sorry for English novelists who are not successful abroad. It's really like working in a graveyard at the moment.

Halpern: How do the American critics compare in your opinion?

Fowles: You have to define what you think of as good criticism. English reviewing, when it is serious and the reviewer is given enough space to do something, is probably more literate, the style is better, and it'll be a lot cooler. English reviewers rarely rave about books. On the other hand, it seems to me that a lot of American reviewing has more naturalness and more heart. If a critic likes a book in the States he'll stake his enthusiasm on it. And he'll be very rude, of course, in the reverse case. On the whole, I think the reviewing scene is healthier in the States. It's more honest, anyway. Every English reviewer marks plus five and minus four, or vice versa. They're great ones for self-insurance.

Halpern: You say that you have been very much influenced by Heraclitus. What is it about his writing that appeals to you?

Fowles: Another outsider. I suppose I have a liking for people who are outside society. Paradox has always fascinated me, Hegelian paradox. The concision and poetry of Heraclitus has always pleased me in some way . . . I don't know why, it's partly an emotional thing. There's not enough of him left, really, to say that one likes him philosophically. But what there is I find extraordinarily modern. Of all these pre-Socratic philosophers, for me he's the one of greatest twentieth century relevance. A proto-existentialist.

Halpern: You talk of outsiders appealing to you. What is the relationship between being an outsider and the kind of writing an outsider produces?

Fowles: I suppose that the usual theory is that you're outside society, therefore outside the accepted art forms of society. But my own being outside society is much more a personal, sociological phenomenon than a literary one.

I don't believe in hermetic art; I think there's everything to be said for writing that wants to get read.

Halpern: Did you do a great deal of research for *The French Lieutenant's Woman?*

Fowles: In the first draft I don't do any research at all. I write little things like *check up* or *develop* in the margin, because I think the skeleton of a novel must be the narrative—I call it the "spine." I let the spine dominate the whole first draft. That means the story must keep going, so I often leave out descriptions of clothes or the mood of a scene or other non-narrative elements, and deal with them later on.

Halpern: In *The Aristos,* the idea of hazard is something that often appears. What part does it play in the writing of your novels?

Fowles: I *do* believe in inspiration. I almost believe in muses. In fact, I wrote a short story last year that did bring the muses into modern life. It's very mysterious where good ideas suddenly appear from . . . I suppose there are all kinds of chemical reactions going on in your head and suddenly a spark flies between two known factors and then a completely unknown factor suddenly appears. You suddenly get a fertile new development. Or on the line-by-line level, you suddenly get to the right image or simile straight off. That is hazard. And because of that it rather dictates the way I write. That is, I never write if I don't want to, if I don't feel like it. Sometimes it can be very difficult. Other writers call it a block, but I hate that word. I simply wait till the muses come.

Halpern: And this waiting doesn't bother you?

Fowles: No. Women have to be waited for.

Halpern: Is there any problem once you've begun a book?

Fowles: Usually when I'm into a narrative the problem becomes physical. The story begins to pour out of me. I wrote a novel two years ago in eighteen days, working sixteen to eighteen hours a day. It can be done.

Halpern: You become, then, quite compulsive once you're into a novel.

Fowles: On this narrative, first draft stretch, I work just as long as I want and can.

Halpern: And after this narrative is finished, do you revise a great deal?

Fowles: First of all, I put the "spine" draft away and try to forget completely about it. The longer you leave it, the better. On the revision draft, though, I work hard. And more or less with discipline. I say more or less because I just don't believe in this business of keeping strict work hours. On the other hand it is sometimes good to revise and re-read when you don't feel like it. A lot of revision is really a form of masochism—what you are today savaging what you were a year ago.

Halpern: In *The French Lieutenant's Woman* you wrote how, once the narrative was started, the characters took over and suggested their own behavior, often in variance to what you as the writer originally had in mind.

Fowles: Well, I suggest that characters *do* do that. But that's not really what I believe. For a time they're just wooden tailor's dummies with clothes on, and suddenly they start up on their own. You get it most of all when you're writing dialogue, and they suddenly won't take the dialogue you're giving them. It's very strange. They are almost present, and they're saying, "I'm sorry, I don't say lines like this." And you get this bizarre experience when you feel they know the line they ought to be saying, and you're searching around in the dark to find it. There's been a masterpiece written about this. Do you know an Irish novel called *At-Swim-Two-Birds?* It is literally about a novelist who sits down quietly to write a novel, and how the characters start knocking on the door and completely messing everything up. But of course in reality the writer has the final say. And on the final draft you have to let the characters know it. Very often by then you know them so well that you are like a really skilled puppet-master. You can make them do anything, almost. You have to guard against that. You have to say to yourself, this is just an assemblage of words, and I can take my scissors and cut it where I want. In other words, you're cutting words, not some real person's skin and flesh.

Halpern: What type of writing do you enjoy reading?

Fowles: I admire craftsmanship. I like to see a literary job well done at whatever level. I go back to Chandler and Hammett. Chandler, especially, is marvelous; his best paragraphs are absolutely tight and hard. Like good furniture.

Halpern: What novelists do you read for enjoyment?

Fowles: I keep reading a fair number of Victorian novels; I read some

French novels; and I keep going, generally years behind, on modern American and English writers. I haven't really read anything recently I've liked very much, except *Ada.*

Halpern: Are there any contemporary American writers you do follow with interest?

Fowles: Most of the American writers I do admire very much are dead. Scott Fitzgerald is for me the best of the century. A very great writer. Updike I don't really like. Cheever I don't get on well with. Malamud I have respect for, I think he's a good writer. But I think *Herzog* is the best American novel since the war . . .

Halpern: What about English writers?

Fowles: Golding I admire very much. A splendid writer. I quite like Kingsley Amis, because he's so English. Alan Sillitoe I admire. And David Storey is very good too. I think one day David Storey may emerge as the most important novelist we've had.

Halpern: I'm curious about *The Aristos.* Would you like to write something else in a philosophical vein?

Fowles: No. That wasn't really meant to be a book of philosophy, but unfortunately it came out rather like that, and it's described like that. The original subtitle was *A Self-Portrait in Ideas.* The notion I had was that if you put down all the ideas you hold, it would amount to a kind of painter's frank self-portrait. I now think the style it's written in is distinctly rebarbative. It's a difficult book to read. My hope was that people would read only little bits of it at a time, but I realize people don't read books like that any more.

Halpern: Was *The Aristos* a reaction to having written two best sellers? To being labeled "a novelist"?

Fowles: Partly, yes. I didn't want to get docketed as a good story teller or as a thriller writer. *The Collector,* you see, was widely reviewed in England as a thriller; it didn't even make the serious novel columns. Which is why I'm certainly tender towards the American critical scene. They at least realized it was simply borrowing something from the thriller form, but that, of course, the deeper intentions were quite different.

Halpern: I have read a dozen or so of your poems. Why don't you spend more time writing poetry?

Fowles: I used to write a lot of poetry. That's wrong. Poetry has to write you. You have to spend time waiting for it. Not writing it. I've never tried to publish much, except once or twice when I've sent out the odd one. You have to wait a very long time for poems; they have to take shape; you have to put them aside; you have to work on them. And I'm still not sure that any poem I've written can't be improved if I leave it another year or two, or another five years. I think of poetry as the area of my writing where I don't cheat—I try and be honest. So I destroy a lot of poetry, too. I can't tell why a poem seems good. Very often one that seems technically—if not perfect—good, for some reason doesn't work. It's not you. It's very mysterious.

Halpern: Is there any novel that comes close to your idea of "the perfect novel"?

Fowles: Yes, I think one is very close. Flaubert's "Un Coeur Simple." I think it is the greatest short novel ever written. There might be a couple of words wrong, but it's very near perfection. And I think *Bovary* is probably the full novel nearest to this concept I have.

Halpern: Let me quote something you wrote in *The Aristos*. "I do not believe, as it is fashionable in this democratic age to believe, that the great arts are equal; though, like human beings, they have every claim to equal rights in society. Literature, in particular poetry, is the most essential and the most valuable." Could you explain why poetry is the most "essential" of the arts?

Fowles: I was, at one time, interested in linguistics. I think our best and our most human and our most evolved tool is language, and therefore it is the art that communicates through language that must be the most important. Poetry is obviously the highest and most concentrated form of that art. This is not talking about the pleasure to be derived. There's obviously equal pleasure to be got from all arts. It's simply that in terms of human society and human culture, this is the one art that we must protect most carefully.

Halpern: What do you mean when you say, "Art is a complex beyond science" *(The Aristos)*.

Fowles: I should really have said good art. But I think art is always stating something that science cannot state as yet. There's always a dimension in art that science hasn't yet evolved a science to describe and analyse. It's a sort of quantum of mystery, which you cannot really pin down by scientific means. An *n* quantity. I simply refuse to believe that literary criticism is more important than literature. A bad novel is humanly more important than the very best criticism.

Halpern: You were recently in the States on a promotional tour for *The French Lieutenant's Woman.* Did you find the people there more concerned with the writer as a personality than with what he's written?

Fowles: Yes, and I don't like this in the States at all. I find that many writers, especially on-campus writers, are more preoccupied with being a writer than actually writing. I think the University is a very bad thing for any writer to get involved with, because in every literature faculty one must be obsessed with looking at past literary ritual, at dissecting past literary technique, at tracing influences, and analysing how it's done. I sincerely believe the best thing for a young writer to do is to get the hell off the campus and go and work it out on his own.

Halpern: And away from any kind of literary group?

Fowles: I honestly think so. This doesn't mean to say that it isn't very useful to know other writers. Like the Ezra Pound-T.S. Eliot relationship. That, of course, can be very fertile.

Halpern: Have you had such a relationship?

Fowles: No, I haven't. Some of my friends are writers, but I very rarely, in fact never, discuss the technical side of writing with them.

Halpern: Is there a difference between the American and English reading publics?

Fowles: Yes, enormous. You see, we have a very strange factor here, which is this. We have the greatest free library system in the world. Even the smallest village in England has a library service. Of my twelve books sold in this country, *eleven* will now go to a public library. So the libraries have an ominously powerful position. They're the great book buyers. This means that writing is economically a terrible proposition in England. For example, if you sell twelve books, you get twelve royalties. One of those royalties will be from a private buyer. That's fine—say five or six friends read it. The other eleven books will go to public libraries, where they'll be read by up to two hundred readers per copy. So, for your eleven basic royalties, you're getting 2,000 or more readers who are not paying anything. And this is crippling. It means that most English novelists can't make a living out of their work.

Halpern: How do you feel about the two films that have been made from your novels?

Fowles: I don't like either of them. I suppose *The Collector* was just passable. It ought to have been made as we originally intended to make it. That is, as a small, cheap-budget, black-and-white movie. In fact, the man I would have liked to make it was the French director, Bresson. He would have done it marvelously. Unfortunately it got into the hands of Hollywood, and that was that. The second film, *The Magus,* was terrible. *Justine* and *The Magus* were the two worst films of the Sixties.

Halpern: What about the script?

Fowles: I wrote the script. My name had the script credit, but in fact I had to alter a lot to please the director, then the producers wanted changes, the Zanucks had their ideas . . . in the end it was a nonsense. And we had the wrong director for it. The casting was wrong . . . everything went wrong. A disaster.

Halpern: What's happening to the film version of *The French Lieutenant's Woman?*

Fowles: This time I've insisted on having a veto on the director. The big men don't like that—it's the writer getting above himself. We could cast it tomorrow, and with the actors and actresses I should like. They want to do it. But I suspect it will never get made. I'm losing no sleep over that. No sleep at all.

Halpern: Would you eventually like to get into directing your own screen-plays?

Fowles: One day, perhaps. What I certainly wouldn't like to do is direct films made out of novels I've written. The longer I go on the surer I feel that the novel has absolutely nothing to do with the film. They're two very different art forms, and there are dozens of better sources for movies than novels.

Halpern: In the firm version of *The Collector* they left out the part where the girl comes in contact with the older artist. That seemed to me an important part of the book.

Fowles: It was all shot. Kenneth More played the artist—an actor I don't like, and I never wanted him to play the part. Anyway, he went to Hollywood and did it. Then, in the cutting room, they suddenly realized they had the thing running over three hours. How they hadn't worked that out before, I don't know. So they cut all his scenes with Sam Eggar. I've never seen them. In the version one sees now, I believe there's still one sequence where you see his head.

Halpern: Is there a particular picture of the world that you would like to develop in your writing? Something that has remained important to you?

Fowles: Freedom, yes. How you achieve freedom. That obsesses me. All my books are about that. The question is, is there really free will? Can we choose freely? Can we act freely? Can we *choose?* How do we do it?

Halpern: An anthropologist friend of mine thinks that the novel is a preface to the cinema. How do you feel about this?

Fowles: No, he's wrong. There are hundreds of things a novel can do that cinema can never do. The cinema can't describe the past very accurately, it can't digress, above all it can't exclude. This is the extraordinary thing in the cinema—you've got to have a certain chair, certain clothes, a certain decor. In a novel you can leave all that out. All you give is a bit of dialogue. It's this negative thing that cinema makers never realize. You don't have to "set up" the whole screen. The delight of writing novels is what you can leave out on each page, in each sentence. The novel is an astounding freedom to choose. It will last just as long as artists want to be free to choose. I think that will be a very long time. As long as man.

John Fowles: The Magus

Rowland Molony / 1973

From *Dorset: The County Magazine* (November 30, 1973), 19–23.
Reprinted by permission of Dorset County Magazine Limited.

Q: You write with interest and appreciation about the West Country. Were you born or brought up here?

Fowles: My ancestors came from various places. I'm a quarter Cornish, and my great-great grandfather was a blacksmith at Yeovil. So, yes I feel very attached to the West Country.

Q: Below us, on the promenade facing the Cobb, is the site of Jane Austen's cottage. Do you feel any affinity with that lady?

Fowles: I love her novels. On the other hand I think her effect on other English writers has been rather dubious. I was recently reading novels for the Booker Prize and was again struck by her sinister latter-day influence—all that tedious and footling analysis of English middle-class social habit. I think that kind of novel is completely out of date now. But one cannot blame her for this, obviously. I don't feel any personal influence, no. I feel more from Peacock. I very much admire Peacock, her contemporary.

Q: Are there any writers that you feel have had a really profound influence upon you?

Fowles: A number of French writers, yes. I studied French at university and French literature has really had much more influence on my life than English. When I was young Sartre and Camus had great attraction both as thinkers and as novelists. Renaissance men like Montaigne and Rabelais also. There are no English modern writers I feel particularly influenced by.

Q: I was going to ask you about that . . . are there any who you feel to be important?

Fowles: I would find that word "important" difficult to define. I can only say who I like. Technically I like Evelyn Waugh; I don't like his ideas, but I think he was a great technician. Graham Greene for the same reason. I rate Golding very high.

Q: Yes, one of your reviewers links you with Golding in originality. Do you share or do you sympathise with that vision of his?

Fowles: I wish I could feel I were his equal, because I think he has produced some very considerable novels. But I find it rather difficult to say what
I like about Golding. It is a feeling of freshness; he does different things.
Somehow he has got out of this horrible English rut of various set kinds of
novels, you know, of which the "Jane Austen" novel is one; and the satirical
novel, another.

Q: There is that very distinct philosophy behind say *Pincher Martin.* What
do you feel about that?

Fowles: Tell me what you think it was.

Q: I'm thinking of that horror, a naked sort of savagery that allows very
little warmth about the human kind . . .

Fowles: You mean that depressive view of human destiny? Yes, that's not
a philosophy I share. It's a sort of Beckett-like feeling. Golding has a perfect
right to exemplify it, of course. But you see, I suspect writers judge other
writers on rather curious grounds. We've somehow got beyond thinking,
"Well, are his ideas right or wrong? Is he being significant or not?" It's much
more involved with technical things, as complex as one's relations with an
old friend. I love that book, *The Inheritors.* And I liked his last one, *The
Pyramid,* which was badly reviewed everywhere. I suppose it's fundamentally on technical grounds that I like him.

Q: *The Collector,* was that your first book?

Fowles: The first I published. I wrote the first draft of *The Magus* long
before that.

Q: By any standards *The Magus* is an enormous feat of imaginative writing. It is a speculative book, both in a moral and a philosophical sense. What
intentions ran through your mind during the period of the writing of it?

Fowles: About fifty thousand, so I can't really answer your question. But
the multiplicity of intention probably explains why for me the thing is a
failure. It tried to do too much. Again, I wrote the first draft when I was 28
years old, much too young to be able to tackle such a project—then I dropped
it for ten years. I wish now I'd waited to my present age. It was always meant
to set questions rather than give answers—like a Rorschach test . . . no "right
reaction", no one correct solution to all the clues. Fundamentally, the intention was metaphysical. Conchis is not meant to represent God, but the human
concept "God"—an important distinction. Urfe stands for Earth—
Everyman. The title *The Magus* was probably a mistake. For a long time I

was going to call it *The Godgame.* Another preoccupation was the battle between reality and illusion. I wanted to see if I could do magic in narrative and descriptive terms. A major influence was Alain-Fournier's *Le Grand Meaulnes*—especially the concept of the *domaine sans nom,* the *domaine perdu.* He wrote about his own book, "I like the marvelous only when it is enveloped in reality," and I tried to keep to that. We both failed. But failing is a prime reason writers keep writing.

Q: *The Collector* illustrated the mental world of Frederick Clegg in a way that drew horrible consequences. Are you ready to explain away the vast differences between the sometimes pitiable, sometimes hateful small-mindedness of "Caliban" and the subtlety and profundity of the artist, "G.P." both of whom find a meeting point in Miranda, purely in a biological sense?

Fowles: You're saying, do I believe that some people are biologically more endowed and more intelligent than others? I think, yes, that is beyond dispute. I don't believe one can argue against it. The curious history of *The Collector* is that all the sympathy it has evoked has really been for Clegg. Only a tiny minority have had any sympathy for the girl, or for the artist, and this has always slightly puzzled me.

Q: Were you happy with the way *The Collector* was translated into a film?
Fowles: No.

Q: Do you have any connections or ambitions in the film world?
Fowles: I have plenty of connections. I've just got rather tough about what I let them do to me at the moment. This last book—I've insisted on having a veto on the director, which probably means it'll never get made. No major studio likes to allow writers that sort of power.

Q: This is *The French Lieutenant's Woman?*
Fowles: Yes.

Q: Will they film it now?
Fowles: Probably not. At the beginning if I'd said I'd sell it outright for X thousand dollars, fine. But in fact I set conditions that weren't acceptable to the studios. It may get made. I'm personally totally indifferent. I think most writers are. It's a nice lump of lolly, but they always screw you in one way or another.

Q: One effect of this latest book, *The French Lieutenant's Woman,* is to draw Victorian minds into the twentieth century. What was it about that age that so drew your attention?

Fowles: I can give a number of answers to that. I think one important one is that I hate historical novels, mainly because you have to start faking the dialogue. I hate hearing Theseus or Marie Antoinette, or whoever, speaking in modern English. The dividing line between being able to use more-or-less modern dialogue and having to start dressing it up is, I suppose, about 1800. I have also always liked the use of the writer's first-person in the novel. It is very, very difficult to do that in a novel set in the 1970s, but of course all the great Victorian novelists introduced their own "I". It's much easier to do if you go back to their age. And the third reason is that the 1860s were in my opinion a crisis period in English history. There is a kind of break there. In fact the twentieth century really began in the 1860s—possibly even a little earlier.

Q: Well, leading on from that idea of the author's first-person in the novel, let me ask you about something which you say in that "liberating" section of the book which I found most interesting, Chapter 13. You say: "The novelist is still a god, since he creates (and not even the most aleatory avant-garde modern novel has managed to extirpate its author completely); what has changed is that we are no longer the gods of the Victorian image, omniscient and decreeing; but in the new theological image, with freedom our first principle, not authority." Is this freedom in your opinion an arrival at long last for the modern novelist at an honest relationship with his creations, despite even a modern assumption of authority by the State? The tribulations of many Soviet writers at the moment would seem to bear this out.

Fowles: I certainly think, in my own personal view of the novel, that this is its most vital function—that is, the establishment of free views of society. That's seeing the novelist as a sort of political being. I think the whole question of whether he can ever establish freedom in his relations with his own characters is very problematic. I don't really accept that it can be done, although lots of people now are trying to give that impression—as I did myself slightly in *The French Lieutenant's Woman*. But there always comes a point when the writer is the man who has the blue pencil in his hand. You are in fact a dictator, and I don't think one can really dodge that. Certainly, I would say that Solzhenitsyn, writers like him, demonstrate the prime function of the novel. A classic example is Rabelais—when you think of the colossal work of demolition he did in those five books. Another writer I like is Diderot, the effect that Diderot's "philosophical" novels had in the mid-eighteenth century.

Q: Can you ever foresee this new freedom being clouded again in the future by self-imposed attitudes and authority?

Fowles: Yes, I think the *nouveau roman* movement in France is a case in question. Writing novels to a theoretical recipe—which just hasn't worked. There have been one or two. . . . Robbe-Grillet's *La Jalousie,* a very fine novel. But most of them have been disasters. The problem for novelists in this country is really finding what kind of freedom to deal with. It's fine for Solzhenitsyn in Russia to be aiming all the time implicitly at political freedom, but that's effectively achieved over here. One reason the British novel is currently so "dead" is that it's very difficult to define what freedom one should be trying to establish.

Q: In *The French Lieutenant's Woman* you quote in a number of places extracts from Marx's writings, sometimes to illustrate that the economics of modern society still produce slaves, sometimes to show how society is compelled to adopt certain universal modes of organisation. The direction of the book does not call for forecasts; nevertheless, are you hopeful of the determinism of the Marxian dialectic?

Fowles: I think that he has been partly borne out by history, though I suppose there are many Communists today who would disagree with that. Where I'm not sure I share Marx's views completely is on the energy and intelligence of the working classes. I have a great distrust of work, of labor. I think this is always glossed over in the Marxist canon. I doubt if most work could ever become glorious and beneficial to the individual. Most jobs are a bloody bore, at all stages of society, and will continue to be so at all stages of human evolution. I suspect that this is the great spanner in the works—the problem of the actual nature, especially the boredom of labor. And I don't think worker control of the production process, nationalization and the rest will in fact ever do anything about that. I don't see how anyone will ever be able to approach many forms of labor with anything but depression, and in that sense I'm pessimistic. But in the general sense of a gradual tendency to the Left in the world, I'm certainly not pessimistic. At this particular moment we're going through a rather nasty little "Right" counter-swing. But then I don't think that's very serious (smiling), that's just part of the dialectic.

Q: You don't see an inevitability about this swing to the Left in the world?

Fowles: Yes, I do. But then there are elements in our century that Marx could never have predicted, such as the nuclear bomb. I think if you could say no nuclear bomb, no pollution, no population menace, then, yes, I would feel politically very optimistic about the human race.

Q: Some literary critics have drawn attention to the 20th century as an age of ideologies, saying that the future of the novel lies in the conflict of these differing visions, and that this replaces traditional subject-matter of the novel: class distinction, wealth and poverty. You have written a highly successful novel contrasting the past and the present—telling a relatively simple story, but embedding it deep in elucidation. We can afford to look back on the nineteenth century with a fair amount of self-satisfaction. The style in which your book is written reflects our sense of emancipation. Do you think there is a future for the novel looking back with twentieth-century enlightenment?

Fowles: I don't think so, no. As a general rule this area is far better left to historians. Personally, if I want to learn about ancient Greece or medieval France I would much rather go to the original texts, however skilled and imaginative the fictional re-creation. I don't think the subject of the novel really ought to be the past, it ought to be the present. Or possibly the future. But not the past. In one way it is much easier to write about the past, of course. It makes the writer's job much easier.

Q: The idea of "long-range" literature—by which I mean that quality of writing which has not necessarily been dedicated to a cause, but which simply contains all the contradictions and paradoxes that an age has shown to the writer, and which survives the centuries because of the breadth of the imagination that recorded it—is always a fascinating talking point. It strikes me that your own work is of this quality, that your attention is caught by all the color and movement in society rather than the need to press a distinct morality. Do you agree?

Fowles: Yes. I think this is a very interesting question. As a matter of fact it is one every writer has to answer. One reason a lot of young novelists get into trouble is that they haven't asked it of themselves. We're really getting back to this business of freedom. I mean "To what extent ought I to concentrate on expressing my political views, and to what extent am I a recorder and entertainer?" The answer is complicated by being British. It's really become very difficult in this country now to write a realistic political novel of any value. I think it's impossible to write, say, a decent socialist novel. You might write a socialist novel that was decent in what it said, but I just don't see how it could be of any great artistic value. I'm talking here in terms of realism. The answer to this is that if you're going to write about political

causes then I think you have to get into the area of the parable and the moral
fable of the George Orwell kind. There the political novel does become perfectly viable.

Q: Engels did say, didn't he, that the further away one hides one's political
ideologies the better it is for the work of art.

Fowles: There again it's a matter of context. I think if I were a Chinese
writer in China I would really be all for the things which so shock the tender
liberals of the West—the things they are trying to do with their arts. Mao's
China is a perfect example of a context where their present sort of theoretical
tendency and attitude to art is probably right. I'm sure in practice it becomes
a bit absurd at times. But here we are, we're stuck in a country which is
getting on for a millenium old, we've seen everything, we've experienced
everything, and you just cannot put over, however decent it is in intention,
simplistic socialist propaganda. In fact you are harming the cause by doing
that, because nobody is going to listen to you. Socialist realism does not even
work in Russia. The Russians have had too many great writers for that stuff
to wash.

An Interview with John Fowles

James Campbell / 1974

From *Contemporary Literature,* 17:4 (Autumn 1976), 455–69. Copyright © 1976. Reprinted by permission of the University of Wisconsin Press.

John Fowles is big, bearded, and burly. His books have brought him, by English standards at least, considerable success, and he lives with his wife in a splendid house in a Dorset village on the English south coast which is almost as many years behind as it is miles distant from the hubbub of London. He was born in 1926 in Leigh-on-Sea and became head boy at Bedford School, later going on to Oxford to read French. Then he took a job teaching on a Greek island for a few years in the fifties and was teaching at a school in England when *The Collector* brought him money and fame in 1963. We conducted the interview before the fire on a winter's day after lunch. Mr. Fowles frowned when he saw the tape recorder but answered all the questions amiably and thoughtfully. He speaks in an English public-school voice, which he punctuates with such gap-fillers as "you know," "I mean," and "sort of," quite often leaving his sentences incomplete and dangling in the air between the two speakers. He answered with impatience one minute and with friendly warmth the next, but in the end his confidence—"I don't need people, really"—is not difficult to believe.

Q: All three of your main novels stop and start a lot before eventually reaching a close, as if unsure of how to end. Is this because you try to give them freedom, or are you in fact in control all the time?

A: Both, really. I do try to give them freedom, yes, but only as a game, because pretending your characters are free can only be a game. The reality of the situation is that you're sitting with a pencil, and at any point you like you can strike out developments in the book.

Q: Do you begin with a preconceived idea?

A: No, I don't. In that sense I do rear them very freely. I start with a general attitude, sometimes just with one scene, rather like a cinema still, and then it develops. I usually find after about 20,000 words that you know whether you've got a book or not because you feel it grip.

Q: *The Collector* seemed to me to be more preconceived than the others. Did you have that idea more or less complete in your head before you began?

A: Yes, that's true. That was a sort of cold-blooded book. That doesn't mean a lot of things don't crop up as you write, though. I mean you have to distinguish two kinds of writing: most important is first-draft writing, which to an extraordinary degree is an intuitive thing—you never quite know when you sit down whether it's going to come or not, and you get all kinds of good ideas from nowhere. They just come between one line and the next. But revision writing's very different—you have to turn yourself into an academic and mark yourself. With this, of course, comes the research. And I find that rather boring.

Q: How long do you normally spend on the first draft?

A: I write it very quickly. I wrote the first draft of *The Collector* in a month. I could write them all in that time but in fact I take longer now.

Q: Why do you find revision so difficult?

A: Well, for one thing, you have to be cold-blooded and ruthless. You can fall in love with passages, but if they are not quite what's needed then you have to strike them out. At the revision stage you've got to be master. In the first-draft stage you don't need to exercise so much control. But it's different for different writers. I know some who cannot move on to another passage until they've got the one they're on right. That's obviously a perfect way of writing, but it's a matter of temperament.

Q: Was *The Collector* your first book?

A: No, although it was the first published. I think in a sense it's a small or narrow book; the others were meant to be much wider. I've always been interested in the Bluebeard syndrome, and really, that book was simply embodying it in one particular case. It's really a casebook for me. It was important for me, though, to prove that I could write well enough to get published.

Q: You didn't have the average writer's trouble getting published, did you?

A: No, I didn't, but as I was thirty-seven I couldn't afford to.

Q: Were you writing as a young man?

A: Yes, I was writing at Oxford, but I had the good sense to know how bad it was.

Q: What sort of thing were you writing before *The Collector?*

A: I wrote *The Magus* before then. I spent most of the fifties, in fact, writing *The Magus.* And I wrote two or three other novels. I kept on changing *The Magus:* it changed enormously in conception. I was very much under the influence of Kafka at the time, and it was a much more Kafkaesque book originally. It was set in Greece, but the backgrounds and characters were much less specific. But a more important influence was the French writer Alain-Fournier. *Le Grand Meaulnes* was a book I loved in my late teens. In a sense, *The Magus* is a reworking of *Le Grand Meaulnes.*

Q: Some critics have said that *The Magus* did not achieve what it set out to do.

A: No argument from me.

Q: None?

A: Well, you must remember it was a young man's first novel and I tried to say too much. It was written by a young man who really didn't have very much experience of life, but who had a tremendous love of narrative. I think the thing that is good in *The Magus*—if one can defend oneself—is that it is readable. When I look back I see that that is what I was really trying to do, but, like all first novelists, I wanted to say all sorts of things about life, and it got too complicated. One thing that worries me now about it is that it's not terribly well written. One day I hope to rewrite it. Also, I don't think it's clear enough. It says so many different things and nothing really is concluded. The original title was *The Godgame,* and, of course, it is about a man's stages of conception of what God is—you know, "God" in quotes. But the sort of thing that disturbs me now is that—you know that trial scene in *The Magus*—in one American university I heard that a group of students are going out into the woods and actually staging that. I mean that trial scene at the time was written as a send-up of psychology—I put in every piece of psychological jargon I could find.

Q: What are your reactions to the kind of status achieved by *The Magus* on campuses?

A: I've nothing to do with it really, but I do think there's a place in the tradition for this sort of adolescent book. I mean it's the same with *Le Grand Meaulnes:* you will not get a serious literary critic to look at that book because Alain-Fournier wrote it at the same age as I was writing *The Magus.* And you can criticize *Le Grand Meaulnes* endlessly, but the fact is that it has haunted generations of young people. One of the things that is lacking in the English novel is that everybody plays it so bloody safe most of the time. Especially young writers. I think you've got to take risks, you've got to gamble, even if later on in life you have to say, okay, I gambled on the wrong horse. But the sad thing I find in young English writers nowadays is that they find some big figure—you know, a Graham Greene or an E. M. Forster—and then they try to write in imitation of them.

Q: A lot of people like to make a link between *The Magus* and the drug climate of that period when it achieved fame, the late sixties.

A: Well, when I was out in California I met one or two people who were on the Leary fringe, you know, who had totally misunderstood *The Magus,* because they were asking me what drug I had used to write it—something I've no experience of whatever.

Q: None at all?

A: I smoked kif once in Tangiers, and it made me terribly sick. Another thing which they took for granted, as many people do, was that I'm very keen on astrology, in which I have no believe at all.

Q: Are you interested in trying drugs as a new type of experience.

A: I'm interested in reading about it; for instance, I love reading those books by Carlos Castaneda, but I've no interest in trying them out for myself. I'm much more interested in experiencing the world as it is. Realism interests me increasingly in fiction—the problems of realistic technique, rather than the drug experience. I drink quite a lot while I'm writing—whiskey I find quite useful—but that soon becomes counterproductive: you soon reach a stage where you think you're writing marvelously and then when you look at it in the cold light of day. . . .

Q: Could you name some of your main influences?

A: Certainly the French writers, Camus and Sartre, impressed me very much, and Gide, although I've gone off him. Lawrence, among English writers, I admired.

Q: Your style of fiction is fundamentally traditional. How do you react to the more pioneering fiction writers of today?

A: I like Robbe-Grillet, who has been mainly responsible for the *nouveau roman. La Jalousie* is especially good. I think it's the best, actually. The French part of me likes it very much, but in places I find it rather boring. There's something new there, though. That doesn't mean, however, that I or anybody else should try to write a *nouveau roman* in English. The English *nouveau roman*—Christine Brooke-Rose—doesn't work, I think. A brave failure. It could be because the French have this extraordinary tradition of rhetoric which we don't have.

Q: What do you think about Beckett's attempts to intermediate?
A: I'm dubious about Beckett. I don't value him so highly as everybody else does. He's written one or two very fine plays, but I've never found his novels terribly impressive.

Q: Do you think he relies on a single formula?
A: Yes, that annoys me about him. Sometimes he reminds me of Kafka, but he's not nearly as good as Kafka. Nor do I like these very short things he's writing. I think Kafka was essentially a playwright who never made it to the stage, and I think Beckett is essentially a playwright, a great monologist, but a novelist?

Q: What do you mean by saying that Kafka was essentially a playwright?
A: In some peculiar way he's not a natural novelist—there are so many things he doesn't know how to do. Yet in these featureless books that he wrote, there's a tremendous dramatic sense, and it seems to me that he developed a marvelous sense of drama from nothing. So in a way he foreshadows Ionesco and Beckett.

Q: Why have you not written in a distinctly modern style?
A: I think you have to have a natural stylistic gift for that. It's no good inventing a style that doesn't come naturally. I naturally write in a realistic way. If I naturally wrote in a gap-jumping, shorthand, allusive way, in the way that we find in Proust or Joyce, then that would be fine, but if I adopted it now, then that would be, in existentialist terms, inauthentic. You're dealt a hand of cards at the beginning, you know, and you can borrow so much, but on the whole it's better to play according to your hand.

Q: Does modern American writing appeal to you more than English?
A: I think it's much healthier, much more alive, and I think technically better than ours, mainly because it's much freer. I have to go back to what I said earlier about this awful thing in this country, of imitating one's elders. Traditionalism can be a hindrance. Another grave block to the writer in this country is the whole academic setup. If there's one gang of people I'd like to see thrown into the sea it's the professors of English Literature. I think they're the most backward. . . . There are one or two: I'm thinking of Malcolm Bradbury at East Anglia—and Tony Tanner at Cambridge is good—but most of them are so backward-looking compared with the average American teacher of English.

Q: Which American writers do you particularly admire?

A: Contemporary ones? I don't really know . . . a name doesn't spring to mind. John Berryman, the poet, was a marvelous writer, wasn't he, but a novelist? There was a time when I loved all the Lost Generation—Scott Fitzgerald, Dos Passos, even Hemingway. I mean one has to admire Hemingway—stunning technician. You can look at a page of Hemingway and it's locked so tight, not a wrong word or a wrong comma.

Q: What do you make of experimenters such as Burroughs with his cut up and permutative writing?

A: Burroughs is an example of a writer who has valuably discovered a way to say something new about the way we think, but I wouldn't for one moment take these experimenters seriously as a contribution to a new kind of writing. I mean I'm glad that one person's done it, and they do add a tiny bit to the whole broad range of literary experience. I think Burroughs will always be a minor writer, though; I don't think he's anywhere near the stature of Joyce or Virginia Woolf, although he's working at the same sort of thing. I don't think there's much future in the way he's doing it.

Q: I take it that you're not in sympathy with the theory that the novel is dead?

A: I think it's bloody nearly dead in this country. It's in a terribly serious state. For a young novelist today it must be a depressing situation to come into. It's just that the whole English establishment's turned its back on the novel, most young people have turned their backs on the novel, and there's a kind of silent majority and all they want is Daphne Du Maurier and Frederick Forsyth.

Q: Why do you continue to write fiction then?

A: Because I happen to have a large international readership, but I don't know what I'd feel if I were the average novelist in this country, selling, if he's lucky, 2000–2500 copies, and very often not getting reviewed, because half the novels, *over* half the novels, don't get reviewed. And the writers are absolutely unable to live on it. And you know this whole general feeling, the telly . . . when do we ever see anything serious about books on the telly?

Q: By "the average novelist" do you mean, say, Sillitoe, or somebody less established than he is?

A: Sillitoe probably sells more than the amount I've just quoted. I'm thinking of two categories, really: serious, good novelists who want to sell much

more, and novelists who perhaps will never be very good, but who deserve
something a little better than the total oblivion they are meeting at present.
Three major London publishing houses didn't publish a single first novel last
year. It's terrible.

Q: That's because there's no revenue.

A: Yes. At 2500 a publisher can hardly break even. I think at 3000 he can.
And now there's this whole business of offset litho, you know, of privately
done editions and so on, but, in a way, that's counterproductive because very
few people are going to read them. My only word of encouragement is that
there still are sums of money to be made—if you strike it lucky.

Q: A curious feature of your work is that such a style as yours should
spring from the environment from which it did, i.e., the angry young man's
working-class novel in England, which was actually anti-experimentalist.

A: Are you saying I'm an experimentalist? A moment ago you were saying
I was a traditionalist.

Q: Your work is basically traditional. But like Benjamin Britten in music
you can be an innovator in a traditional vein. But I wanted to ask you about
the literary environment in which you began writing.

A: I'm not against the working-class novel; I mean I'm very glad that it
happened, but I've always argued that it was a kind of dead end. Once you've
done one good novel about the working class, it becomes a very difficult field
to go on with because culturally—this is not being snobbish—but culturally
it is limited, the situations are limited. And the thing with the middle class is
that there are far more situations, middle-class people are far more complex
than working-class people, and therefore, in a sense, it's just giving yourself
more room. Another thing I think is that because these working-class novels
that Sillitoe and all the rest wrote are sociological, this raises another question
of whether modern sociology doesn't do all that better—can't it all be done
better by the television documentary, and I think possibly the theater, than
the novel? In a way, Zola, who started all this, is another kind of dead end.
Zola is a bit like Burroughs in that way. There's just so far that you can go
in the strict world of working-class culture.

Q: Are you saying that the working-class novel was a flash in the pan
rather than the basis for a new subculture?

A: I think it's dead. I mean this isn't an argument against the working
class, for God's sake, you know, if some young writer knows his own envi-

ronment best, and that environment happens to be working class, then of course he should write about it. But I can't imagine a whole school that catalogues itself as "The Working-Class Novel." I just can't see that happening. Of course, there's nothing to stop somebody doing the same thing for the Scottish working classes. There are things there. For instance, I'm very interested in this Communist miners' enclave in Scotland. I should think there's interesting stuff to be written there, not just reproducing that North-Country English style either.

Q: What are the differences for you between writing in the third as opposed to the first person?

A: I find the first person much more natural. I never think of writing a book in the third person, although *The Ebony Tower* and *The French Lieutenant's Woman* are both third-person books. It usually just turns out that way after having been in the first person originally. I never feel quite at home as the omniscient narrator.

Q: Do you subscribe to Sartre's dictum that the novelist cannot be God, should not be the omniscient narrator?

A: You can't. It's silly to say the novelist isn't God, cannot pretend to be God, because the *fact* is that when you write a book you are potentially a tyrant, you are the total dictator, and there's nothing in the book that has to be there if you want to knock it out or change it. Then you have a comparatively free choice about it, and it's very difficult for a character in the book to stand up and say, you cannot do that, or, I demand that that line be changed.

Q: I think what Sartre was getting at was that to act as the omniscient narrator is to destroy the autonomy of your characters; they have to find their own roles, and the novelist cannot be continually stepping in with evaluative statements. Wasn't there something of this in what you were doing in *The French Lieutenant's Woman?*

A: Yes, well, I only made it explicit in that book. But this does happen: people in the book do suddenly seem to do things which one hadn't imagined or couldn't have predicted in any way.

Q: You've written somewhere that "Camus and Sartre have in their own way been trying to lead us to a Victorian seriousness of purpose and moral sensitivity." Was this notion part of the original inspiration for the *The French Lieutenant's Woman?*

A: No, not at all.

Q: How did it start?

A: From an obsessive image of a woman with her back turned, looking out to sea. It didn't begin as a historical novel, and the reason it turned historical may be that I have collected Victorian books all my life. I have a poor academic knowledge of the age, but I do know quite a lot about the byways of Victorian life just because I happen to collect Victorian books. So I didn't have to do much research, although I did have that very useful book by E. Royston Pike, *Human Documents of the Victorian Golden Age,* which in my opinion is the best of all anthologies about the nineteenth century. Another thing which I used a great deal was *Punch. Punch* was a great magazine in Victorian times, and that does all your work for you: you get your food details from it, and all your clothes details, and a lot of dialogue. That's another curious thing—the dialogue in *The French Lieutenant's Woman.* You see, the dialogue there is not absolutely true to how they spoke in that age, but the dialogue they actually used in the 1860s seems a little too modern to us. So I had to archaize it, to stretch the more formal elements to get it to sound right.

Q: By bringing in Rossetti at the end, did you mean to signify something about the age as a whole, using his *fin-de-siècle* decadence?

A: The Pre-Raphaelite movement was one of the key movements in working out that awful strait-jacketed, puritanical aspect of the Victorian age. But you see, the sense of purpose of the Victorians was at its finest before the Victorian age began, that whole movement between 1810 and 1830 when there was a really solid corpus of progressive thinking in this country, and it climaxed in the 1832 Reform Bill. But by mid-Victorian times, that had become terribly pious and phony; it was a mask you wore over your face—"I'm a serious, deeply principled man." And that was when the Rossetti thing came in. I mean you can't pin that sort of thing down obviously, but certainly I think Rossetti's a very good symbol of a breakthrough.

Q: A breakthrough in what way?

A: Standing up against the age, really, and saying, there's something sick about this age, and we've got to become more human, more sensuous.

Q: Why did you make two endings in *The French Lieutenant's Woman?* Was it an allusion to *Great Expectations?*

A: No. It's been pointed out endlessly since, but I definitely wasn't conscious of it. I'm sure it's been done lots of times in novels and in films.

Q: In all of your novels and in the longest stories in *The Ebony Tower,* the female characters have had the edge on the men in terms of awareness and knowledge of themselves. Do you believe in some sort of female principle?

A: Yes. I feel that the universe is female in some deep way. I think one of the things that is lacking in our society is equality of male and female ways of looking at life. I've always disliked the dominant theme of machismo as in Hemingway and the whole of American society. This sort of deep thing in one's writing really doesn't come out in one's conscious mind: it comes out in how one was born, the culture one was brought up in. Which is what I was trying to say in *The Collector.*

Q: Are you conscious of the fact that in all your novels the men have been, so to speak, blind at first and have come to a greater awareness of their real selves in the arms of the women?

A: Yes, especially in *The French Lieutenant's Woman.* This is the sort of existential thesis of the books—that one has to discover one's feelings.

Q: You've borrowed a lot from existentialism, haven't you, but were you ever committed in their way to that sort of writing?

A: The sort of novel that Camus and Sartre wrote—it's like the *nouveau roman*—I don't think you can do it in English. It's something that's grown out of the texture of the language; it's dependent upon being able to write in a very metaphorical way and having that tradition behind you. I don't think the English tradition, which is inherently pragmatic and realistic, can do it.

Q: Have you avoided trying to do it for that reason alone, or does it not interest you to embody such a philosophy in a novel?

A: It may do, it may do. But I'm interested in the side of existentialism which deals with freedom: the business of whether we do have freedom, whether we do have free will, to what extent you can change your life, choose yourself, and all the rest of it. Most of my major characters have been involved in this Sartrian concept of authenticity and inauthenticity.

Q: Can you illustrate the contrast for us by using Nicholas and Alison from *The Magus?*

A: Alison, for instance, was supposed to be someone who is choosing herself, who has very little *mauvaise foi.* The contrast between her and Nicholas is absolutely deliberate; he was meant to be a typical inauthentic man of the 1945–50 period, when all this hit me.

Q: So in fact, like the characters in *The Collector,* and Charles and Sarah from *The French Lieutenant's Woman,* Nicholas, too, was historically determined.
A: Yes, although it's not so clear as in the other two.

Q: And the novel is all the time moving towards a reconciliation of Nicholas to his real self?
A: Sort of getting near it. I didn't mean to suggest that by the end he was authentic. But that last chapter in *The Magus* is certainly about achieving authenticity, and for someone with any knowledge at all of what the existentialists were doing in that period, that last chapter is not a problem. I've seen some wild American interpretations of it, but there's a man called Robert Scholes who wrote a very good essay about it—you know, I could have written it myself.

Q: Where is that published?
A: In an academic magazine called *Hollins Critic,* December 1969.

Q: Did you make the same contrast between Charles and Sarah in *The French Lieutenant's Woman?*
A: Yes, in a much more English context. They were both meant to be determined by history and challenged with choosing themselves.

Q: What about *The Ebony Tower?*
A: The original working title for that book was *Variations,* so you see, the same themes in a way are at work there, too. I don't think this business of dominant themes is conscious on the part of the author; it just happens that way—it's bound to happen that way.

Q: You say the working title was *Variations.* Does that mean that the stories are variations of each other, or on past themes?
A: On past themes, I think. I mean two girls under the wing of an older man in the title story is obviously going to recall *The Magus.* But I don't think *The Ebony Tower* is only a reworking of *The Magus,* not at all.

Q: When did you begin *The Aristos?*
A: In my twenties. I began it at Oxford. That book is very arrogant, but there are things in it which I still feel and believe.

Q: How did you come to publish it in 1965 "against the advice of almost everyone who read it"?

A: Well, it's one of those books you have for years, and you add to it, and change it, and I felt. . . . Probably it's the awful French influence on me, not altogether good. . . . It's the sort of book a French writer would publish naturally, and in a way I'm glad that it's at last able to breathe.

Q: In what way was it against the advice of your friends?

A: Well, I mean my publishers didn't say, we're not going to publish this, but they said, don't you think it might be better to wait, rewrite it? But you have to use the iron fist with publishers occasionally. I wouldn't want to get into this American situation where your publishing editor dominates your life; almost as soon as you write a page you have to send it to him.

Q: On the basis of that book you've been accused of elitism.

A: That's a misunderstanding. I have never used this word "elitism." Elitism has come to mean, in New Left terms, a small group who are privileged in economic terms, hasn't it? And I have never supported that. Biological elitism I certainly believe in—I don't see how you can dispute it. I mean you could get everybody in this country absolutely equal educationally and you would still end up with gross differences in intelligence, perception, memory. I'm not defending this; I'm simply saying that it is a biological fact about life. Ninety-nine percent of humanity are not of the artistic, moral, and intellectual elite; they're not particularly moral, they're not particularly artistic, and they're not particularly intelligent.

Q: This has obviously influenced your novels as well.

A: Yes it has.

Q: *The Collector* springs to mind most readily.

A: Yes, but please don't get me wrong—I'm not a Kingsley Amis or a John Braine. I have no sympathy with the political Right at all.

Q: In *The Aristos* you qualify yourself as a social democrat.

A: Yes, I mean I don't hold much brief for Wedgwood Benn or Michael Foot, but there is a feeling that they are trying to get British Socialism, which has gone completely haywire, back on the rails. My view is that capitalism must outgrow itself. In one way that's why I rather welcome this present energy crisis. The idea of a complete violent overthrow of capitalism in this country tomorrow is absolutely ludicrous, because there's a massively powerful fascist element in Britain, and a potential disaster could occur.

Q: Have you ever tried to write an explicitly political book?

A: No. I have no faith in socialist realism. I sincerely hope the Marxist element in this country will grow, but I don't think you can put Marxism across in a novel.

Q: Why do you continue to live in this country?

A: Because English is the language I use. Also, I don't despise Britain—I think the standards of civic decency in this country are superior to most other countries. And I like the weather in England. I lived in Greece for a long time and grew to hate it, that interminable sunshine.

John Fowles on Islands and . . . Hidden Valleys

Aaron Latham / 1977

From *The Washington Post Book World* (October 16, 1977), E1, E4.
Reprinted by permission of Aaron Latham.

On the plane on the way to New York City, I decided to begin the interview by asking John Fowles to name his favorite Shakespeare play. I hoped he would choose *The Tempest* with its magician-hero Prospero. If he did, then I would feel better about what I thought of as my Prospero theory. But what if he said *Hamlet*? I wouldn't know what to ask next.

I met John Fowles in the Dorset Hotel. He had arrived from England three days earlier to preside over the publication of his new novel, *Daniel Martin*. My theory had to do with why he had written the book the way he had written it: for it seemed to me that he had deliberately authored an anti-bestseller. It was as if he felt his previous novels—*The Collector, The Magus, The French Lieutenant's Woman*—had been too popular.

"What's your favorite Shakespeare play?" I asked.

"*The Tempest*," Fowles said.

Relaxing a little, I took the time to study the 51-year-old Fowles. He wore a T-shirt, looked sleepy, and was a few pounds overweight, all of which made me like him. Since Fowles's book-jacket photographs are among the handsomest in literature, I had been afraid he might look like a local TV anchorman *manqué*, which is not how Prospero should look.

Why did Fowles prefer *The Tempest*? Was it because the play is about an island?

"The island imagery appeals to me," he said. "Islands have always attracted me. It's like a sexual preference, it goes so deep inside you."

And of course islands run all through his books. In *The Collector,* the isolated house where the girl is held prisoner is a metaphorical island. *The Magus* is set on a literal Greek island. The village of Lyme Regis in *The French Lieutenant's Woman* is a kind of island in time and place. And *Daniel Martin* climaxes with a journey to an island in the Nile.

Daniel Martin's other passion, besides islands, is for hidden valleys. Was there a connection between these two loves?

"Of course," Fowles said, "the hidden valley is an inland island."

Was *Daniel Martin* not only about islands but also a kind of island in itself? Or perhaps a hidden valley? Had he written a difficult book to separate the serious explorers from the many casual readers who had picnicked off his easier fiction?

"*Daniel Martin* is a journey into the hidden valley of me. I think it's a selfish book in a double sense. It's selfish in the more old-fashioned sense: self-indulgent. But it's also more about self. I think every novelist should write one selfish novel."

Was this new "selfish" novel in a sense a reaction against the success of his earlier books?

"I know I could turn out a best seller a year." Fowles said. "I know I can hook people. One rule I determined in this book was: I wouldn't use any of the simpler or more obvious tricks of narrative. I conceived the book as not a linear narrative but a landscape."

Prospero had decided to lay aside the magic cloak of his narrative gift. The magician was going straight. It was like the end of *The Tempest.* His career followed the curve of the play. But why? What had motivated him?

"*The Magus* was a deliberate games novel," Fowles said. "And there were games in some of the others as well. I felt that had given a false image of what's important in my life. Nature. Humanism. Humanism is literally what it says—respect for human life."

He thought a moment, glancing out the window at my idea of an enchanted island: Manhattan.

"Most writers know who they are by 50. I don't. Every book I write is an attempt to discover who I am."

What had he learned writing *The Magus*?

"I discovered what the novel is capable of and what I'm capable of. I was like a chimpanzee who had been let into a room with all these tools. That's when I learned that I can tell stories that involve people, hook them."

In writing a book about a Prospero-like island magician called the Magus, John Fowles had discovered his own Prospero-like powers—his cloak.

I asked him a question you should never ask an author: What did *The Magus* mean?

"The basic scheme was the old man in the book showed the young man all the various masks that human beings put on the face of God. From super-stition right up to psychiatry. But there's a basic fault in *The Magus*: if you're creating a myth you shouldn't do it in realistic language. I've just rewritten it. I knew I could write it better now."

The revised *Magus* with its more mythical language is currently a best seller in England and will be published in America next year.

What had Fowles learned from writing *The French Lieutenant's Woman*?

"That was basically a stylistic exercise," he said. "Twisting language to try to make it sound Victorian." The magician had learned to perform a new trick.

Which of his novels did he like best?

"I've always had a very special feeling for *The Magus*. It's my most failed book in academic terms, also the richest in human terms, by pure fluke."

Why were his novels all so different? Couldn't he make up his mind?

"I've never gotten much satisfaction with repeating formulas, but I don't blame people like Le Carré who do turn out recipe novels," Fowles said. Then he went ahead to blame: "He is the best at the spy thriller genre, but his books seem to me to be fairy stories. Not about reality. I find the whole genre profoundly antihumanistic. I think the women in Le Carré are awful. His father is Raymond Chandler and his grandfather is Conan Doyle."

Who were Fowles's own literary grandfathers?

Two were English: Thomas Hardy and D. H. Lawrence. And two were American: Henry James and Herman Melville. He especially admired Melville's *Pierre,* which he called "a failed novel," and which he seemed to equate with *The Magus.*

Was *Daniel Martin,* a book about a writer, autobiographical?

"No," Fowles said. "I hate producing recognizable portraits. But it is about the spirits of certain old friends."

He went on to say, however, that the book was based on other spirits as well.

"Behind the character of Jane in my book is Jane Austen. Castrated, sterile, in-turned."

So he wasn't an admirer of Miss Austen?

"She was our greatest novelist but one of our worst influences. You could say something of the same thing about James Joyce. They both had a bad effect on lesser writers who tried to imitate them."

Would he care to name names?

"Elizabeth Taylor [the novelist] would have been a better writer if Jane Austen had never existed. And William Faulkner would have been a better writer if James Joyce had never existed."

But didn't Fowles's passion, islands, have a lot in common with Jane Austen's world? Weren't they both in-turned?

"One of the things I like about islands is the contrast between openness and closedness. Standing on an island beach looking out to sea, one has a feeling of openness. But from a distance islands appear closed, mysterious."

Was there a connection between his love of islands and his being English?

"Probably."

What is an island psychology?

"Going rather deep, you must voyage. You must experiment. The voyage dominates a lot of English art."

In a sense, each of Fowles's very different novels has been a voyage into a new sea, but the destination is always the same: another island.

Interview with Author John Fowles

David North / 1977

From *Maclean's*, 90 (November 14, 1977), 4, 6, 8. Reprinted by permission of *Maclean's*.

What does an internationally renowned, 51-year-old novelist worry about when he's 3,000 miles from home, promoting a new book in North America? Wearing his fingers to the bone autographing copies for students? Not being late for that literary luncheon? Saying the right things to all those boring critics? Some such matters may have been on the mind of John Fowles (*The Magus, The French Lieutenant's Woman*) when he made a 48-hour stopover in Toronto recently, to help launch his latest and most ambitious novel, *Daniel Martin* (published in Canada by Collins Publishers). But what Fowles was really fretting about, amid all the ballyhoo, was whether he could get back to harvest the potato crop in the garden of his Georgian home at Lyme Regis, in Dorset, before the frost got it; and cursing the luck that was to keep him in London for a further week on his return to Britain. While in Toronto, however, he did manage to talk to *Maclean's* David North about his life and times as a best-selling novelist.

Maclean's: A lot of readers look to novelists for entertainment, much as they watch television or go to the movies. Is that how you see yourself, as an entertainer?

Fowles: I am not ashamed to be thought of as an entertainer. I think that's one viable function for the novel. An equally viable one, I think, is criticizing society, another is didactic teaching. I think at the moment the novel actually has got too obsessed with entertainment because that's where the money is, and I hate this American phrase, "the recipe novel." I have just been in New York and that's certainly what all the editors are looking for there. They want novels that are written according to a recipe. Very often the editor seems to do as much writing as the actual writer. This seems to be a dangerous encroachment on something very important about the novel which is that it is one person's view of life.

Maclean's: A lot of people are writing off the novel as an art form. Do you think that's the reason—formula writing?

Fowles: I think a lot of formula or recipe writing really is bastard television, and it's written to sell film rights, not on publication but before publication. That is one danger. But I don't see any chance of the novel dying. There's no evidence in libraries or in book shops that poetry or the novel is dying. I think that the novel and poetry are very close in a way because they are both one man's view of life.

Maclean's: When did you actually start writing?

Fowles: Rather late compared to most writers. I should think in my mid-twenties. I tried to write a little in my last year at Oxford, but I was of the war generation and went late to Oxford in any case. When I left Oxford I taught in a French university for a year and then I went to a very weird boarding school in Greece where I taught English. It was very much like an Evelyn Waugh school. I used it in my novel, *The Magus,* but for libel reasons I couldn't really tell the truth about that school.

Maclean's: Is it still going?

Fowles: Only two months ago, the present English master came to see me, and he assured me it is much reformed.

Maclean's: But you haven't been back to perform an autopsy?

Fowles: I have never been back. The Greek educational system is a peculiar law unto itself so the school is not, I think, very exceptional in Greece.

Maclean's: What made you decide to start writing? What drove you to write?

Fowles: My view of this is heretical. I think writers are made genetically. You have to have a certain natural gift in your brain (with words) obviously. I think you also have to have a sense of loss implanted when you are very young. In other words, I think writers are quite literally born, therefore, I do not believe in creative writing. The Freudian theory of this, that I would apply to all artists, is that some people have had a very peculiar experience after the loss of their mother and the discovery of their own separate identity. Young infants really don't have clear frontiers between themselves and their mother. With some people it's the kind of fluidity of this experience, the changing of shape and the supreme happiness from the sort of union with mother that probably dominates their adult lives, unconsciously of course. All this goes into the unconscious. Although I am not a total Freudian, I find this very convincing because I think what is interesting about the novel is the obsessive repetitive need in true novelists to go on telling stories. We always

have to be telling legends, myths, which very often try in some way to make
the world more perfect. Obviously, there is some dim memory somewhere of
a more perfect, happier, magical state, and we are all trying to get to that. It's
very obvious in novelists like Thomas Hardy who was totally fixed on his
mother. All the women he fell in love with all through his life even had his
mother's physical features.

Mclean's: How do you organize your writing? Do you, like some writers,
churn out a regular 1,000 words a day?

Fowles: Absolutely not. It's not that I sometimes don't wish I couldn't do
that, but it's partly because a novel for me is a kind of voyage, let's say a
sailing voyage, and I rather rely on whether the wind is there. If the wind is
there then I will write hard. If the wind is not there, and I go into doldrums,
then I don't worry. American writers call it "writer's block." I think it's
usually a signal that it's best to stop and it doesn't worry me. It's just like
being becalmed and I do other things.

Maclean's: How do you, in fact, spend your days?

Fowles: I suppose I live a rather 19th-century pastoral dilettante's existence, perhaps rather like a lucky 19th-century vicar who has a parish he
doesn't need to worry about. My parish is my garden, I do a certain amount
of gardening, but I spend an enormous amount of time just wandering around
it doing nothing.

Maclean's: Afternoon tea on the lawn?

Fowles: No, nothing formal like that. It's a wild garden, I have a fine rich
natural life in it which I encourage, and it's just really my birds and the
insects and the plants. I am a terrible seed stealer. Everywhere I go in the
world I pinch seeds and take them back and that sort of thing. I read a lot
too.

Maclean's: Does it help your writing to live in one of the most beautiful
spots in Britain?

Fowles: I don't think so at all. I do have a marvelous view in front of my
study window. A number of writers have stood by me and said, "How on
earth can you write in a place like this?" I remember Peter Ustinov once
telling me that he had gone to Sicily to write a book. He had a marvelous
18th-century Sicilian room with a superb landscape of the sea, and he hadn't
written a word. In fact he spent the whole time just admiring, staring out of

the window. I told him what was wrong was that, of course, he went there for a holiday.

Maclean's: Are you a tidy worker or do you litter your desk with paper and stuff?

Fowles: I think the untidiest writer I know of was Charles Dickens. If you've ever seen a Dickens galley with corrections . . . unimaginable. I am rather like that. I am not tidy.

Maclean's: Can a novelist be a family man?

Fowles: I think it's an enormous advantage for novelists not to have children. But I think novelists need a particular kind of wife. It's a peculiar profession being a novelist's wife, and I am very fortunate in having a very expert wife. But I think if you get too involved and too worried about your family that must handicap your work. But my wife does have a daughter by a previous marriage, so we are not familyless.

Maclean's: Where do you get your ideas?

Fowles: In all sorts of ways. It's difficult to be very specific about that. I read a lot in the past, and I am a great collector of 19th-century books, 18th-century books, even 17th-century books, and I have a bad memory. I have a very distinguished, or I had, sadly, a very distinguished Russian fan who was the great neurologist and memory expert, Professor A. R. Luria. I wrote him once and said, "I can't understand. I know when I have to recreate a scene my memory is good, and all sorts of things come back, but I forget authors' names and dates, and I'm appalling like that." He said in his experience, and he had probably more experience of memory than anyone else in the world, this is absolutely normal of writers and artists. Our memories work laterally. They don't work logically. If you say what is the date of something, you know, we are stymied, but we will remember tiny relevant facts. For instance, I could write a very good description of the Battle of Waterloo. I have collected one or two old books on the Battle of Waterloo and if you asked me to give a good sort of academic answer to the question, "How did the Battle of Waterloo happen?" you know, I'd be terrible. But what it was like actually to be in the battle, I think, I could give a good account.

Maclean's: How do you do your research?

Fowles: I don't believe in research. I believe in my fallible memory. I think if my memory forgets details about a place or a mood then it probably suggests that the reader doesn't want those details. I am very suspicious of writers who say "I've got to set a scene in Toronto, Canada, therefore I must go to Toronto, Canada." It's quite enough for me that I have once spent two days in Toronto. I would never, if I wanted to write a chapter on Toronto, come back to Toronto to research because the things I would have forgotten probably should have been forgotten for literary reasons.

Maclean's: Do you work on one book at a time, or do you have several on the go?

Fowles: The first book I wrote was *The Magus* which was published second. This last one I broke off to write a collection of short stories called *The Ebony Tower.*

Maclean's: When you have finished a book what's your chief emotion—relief, elation?

Fowles: Depression. Every writer, I think, feels depressed. I think of it in temperature terms. When a book is being written it's warm, and somehow when you've got the final galley it's cold. You can't alter it any more.

Maclean's: You do rather enjoy tinkering, don't you? I was astonished to read the other day that you had completely rewritten *The Magus.*

Fowles: Not completely, I have partially rewritten it.

Maclean's: Why?

Fowles: It was the first book I wrote, and technically it never satisfied me. I've learned more about the tricks of the trade since then. I wanted to put in one or two new scenes, and I wanted to clarify one or two things a little bit.

Maclean's: What did the publisher say when you told him he'd got to print another edition of it?

Fowles: I wanted it to be slipped into the normal reprint cycle. But my English publisher said, "This book is going to sell." I said, "Nonsense." And he said, "Alright, do you want to bet?" Because he is a very good publisher, I didn't take his bet but, in fact, it has been, I think, a best seller for 10 weeks in England. That amazed me.

Maclean's: *The Magus* became rather a cult because it coincided with a particular era. Did that bother you?

Fowles: Some rather mad things happened in the United States in the Sixties. One university, I was told, used to put on the trial scene, and I had quite a lot of cranks after me. I think that's finished now.

Maclean's: In rewriting *The Magus* were you trying to lay that ghost?
Fowles: No. Because I think it was always based on a misreading.

Maclean's: How do you feel about your readers?
Fowles: The readers' reaction is much more important to me than the critics'. That takes many years to come in, though. Especially with a complicated book like the new one.

Maclean's: Which of your fellow novelists do you most admire and why?
Fowles: I like Joseph Heller in America. In Britain, I like David Storey. I think Margaret Drabble is a good writer. I like Alison Lurie, another American woman writer, and I like Joan Didion, another American woman writer. On the whole I think women writers are rather better today than men writers.

Maclean's: Do you know why that should be?
Fowles: I think women writers are generally more honest, and I think they are closer to the ground. I think they are less obsessed by best-selling and the whole recipe novel side of the business. I find them on the whole more serious than most men novelists. I did like Joseph Heller's last novel *Something Happened.* Of course, in a way, it seemed to be a sort of feminine novel. He'd probably be deeply insulted.

Maclean's: The novelist is sometimes compared to a skilled lover. He builds up the excitement, it is said, by every technical art before allowing the reader the satisfaction of a conclusion. Do you think perhaps this is why women writers are so good?
Fowles: I think that might be one reason. I mean, I don't think of women actually as very good at suspense. There are very few good women thriller writers, but that for me is a mark in their favor. I think they are much better at the domestic side of things. I mean daily realities. Men writers get bored with daily realities. Someone like Margaret Drabble is terribly good at that. But I personally wouldn't use the sexual analogy. I think I'd rather use one of cooperation, because another reason I think the novel will survive is that the reader has to work in a novel. In a film, you are presented with someone else's imagination exactly bodied out. The marvelous thing about a novel is that every reader will imagine even the very simplest sentence slightly differently.

Maclean's: And at 300,000 words in *Daniel Martin* that's quite a feat of imagination. Do you have any mercy on your readers?

Fowles: I am not writing for reviewers. Reviewers have said the book should have been shorter. A lot of them said, "Why wasn't it shorter?" Somebody in America said that there's nothing wrong with this book that a good editor couldn't have cured. That, to me, that is just a weakness in reviewers. I mean, it's possible that the book is too long, and there may be literary reasons why it's too long, but I am writing for readers who are prepared to spend a week or two weeks reading a book.

Maclean's: And you are prepared to take the risk that the 300,000 words may be just a few too many?

Fowles: Absolutely. I mean, I know I have a gift as a writer. I can, if I want, keep people turning pages as fast as I want. I know how to tell stories. But people who read that book have got to look for other pleasures. You know, this book is what one 20th-century man feels about his century and generation in one particular country.

Maclean's: What in your view is the chief distinction between fiction and the real world?

Fowles: Well, it's a metaphor for reality, and this is why I think poetry and the novel are so close, because all novels are really metaphors for reality, and I personally would not distinguish between the reality and the metaphor and reality and reality. I think once the thing is written it assumes a certain reality. I suppose you could say some of Shakespeare's great speeches are unreal, but that seems to be an equally important reality, a mental reality.

Maclean's: So it's not really an illusion?

Fowles: It's illusion at one level. If you are talking in terms of, for instance, 20th-century empirical philosophy, of course it is an illusion, but personally I don't think so . . . I am not much in favor of the documentary novel. I think that really is rather a bastard form, and I have never really liked extremes very much, extreme naturalism, writers like Zola. I suppose my greatest liking is for the average stream—the Voltaires, the George Orwells, the allegorists. Certainly there are, I think, allegorical realities surely as strong as many forms of actual reality.

Maclean's: What, therefore, would you say were, not necessarily in order of priority, a novelist's duties toward his readers?

Fowles: I think I would doubt your question. I think a novelist's first duties, oddly enough, are really toward himself. To be honest to his own imagination, his own total knowledge of existence. That's the prime duty to me.

You always write for yourself first, to discover yourself first. Then there are, I think, lesser duties down the line. I personally feel that my duty is to write for an educated majority. That's not an avant-garde minority; in other words I think we've seen quite enough of avant-garde art in the 20th century, so in a way in this book I am going back a little from that.

Maclean's: That seems nicely to combine acceptability as an artist and profitability as a journeyman.

Fowles: It does. I must say "Guilty" if that's said. But I've never written to make money. I never was more amazed than when *The Collector* was a best seller, and I didn't think *The French Lieutenant's Woman* would ever make it.

Maclean's: How many copies of all your various books have you sold?

Fowles: I am not very interested in that side of my life. I honestly couldn't give you a figure. I think *The French Lieutenant's Woman* is coming up to three million in paperback. *The Magus,* I suppose, must be somewhere near there.

Maclean's: And the money, are you interested in that?

Fowles: I am economically free to write, but, for a best-selling author, we lead very simple lives. We really have no expensive tastes. We don't go in for a car. I don't even drive. I refuse to pay high prices for antiques. I wouldn't want to live with valuable things around me. And if they are very beautiful things I think they ought to be in public museums anyway.

Maclean's: What, then, would you say is the greatest benefit you've derived from your success?

Fowles: Freedom. I am fortunate to be a very free person. I work when I like. We could live where we like, travel when we like. Nobody tells me what to do. Everyone else today has to work in some form of organization. I sometimes feel I am from another planet.

Maclean's: I would have said that *Daniel Martin* is probably by far the most ambitious book you have ever written, would you say that?

Fowles: I would say it is ambitious, and it is risky. I know that book is going to be misunderstood, misinterpreted and all kinds of things but, again, I think if you are a novelist you have to put yourself out on a branch.

Maclean's: How seriously are we to take some of the hates expressed in the book? The commercial cinema, for instance.

Fowles: I've had a bad time with the commercial cinema. I think the commercial side of Hollywood has done America more damage than anyone at the present moment actually realizes. It gives such a false image of what America is about, and anyone who has been in that world knows that the decisions are taken on such absurd grounds. Art hardly ever comes into it.

Maclean's: And the North American, I am quoting here, "heresy that size and looks are everything"?

Fowles: I don't like to lump Canada in. I have been here for 48 hours . . . I think, if I talk of the United States, yes, I think their addiction to size is insane and evil. Even in the kinds of things like the portions in certain restaurants. At the end of a meal in a New York restaurant you always see the plates half full because nobody can eat it all . . . and the waste of electricity, the absurd cars. But America is difficult because I noticed in Boston compact cars now seem to be in the majority, but for some ridiculous reason that is not so in New York.

Maclean's: You write in *Daniel Martin* about the printed word and I quote: "It's only the spoor of an animal that has passed and is now somewhere else in the forest." You have already said that *Daniel Martin* is your major work so far. Whereabouts in the forest . . .

Fowles: Well, no . . . Whether it's my major work I don't know. Technically I shall never beat *The French Lieutenant's Woman.* I think that that is a very good craftsman's job at imitating certain tones of voice. I don't think I'll ever write a book as good as that. I am talking on this technical level . . .

Maclean's: Alright, so I come back to my question: whereabouts in the forest are you?

Fowles: I don't know at the moment. I shan't know because you write books to find out where you are in the forest. I shan't know until I have written another book. I really meant by that that in a way, as soon as you've written a book, you know it's not enough. It doesn't really say what you wanted to say, and for some peculiar reason, until it's published and you see it in print and it's reviewed, criticized or even praised, it's only then that you see what was wrong with it very often, and that's why you have to write another novel.

John Fowles: An Exclusive Interview

Tony Graham, Hilary Arnold, Sappho Durrell,
and John Thackara / 1977

From *Socialist Challenge* (December 15–31, 1977), 17. Reprinted by
permission of Tariq Ali.

The works of John Fowles are probably more widely-known across the world
than he is. Among his books can be found *The Collector* (1963), *The Magus*
(1966) recently revised, *The French Lieutenant's Woman* (1969), *The Ebony
Tower* (1974) and *Daniel Martin* (1977).

The left has, in general, been somewhat lax in assessing new developments
in literature. While it is true that the future of the novel, the relationship of
politics to literature, and similar questions will not be found at the head of
every trade union agenda, it would be wrong to permit ruling-class ideo-
logues a free hand on these matters.

Fowles' latest book, *Daniel Martin,* serves as a useful example of this
point. Before the book publication, Fowles described it as a "homage to
Lukács." Much of the book is devoted to uncovering the myth of "Englishness" through stripping off the social and psychological layers that have
clothed the British Emperor of the twentieth century. Now revealed without
his clothes, he has summoned his mandarins to launch a counter-attack. The
"literary establishment" and media have joined hands to ridicule and demean
Daniel Martin. Socialists would do well to read the book and draw their own
conclusions.

*A general statement in novels seems to be that the central female charac-
ters are repositories of "right feeling," emotion and self-awareness, whilst
the central male characters are repositories of culture, imaginative artifice
and self-indulgence. In an essay, "Notes on an Unfinished Novel," you wrote:*
**"My female characters tend to dominate the male. I see man as a kind
of artifice, and woman as a kind of reality. The one is cold idea, the other
is warm fact."**

*In bringing these two polarities together you show that the former, the
female characters, can have a positive effect on the latter, the male characters, but you do not, despite the fact that you bring them to a point of mutual
recognition, resolve the inevitable conflict and tension that exists between*

59

them. Do you believe that the two are irreconcilable, and have you ever
considered exploring beyond the impact of mutual recognition?

The two perennial incompatibles in the human condition seem to me the
desire for personal freedom and the desire for social equality. The battle
between the two desires is less destructive when the female principle dominates or has at least some sort of parity, as during the escape from the Dark
Ages, the Renaissance and our own time.

Male-principle societies are much more strait-jacketing. More conforming,
besotted by law and order, suspicious of heresy—right-wing in short. Eve
welcomes change, Adam—even Marxist Adam—fears it. Socialism has still
to shake off the handicap of having been largely conceived and formulated
by men and in a male-dominated age. Comte is a classic case of onesided-
ness, as the feminist J.S. Mill was quick to point out at the time.

One thing I don't like about certain aspects, or phrases, of socialism is the
inflexible male-aggressor tone—the preserving of traditional structure and
creed at all costs, and the low value put on the characteristic female gift for
personal judgement and feeling and for the practical as against the ideal. For
instance, certain familiar uses of parroted invective and esoteric jargon seem
to me good deal less socialist than just primæval male.

On the other hand I am equally suspicious of extreme liberationist attempts
to prove that the only difference between women and men is psychological.
I believe that it is vital that women retain their ability to think, feel and act
different from men, however much they may share intellectually the same
social beliefs. This is what has to be mutually recognized.

The "tension and conflict" that must result is inherently fertile—not of
course when it springs from the attempt to impose or cling to outmoded roles,
but because the give-and-take democracy of the good male-female relationship is the basis for all other democracies. This is one reason why more
women are urgently needed in government and parliament—not the sort who
ape male attitudes, but the ones who can modify and see through their always
incipient conservatism. I have absolutely no belief in a time when the two
sexes will live in unending harmony.

What concerns me as a novelist is achieving the point of recognition both
of the difference and of the mutual need. What happens beyond that point is
not in my view a right subject for ordinary novels until this recognition is
publicly established. Till then, alas, it stays in the domain of science fiction.

You have implied that you "do not understand" the women you incorpo-

rate as central characters in your books. At the same time they are an essen-
tial device in your books and act as the conveyors of "radical" ideas. Why
do you feel unable to analyse and express their development and their moti-
vations?

What I really meant is that they are not to be understood by traditional male standards. Like most male artists, I have a strong female component in my character, just as most women artists have a strong male one.

This may help us in creating characters of the opposite sex, but of course we're always, finally, no more than sympathetic visitors in a foreign country . . . not natives. If my women characters seem short on motivation and analy-sis—I suppose most notoriously in *The French Lieutenant's Woman*—it is because I am writing from the standpoint of this male "visitor." The art of the novel is also very much bound up with the art of leaving the reader to fill the gaps.

I could have analysed Sarah Woodruff more than I did. But not to do so was a conscious decision. One strong reason was that I think women are far less amenable to analysis than men—for a number of historical and biological reasons, but primarily because the ill wind of their past exploitation has brought one good: a kind of common exile that permits them to stand outside the ritual games and role-mania of the average male. Sarah Woodruff was deliberately created to suggest this "beneficial" side of the historical exile—which is closely linked to the presently needed "gifts" I mentioned just now.

Contrary to what many of the critics have said, we felt that the distinction in the novel between Daniel Martin and his "ill-concealed ghost" was beau-tifully sustained.

There were only two places where the relationship between them seemed, stylistically, to break down: the first was the decision of the orchard and the second in the concluding paragraphs of the book. Why, at the two most cru-cial points of enlightened dilemma does the author need to stand between Daniel Martin and his [DM's] own intentions?

I can't really answer this. They are two points where author and character converge. I certainly didn't mean to stand "between" Daniel and his future, but beside him or with him. Fraternally.

In a recent television interview, you described yourself as a socialist on several occasions, denied being a "political being," and said that should the equivalent of the French "Les Verts" party [a radical ecologist movement] exist in Britain you would feel closest to it. Could you clarify the relationship among these statements?

The notion of "scientists and sociologists" being the only people able to take correct decisions in a complex industrial society is something else you mentioned. How does this idea square with the more serious question of which class controls the levers of society?

I have all my adult life been torn between a biological and political view of society. I am not a political being because I don't enter actively into politics. I would count myself a socialist, or a radical, because I would much rather see a government of the left in any country than one of the right.

But the other side of me cannot stomach the belief the left shares with the right: that ever-increasing industrialisation is the only solution. However high the wages, however great the worker control, I can see along this road only enduring alienation. The worker can own the means of production. But he will never happily own the repetitive and life-stultifying daily boredom of much actual production.

This is certainly far worse in a capitalist society, but I don't think the removal of capitalism alone will marry man to his full humanity. The prime problem of our world is biological rather than political. The chase, East and West, after higher wages, mounting consumerism, is just opium to dull the basic horror of gross overpopulation and its concomitant gross under-education.

I loathe the Labour Government's current attempt to indoctrinate school-children with the notion of production as the supreme good, i.e., to turn them into brainwashed work-donkeys who can be fed synthetic carrots. This fits in perfectly with their philistine contempt for the arts in general. They don't want ordinary people to live culturally richer and more thinking lives. The only viable supreme goods are the healthy form of those two basic incompatible desires in each of us: self-knowledge and concern for others.

Increased access to money will never break the hegemony. Any socialism that devotes almost all its time and energy to solely economic gain is cutting its own throat: feeding more of the same old poison. In every class, richer men seldom discover an increased desire for social equality. Far more frequently they turn embryo Tories—example: the Labour Party in South Wales.

A true socialism has to find new ends and ambitions for mankind; not the vicious spiral of ever-increasing manufacture and consumption, all pleasure in existence reduced to buying and spending. Only a massive disintoxication will get us through the straits ahead. I don't believe politicians alone will ever dare institute it, since they keep power by continuing the intoxication.

Who should theoretically control society is less important to me than what actually controls it: money, greed.

That can be countered only by an intelligent socialism—but intelligent enough to take account of conditions its founders, from Rousseau on, could not have foreseen—principally that vile joker in the biological pack, overpopulation.

You have said before that you see yourself, in part, as a writer with a didactic role to play. Understandably, you are keen for your work to speak for itself.

However, it would be helpful if you could comment on your attitude to the relation between politics and literature—particularly in the light of the damage done to this question by the dogmatic Stalinist school of art.

I doubt profoundly whether the novel is the place for political propaganda, except perhaps in its satirical-fable form, or for serious political analysis. Other modes and media are now far more apt for direct effect. I am intensely opposed to all externally imposed interference in the arts. This was the most damaging of all the doctrinal blunders of the Stalinists. All serious artists are born contrasuggestibles, odd persons out. But no society can stay healthy without their criticism.

Would it be fair to say that you are less critical of Samuel Beckett's vision and James Joyce's form than of those writers and critics who have sought to transform these into a rule of thumb for the modern writer?

Yes. All three are great writers, and all three have had disastrous effects on countless lesser ones. I think there is a close parallel with the Romantic period, with Chateaubriand, Byron and their brood: there too we see the retreat of genius into convolution, self and *angst,* followed by an endless swarm of inauthentic scribbles trading on a fad . . . and the first dose of modern fascism in the outside world.

Furthermore, would this explain your sympathy with George Lukács, who cogently argued that the tragedy of modern art was its movement away from its real social basis?

Yes, very much so. The interesting question is to what extent "real social basis" implies stylistic and thematic realism. I have very little time for the fashionable theory that you can't criticise a society unless you first smash the traditional art forms. Unfortunately that only too often also smashes the common sign-system between artist and general audience. Which leaves him preaching to a converted elite.

"I believe that it is wrong to interpret the works of a major writer on the basis of their own theories. If these works are important it is almost always because they can achieve a form which can render the conflicts of their times at the fullest range within the given historical reality." Does Lukács' comment concur with your own distaste for "revealing" your own "theories" to the media?

The key word here is "interpret." In the strict context "to interpret the works for their social value") then obviously Lukacs is right. On the other hand there is a place for examining how the artist *thinks* that he (sic) achieves his (sic) socially valid form. I know the engine for my own books is an unresolved psychological dilemma—almost a dialectic.

It has little influence on the general tenor of *where* a book goes, but it can affect narrative shape and confrontations of character quite deeply. It is *why* the book goes, if it does. I don't see a conflict here. Lukacs was talking of external value. I speak of internal mechanism. The first is clearly more important than the second—the ship is its voyage, not its construction plan. But if the design "works," there must be some value in knowing the designer's own view of its genesis—and by no means, in literature, just because it works as he intended.

It may be very useful to find out why it works as he didn't intend, as Lukacs himself showed in his examination of Walter Scott. I suspect a very interesting case for some future Lukács is Evelyn Waugh, where overt beliefs and actual effects seem to me highly contradictory. I am not quite sure why the left's favorite literary devil is also very arguably the one who did the most damage to his own side.

Staying Green: An Interview with John Fowles the Novelist

Devon McNamara / 1979

From *The Christian Science Monitor* (February 1, 1979), 20, 21. Reprinted by permission of Devon McNamara.

John Fowles has been called the most important novelist now writing in English. In 1977, *Daniel Martin,* a profoundly moral book about the rebirth of love, and, in his words, "intended as a defense and illustration of an unfashionable philosophy, humanism," illuminated an already illustrious career which includes *The Magus, The Collector, The Ebony Tower,* and *The French Lieutenant's Woman,* a best seller in America for over a year. Born in Essex, England, Fowles was educated at Oxford and taught in France and Greece before turning to writing full-time. A shy, humorous, scrupulously courteous, gentle man, this master storyteller gives few interviews, but was willing to talk with the Monitor in Dorchester, where he also spoke with a group of American students, not far from his home in Lyme Regis, Dorset. Fowles told the students of the great psychic energy involved in novel writing— *Daniel Martin,* now a best seller in the United States, took seven years—and noted: "If you wonder whether you should be a novelist, the answer is no, but if you find you can't stop writing, the answer is yes." In addition to literary critic and translator, Fowles is honorary curator of the local museum in Lyme Regis. Devon McNamara put the questions to Mr. Fowles.

Daniel Martin is a rich novel of middle life, about returning to one's true geography, where one comes to know the place for the first time, to use the poet T. S. Eliot's phrase. Since your work is deeply rooted in particular landscapes, your native England, Greece, France, I can't help wondering: are you as interested in place as in people? A naturalist rather than a literary personage?

Nature is very important to me, both as a "retreat" and as a sort of bible, a place for aphorisms and texts, especially in its behaviorisms and evolutionary adaptations. I'm a nature-needer rather than a nature-lover or naturalist in the field sense of the word. I have no desire at all to be a "literary personage," whatever that means. I can usually establish a much richer and better relationship with the surrounding nature, wherever I am, than with the surrounding human beings. I think that's mainly because the only kind of relationship I value is the one-to-one, and that's much easier for me to make with a nonhuman object. Knowing the place for the first time is for me a repetitive process, not some sort of single climactic event. There are always knowings for the first time, on even the simplest or most familiar return . . . if one knows how to look for them.

Do you see the novel as a civilizing force? Your screenwriter-turned-novelist hero, Daniel Martin, says the word is the most imprecise of signs but that therein lies one of its virtues.

The novel *can* be a civilizing force. It has the potential, at least. In my view it civilizes best by refining feeling or demonstrating what I called "right feeling" in *Daniel Martin*. This seems to me more its function than advocating specific moral or political attitudes, whose proper medium lies elsewhere. After all, its basic context is one-to-one—one writer meets one reader, however many copies are sold. All sorts of relationships are legitimate inside that context, but not a hectoring one. The novel is also a very important "nature reserve" for language, and encourages the pleasure uses of language—being able to create images from printed symbols. What terrifies me is an increasing lack of ability in children to do this . . . words losing their colors, their histories, their echoes, their emotive values. The metaphor is the miracle of higher civilization.

One of your fascinating characters, "Herr Professor," says the Egyptians perceived how the greatest tool of knowing is the symbol that allows you to bring what is not present before your eyes. Two of your books have been filmed, *The Collector* and *The Magus*. What did you think of the translation of these metaphors into cinema?

I found the film of *The Collector* disappointing, though I have respect for William Wyler personally and for much of his other work. The movie of *The Magus* was disastrously awful. I do find something distressingly amoral in the very nature of film and TV—possibly because the photographed image denies the spectator virtually all use of his own imaginative powers. Whereas reading requires a constant use of the reader's imagination. Also I find films generally fat and flabby, the result of all the details the movie frame has to include which the poem or the novel doesn't.

And actors can limit a character for readers if they see the film first, can't they? Yet do any of your characters reveal the full depth of *your* own feelings?

My characters never show the depth of my feelings and they would be wrong if they did. You have to leave a space for the reader's feelings to meet yours. Half the art of the novel is leaving-out—what you don't say, or explain, or make clear. Americans are not very good at understanding this, despite many great American poets and novelists who have understood it perfectly.

One of the great, energizing images of all your work might be called the green world, a kind of Eden, the childhood which we lose but which never loses us. Daniel Martin says, "Ban the green from your life, and what are you left with?" Yet how are we to stay green?

I think innocence and greenness seem unattainable only in a culture sick with complexity. I do not regard present Western capitalist society as free at all, mainly because its only real freedom—to choose how one lives and which ends to follow—is available to so very few. Nine-tenths of the energy and resources of such societies go into making humans think what they don't believe, buy what they don't need, race with the other rats, and so on. Admittedly our societies are much subtler, softer and silkier than the Communist brand—much more a skilled seduction and corruption job than jack-boots and party tyranny. The fact that we do at least allow the possibility of individual freedom does give us a moral edge, but I think it is rather less than Western propagandists generally claim.

You spoke to the American students about the self-destructive nature of a fashionable despair . . . are you optimistic about the survival of civilization?

I don't have much time for the notion that life is black, absurd, futile— especially when it becomes synonymous with intellectual chic. Though I admire Kafka and Beckett as handlers of language, I think they are poor philosophers and prophets. Some very rough times may be ahead for humanity in social and biological terms, but I don't feel particularly gloomy about them. I'd say the chances were about even that we shall come through to a saner world.

All your characters seem to want freedom, and I like one of your definitions of God as the freedom that allows other freedoms to exist. It seems an excellent definition of art, as well. Are artists the freest members of our society?

Yes, I think artists are probably the most free in present society—or can be, if they choose. A lot do not, usually for reasons of vanity or greed. Being free (or comparatively free) is a very difficult art, partly because the entire weight of our educational systems has long been devoted to teaching young people to conform to society and to the supposed social gods who demand the making of money, obedience to superior cogs in the machine, who regard leisure as something that has to be earned by hard work, and so on. Choosing to do only what one wants to do, even to being bone-idle, requires faculties and knowledge almost gone from the world. Working slaves can never believe this. A week of the sort of life I lead would drive most executives insane with its apparent aimlessness, its endless chain of sideways inconsequences, its lack of structure. Their natures are conditioned to the machine, my machine is conditioned to nature.

What about time? The hero of *The French Lieutenant's Woman* says most people accept an illusion about it, that it's a "road—on which one can constantly see where one was and where one probably will be—instead of the truth: that time is a room, a *now* so close to us that we regularly fail to see it." Your characters experience dislocations in time . . . one says, the past lives by love.

Novelists need a sharp sense of time in one sense—of being able to re-create a period—and a dull sense in another—that is, in their sense of what is meant by the "present." I have always felt it very easy to feel present in other people's presents, however remote chronologically. One can't acquire this gift, of course—one is born with or without it. It means a way that we can "feel" the past alive; a very useful experience when one is trying to bring a fictional past into life.

The French Lieutenant's Woman is a re-creation of Victorian life. You talk about money in that novel, and your hero rejects the "notion of possession as the purpose of life, whether it be of a woman's body, or of high profit at all costs, or of the right to dictate the speed of progress."

I think the lust to possess is the single nastiest aspect of Western man—or rather the confusion between the lust to possess (evil) and the lust to experience (good). I loathe it above all when great art is involved. Millionaires who put Rembrandts in bank vaults are beyond contempt.

There's a great struggle with the female principle going on in our culture right now. Adrienne Rich, the American poet, writes of getting to some spot where she could look back to earth, "the wildwood/where the split began," where the sexes got separated from each other. Does the idea of being man-womanly and woman-manly, as Virginia Woolf put it, make sense for you as a writer?

Like most male artists, I have to live with a strong female anima; just as most women artists have to live with a strong male one. I have not the least desire to get back (or forward) to some unisex utopia. Gender difference is a vital source of energy, and profoundly civilizing in evolutionary terms. Liberationists who think this polarity or tension is a mere result of historical male chauvinism are profoundly wrong. It has been vilely exploited by man, but that's not the same thing.

What about books? Have they influenced you?

At my age the major influence on a writer is always his own past work. Influence-tracing is one of those stupid rituals unimaginative academics go in for. Hardy influenced me years ago. So did D. H. Lawrence, André Gide, Flaubert and a hundred others; and so did every book I have ever read, one way or another. All the late-acquired tastes and fads, in any writer, seem to me profoundly trivial beside the mystery of what turned him or her into a writer in the first place.

I wonder about the systematic academic study of literature. As a matter of fact you'd become a dissertation topic yourself.

It seems to me the academic study of literature is obsessed with tying on labels and price tickets and the dissection of corpses. It's as though biology had not moved on from the Linnaean system. Biology's now concerned with how the living creature functions socially and individually. But the academic approach to literature still hasn't taken that step.

You have published "A revised version" of *The Magus,* a novel for which you were much celebrated in the '60s, and in the introduction you say *The Magus* represents a basically adolescent longing to transcend words, to write something beyond the literary. Doesn't that longing keep us "green"? In that sense it must be your real "first novel."

It all depends on what value you attach to "adolescence." Most of the great lyric poetry of the world has been written by adolescents, or people who have only just left that age. Unfortunately the novel is much more earthbound than poetry and needs the kind of linguistic skills few of us acquire before our fourth decade. Instead of transcending language, most first novels are crushed by lack of knowing how to use it. I set out to revise *The Magus* much more heavily than I finally did; but then decided that staying green was as good as growing wise.

John Fowles

Christopher Bigsby / 1979

From *The Radical Imagination and the Liberal Tradition: Interviews with English and American Novelists* (London: Junction Books, 1982), 114–25. Reprinted by permission of Christopher Bigsby.

CB: Does the novelist's desire to transform the real coexist with a political desire to alter society, or is it a sublimation of it? Have you been tempted to political action?

JF: No. I make what is perhaps a peculiar distinction between desires and dreams. I have a dream of an altered society, and cherish that but don't lose much sleep over desires I know I can't fulfil in practical terms. The most useful working quality in any politician is a lack of imagination. Novelists are ruled out. In any case, the novel is not the literary medium in which to advocate political action of a direct kind, simply because it never works. It has of course in the past helped remedy various social outrages. But I think its main power, in this context, is in enlarging or focusing sensibility— changing climates a little, not inspiring action directly.

CB: While hardly a recluse you don't throw yourself into the public arena or even play a public role in the literary world. Do you feel in some degree an exile from contemporary England or from an English tradition in writing. Are you buying your freedom with isolation?

JF: I feel exiled from many present English conceptions of society, social behaviour and so on. I think the notion of an English "literary world" exists only in the kind of people who run literary organizations. We have no "community of letters" that I have ever discovered. I feel in no way whatever exiled from the English tradition in a broad sense, though by the hazard of existence I am probably a bit more at home in French literature than most native writers today. I do find a lot of contemporary English fiction abysmally parochial, and of no conceivable interest to anyone who is not English and middle-class. I buy freedom with isolation in this sense.

CB: And you see the novel as itself an instrument of freedom.

JF: It is certainly an instrument for freedom—if self-knowledge is freedom—for the writer. But even the form itself, mainly because it is not a community art and because it is in economic terms cheap to produce, is potentially a freedom. Communication through printed symbol requires almost as much effort and "creativity"—and as much sensitivity—from the recipient as from the sender, though much of this takes place in the reader at an unconscious level. In a sense all art is inherently totalitarian. Someone is trying to stamp his or her own sensibility and philosophy on someone else. The fact that the novel is handsomely the most despised of the contemporary major art forms in this country is of course painful for all of us who write fiction, but I suspect it also proves that the novel allows a greater freedom of reaction, and far more than the other narrative forms like the play and the film. There the audience is awed by spectacle and cost and has all the moment-to-moment imagining done for it by the visual image.

CB: The central character of *The French Lieutenant's Woman* sees himself as a liberal. If I'm right in thinking that your own convictions are liberal/ socialist, what is the difference between your own liberalism and his?

JF: A century of intellectual ferment. My sympathies lie in present terms with the left wing of the Labour Party, though I have some quarrels even there.

CB: You have implied (in "Notes on an Unfinished Novel" and in *The French Lieutenant's Woman*) that we live in an age which is out to exterminate both the individual and the enduring. Isn't it arguable that in former ages freedom was simply a class prerogative and hence was illusory for the mass of people, and that there is now a swing back to respect for the enduring— indeed to a form of conservatism which is political as well as cultural in form?

JF: A key phrase for me here is Gramsci's "cultural hegemony"—the very cunning and sophisticated systems of brainwashing that so-called democratic Western societies have evolved to keep the ordinary man and woman passive and sheeplike. Of course economic and cultural freedom was and is largely a class prerogative, but how you should think conservatism can remedy that is beyond me. In a historical sense I am not at all sure that for most people the political and economic non-freedom of this country before the Industrial Revolution was *culturally* worse than the alleged freedom since. People who are shocked by this should read Pastor Moritz's *Journeys in England* of 1782.

CB: Of course I don't think that conservatism can remedy this. In many ways it's the root of the problem. What I meant was that far from living in an age which is out to exterminate the enduring we seem to be living in an age with an undue respect for the enduring—at least in political terms. Right-wing conservatives struggle to sustain an England which has long since disappeared; left-wing socialists still believe in nineteenth-century economic theories and seek to preserve a model of England based on the political realities of the thirties, and a model of union structure based on the craft guilds.

JF: I didn't fully take your point. By "enduring" I didn't of course mean what are merely by-products of class or personal selfishness. I was thinking more of things like built-in obsolescence, exploitation of natural resources, contempt for craftsmanship . . . and of certain values on the more intellectual side, such as a historical sense, community feeling, self-reliance, all the qualities that the over-powerful state, whether left, right or centre, tends to sap and diminish. The trouble is that many of these "qualities" are simply forces, like electricity or nuclear power, and capable of serving very different ends. A historical sense can become a blindness to the present: community feeling, community brainwashing, self-reliance, a justification for economic greed, and so on. No doubt the threat to these ancient and potentially good values is simply the cost of social, economic, and technological advance in other ways. I still think it is a cost that the political left in particular persistently under-rates. My general sympathy for the left does here get trumped by my biological beliefs. But then socialism's weakest point has always been in its attitude to nature and the natural sciences, which is far more damaging to it than its other and notorious inability to come to terms with art. The recent rise of the "Green" parties all over Europe is in my view a direct result of this.

CB: It seems to me that there is a continuing debate in your work about the reality and extent of individual freedom. Your protagonist in *The French Lieutenant's Woman* is a Darwinian in a tussle with social determinisms—that is, he seeks a freedom of action which, in a fundamental sense, he doesn't wholly believe in. On the whole you seem to insist on the reality and even the moral necessity of that freedom. How do you relate that to your strong interest in a natural world which is contingent and determined?

JF: For most of my life I've been more interested in the natural sciences and in history than in literature. Behaviorism and evolutionary adaptations, in both human and non-human nature, fascinate me. My only sustained interest in the study of fiction concerns my own natural history (and behaviorism) as a writer, oneself as guinea-pig. I simply don't know the answer to the old enigma of free will. In many ways I get more and more dubious of its exis-

tence as I grow older, and (for instance) now regard many past and supposedly "free" decisions of my own as clearly conditioned; and especially in
terms of choices taken during writing as regards character destinies and
courses of events. But I am convinced there are degrees of being conditioned
and that there is an area where many people—if society allows—can achieve
moments or periods of comparative freedom. I think it is very necessary to
cling to that, until science can categorically prove that all is conditioned. I
now think of existentialism as a kind of literary metaphor, a wish fulfilment.
I long ago began to doubt whether it had any true philosophical value in
many of its assertions about freedom.

CB: Again and again I'm struck by the lyricism which you find in the
natural world and which often stands in contrast to the prosaic formulae of
human relationships and customs. And yet isn't that lyricism a false standard? The natural world is beautiful, calm, and restorative precisely because
it lacks the anguished self-doubt and personal and ideological conflicts of the
human world; it lacks that drive for meaning and purpose which provides
both the irony and the impetus for change in human affairs.

JF: Nature may lack some of the things you name (though surely not
"personal conflict"), but you seem to be putting an extreme case, where the
nature-lover attempts to turn *enfant sauvage*—or retreats to the blue lagoon.
I hold no brief for that. Of course the "restorative" in any aspect of existence
may finally be dangerous, but I can't see why one must distrust a central
experience because of a potential danger in it. Even if nature itself is
"amoral," our actual human relationship with it creates all sorts of moral
problems, such as this one you've just raised. Nor do I understand at all what
you mean by nature lacking "a drive for meaning and purpose," which seems
to imply there is no connection between human and non-human (or self-
conscious and instinctive) drives. I see no hard frontier there, especially in
matters like territorial impulse. A great deal of human behavior (in ordinary
conversation, for example) is quite unconsciously territorial in its characteristic sequences of assertion, backing-down, "distraction behavior" and the rest.
Human males don't actually perch on their rooftops endlessly rehearsing their
favorite operatic arias. But certain tunes have them—and most women—by
heart.

Nature is above all for me rich in similes and metaphors of man. It is the
poetry to the "prose" of human behavior, but not just lyrical poetry. I would
claim my own experience of nature informs my work in many different ways.

I've never been too fond of the strictly lyrical approach, in fact, except in a few poets of genius, and one or two prose writers like Thoreau and Jefferies. Even those last two I much prefer for their philosophical or quasi-religious understanding of nature.

CB: You clearly try to get your reader to enact his or her own freedom, particularly in *The French Lieutenant's Woman,* by making him collaborate in imaginatively developing possibilities. For although all readers are in some degree inventors and can ostensibly project the narrative lines along parabolas of their own choice, you have yourself created those possibilities. That is a problem also in *The Magus* and is recognized as such by the protagonist who is uncertain as to whether his options have not perhaps been created for him by hypnotic suggestion or sheer conspiracy. How real, then, is the freedom which you offer. And, by extension, how real is the freedom which you seem to believe the individual has in a world surely shaped by hereditary and environmental forces of an unpredictable and unquantifiable kind?

JF: Good question, and one I was very aware of during the writing of *The French Lieutenant's Woman,* as a close reading of some passages will reveal. In an internal sense, textually, I do not think a novelist can offer freedom to his readers, however aleatory his technique, however many forks he offers, however many "clues" he suppresses. This is especially true in narrative and character terms. On the other hand, I think there is some sort of metaphorical truth in the use of alternative situations—that is, it suggests to the reader a possible method of escape in terms of her or his own life and its fictions and realities. It can't of course offer the actual escape itself. This isn't quite pure theory on my part. I am fortunate in getting plenty of letters from readers, and some at least have understood this function (the exemplary intention of the device in the book) rather better than the many academic students of the text.

The feedback from readers is in my view most important for a novelist—even when it is hostile—and I suspect most British novelists suffer increasingly from not receiving it. One can discover a great deal about contemporary sensibilities, needs, lacks, yearnings, from such letters and all this fertilizes one's work. If one's only feedback is from reviewers—especially English reviewers—one is seeing only half the reality. I know Doris Lessing feels exactly the same about this. It also partly accounts for my being something of a hermit in everyday terms. But I am a hermit who receives several hundred letters a year, and often very human and revealing ones, from complete strangers.

CB: Why do you associate freedom with women in your work?

JF: Because there is abundant historical evidence of a connection between periods of political and cultural progress (such as the Renaissance) and wider recognition of the feminine principle. I don't think it is worth arguing whether enhanced status for women follows an increased general liberalism, or vice versa; what is clear is that, once in motion, the two things feed each other. I can't see history as being solely determined by public events; I should have thought most public events are determined by social climates.

CB: Couldn't it be argued that the woman born out of her time, like the heroine of *The French Lieutenant's Woman,* and hence able to operate as the agent of change, may simply seem free because the rules she obeys are not yet socially enforced?

JF: Very possibly, but I don't see why this diminishes such a woman's value as precursor.

CB: No, but it may limit her value as an image of freedom if she simply stands for a different set of constraints.

JF: This seems to me a very idealistic objection. I don't see how any human can do more than predicate, in theory or behavior, a more humane future social system. Inevitably that system, if it comes into being, will one day reveal faults and constraints of a different kind. I cannot conceive how any "agent of change" could ever achieve a total, once-and-for-all freedom. Human examples and images of personal freedom must surely always be very comparative—adulterated by what is being escaped from, and therefore adulterating what is being escaped to.

CB: Both Sarah, in *The French Lieutenant's Woman,* and Lily, in *The Magus,* use sexuality as part of the process of moral education. And yet aren't they both guilty of an immorality more fundamental than a matter of sexual ethics in that both, in manipulating the other, become violators of what Hawthorne would have called "the human heart," that is, they break some kind of moral contract.

JF: It has to be an excessively fastidious morality that condemns an oppressed race, class or sex for using the same weapons as its enemy. It is certainly not an evolutionary morality. Nor do I see how a contract that allows me an unfair privilege and denies you a just right can be termed "moral." Whether or not there was a heuristic, liberating and "good" motive behind my imaginary Sarah seems to me not very important beside the fact that many such women, with such motives, have really existed.

CB: That strikes me as a little disingenuous. After all, the conspiracy in *The Magus* is directed to bringing home to the protagonist his selfishness— the fact that he violates the emotional integrity of others for his own purposes. My worry about Sarah and Lily is not that they use sexuality (as you rightly say, in a sense they are simply turning a weapon back on the sex which has always tended to see this weapon as its own prerogative) but that in doing so they become guilty of that same moral failing which Lily at least had set out to purge from the protagonist.

JF: Perhaps what is really revealed here is my intense dislike of general moral principles, or arguing solely from them. I've always found what one might call the algebraic side of ethics—"All actions of type *y* are bad"— distinctly scholastic. Particular cases are very different. I'm not denying that inductively achieved moral principles are usually unjustifiable, and so on. *The Magus* was of course a deliberately artificial, model-proposing novel, and a good deal more about fiction than any "real" situation, and I shouldn't go to the stake for Lily's morality (or her master's). Sarah in *The French Lieutenant's Woman* was always intended to be a sort of borderline case. I've long reached the conclusion that one principal function of the novel, or at least of my own novels, is to present such borderline cases. *Daniel Martin* was very intentionally conceived as such a one. I had during the writing harbored the notion that he would end by some fairly serious political "com- mitment"—perhaps to one of the Marxist parties—but realized when it came to it that bathos was needed. So put him in the Labour Party. On grounds of "pure" principle, I think he has no case at all. But do any of us?

CB: You imply that Charles's defect in *The French Lieutenant's Woman* was that he failed to recognize the power of passion and the imagination. Is this a critique of liberalism, which finds passion as difficult a subject as mystery?

JF: Yes. Of humanism also.

CB: You have said that you see man as a kind of artifice and woman as a kind of reality; the former as cold idea, the latter as warm fact. Isn't that a form of sentimentality, almost setting one up as the ego and the other as id?

JF: I don't think so, but on the contrary something true of the two sexes, for both biological and cultural reasons. There are of course many gradations from female males (no male novelist needs to be told why Hemingway felt obliged to wear such a *macho* face in public) to male females; and in the worst times of exploitation, such as the Victorian period, women have largely worn male faces and gone in just as stupidly for social status, kowtowing to authority and all the rest. But I still think that most men, and still today, are over-obsessed by order, logic and theory—that is, by various abstract games systems that allow them to compete more or less ritually for artificial status—and women by the contrary qualities, which also have their faults. I am not talking of values, or saying that in some way female qualities are *ipso facto* "better" than male ones, or denying that logic and order have important virtues, but in terms of essential and mutually indispensable natures.

CB: You react in your novels against social coercions and yet fiction is also a coercer, perhaps never more so that when it falsely pretends to surrender that power—a lesson clear enough from *The Magus.* Have you ever been tempted by more radical disjunctions of your narrative—the box novel, the novel organized by chance principle? Is it a resolvable paradox?

JF: No. The purest aleatory technique and end product must always be caused by an original conscious and non-aleatory decision to write so. I regard all this as twentieth century rococo; I'd be happy to regard it as amusing nonsense . . . if only its creators would. The shock disjunction is the oldest trick in the world in one profession: that of the clown. The Monty Python group owe their success very much to their brilliant use of it.

CB: Some of your more sympathetic characters are deceivers. Their deceptions are justified by the fact that they deceive in the name of moral truth. Isn't that a very dangerous principle to endorse?

JF: If you take the novel as a straight reflection of reality, or desirable reality. I think of it much more in metaphorical or parable terms. And even if it is a dangerous principle, I must point out that it is deeply imbedded in the evolutionary system, which might be described as the triumph of intelligence over deception.

CB: Do you believe in evil? I'm thinking in particular of the German torturers in *The Magus.*

JF: Only as a very loose and vague (but useful) word applied to certain kinds of moral reaction to certain kinds of human behavior. In a supernatural or religious sense, not at all. The exploitation of the Devil-myth by some contemporary writers and movie-makers does not appeal to me one bit. That is evil.

CB: There is a strong narrative drive in your work, a commitment to narrative, and yet there is an almost equally powerful urge to disrupt that narrative.

Is that the outward expression of a debate in your mind between a liberal belief in causality, character, life as a process of discovery, and a sense of the contingent.

JF: I'm afraid I give good story-tellers far more credit than they deserve by other literary standards: and devalue writers who depend more on stylistic gifts than narrative ones. I don't defend this; it's simply the way I am. I do like the part hazard plays in evolution—and ordinary life—but nine times out of ten I break up or jump-cut straight narrative purely for fun . . . and also because readers seem to enjoy it, even if reviewers don't.

CB: The narrator in *Daniel Martin* says that the desire to create imaginary worlds is strongly linked with the notion of retreat. Do you see writing as in some ways expressing a failure of moral will?

JF: Not at all. A lack of politically activist will, perhaps. Novelists are all egoists, narcissists, parties of one, from the greatest to the least. But that is our principal social function—not to join, not to be what the contemporary state considers safe citizens. That can take rather more moral will, patience and courage than most non-writers ever care to realize.

CB: Yours was a generation which was confronted with matters of public policy which seemed to demand a personal moral response in a way which, perhaps, had not been quite so true for previous generations. *Daniel Martin* seems to suggest that a generation had failed in its responsibilities. What was the essence of that failure? A failure of action or imagination?

JF: Both, but I suspect they are only symptoms of the underlying cause, which was, and remains, a retreat into the self—a deep conviction that personal destiny matters more than public destiny. My generation developed (or had developed in us by world events 1939–49) a deep cynicism about anything that smacked of ideals and absolutes, indeed about all existing social and political theory. Our tacit motto became the old Navy catchphrase, "Jack's inboard." If I'm all right, to hell with you. Our self-fascination was certainly also aggravated by the fall in international status. This new treachery of the clerks has bred the dominant public spirit among the British intelligentsia during these last two decades: that of satire and sour grapes, of carping, complaining, cutting down to size, while I suspect the inward spirit—the underlying ethic, or lack of it—shows some curious parallels with seventeenth-century quietism. I am not suggesting that our self-defensive scepticism in public matters had not brought about some healthy demolition. One could argue that the main failure of my generation is not that we did not resist all this, but that we did not push it farther and destroy more. Instead, most of us in the professional middle classes have settled for Toryism, defence of a doomed system and comfortable fifth-rate lives. I think the bill is beginning to come in now.

Of course generations of moral failure—I'd rather say who fail to adapt to their historical situation—are commonplace in history, and perhaps because of our puritan conscience, especially familiar in British history. I don't think we're any worse than, say, the generations in power 1660–89 or 1890–1914.

CB: Although you seem to imply that the present younger generation displays a kind of honesty, at least in its idea of human relationships. Couldn't this be a form of sentimentality?

JF: A lot of it may seem sentimental to the jaundiced eyes of my class and generation. But I see sentimentality as an excess of a good thing, not of an already bad one. For me the Romantic Movement and the French Revolution are the same phenomenon. The best thing that could happen to the 1980s is the 1740s—a dawn of a swing on that old mind-heart pendulum.

CB: I know that you have said you were influenced by Zen in the sixties. Is that principally in the need for a sensitivity to the nature of your surroundings or in its concern with pursuing a transcendent self?

JF: I was at that time becoming far too science-besotted in my relationship with nature. Zen rescued me from that. I have no interest in its theology. I dislike all transcendental religion, and especially the oriental kind. However, I greatly admire some Zen "aids" to experiencing and seeing. I try now to experience nature in both ways.

CB: You are constantly debating the significance of first and third person narration in your novels, as much as in your critical essays. What is the significance of that problem to you?

JF: Whichever person I start a novel in, I very soon begin feeling its restrictions, and remembering the liberties of the other. I think I'm settling towards the third now. The omnipotent power of gravity in the novel form is realism. I resist it less and less.

CB: What do you mean by realism?

JF: What is generally meant by the word. The attempt to reflect life, both in style and content, as it is *seen* by the majority; though not necessarily, of course, as it is *valued* by the majority. I suppose I mean something like "traditional technique but original vision," which on the first ground would exclude Kafka and the later Joyce. For me Flaubert would serve as a paragon of realism or Lukács's hero, Thomas Mann. I don't in the least mean by this that I am in some way opposed to innovative technique. I am very certain that Joyce is the greatest novelist of this century. The liberty to express oneself as one pleases is the fundamental right of every artist, and I have no time for any literary theory or "party" that challenges the general principle.

I suspect the crucial thing, in the novel, is how the novelist conceives of audience. My own preferred contract is in the middle ground, and I am not ashamed of being widely read, since in my view that must always be an implicit hope in this particular choice (just as there are equally legitimate choices of audience that must exclude it). To the extent that liberalism is a teaching or converting belief, then I think realism must always hold a powerful attraction to "liberal" writers; conversely, the always lurking suspicion of elitism in experimental or highly intellectual writing (in the novel) will repel them. So will strict "socialist realism," in another direction.

I don't think one has to argue with the neo-Marxist view that the novel is an adamantly bourgeois form. This is just a way of saying that all art is elitist of its nature—beyond the majority in creation and very often beyond the majority in comprehension. All would-be egalitarian theories of art have their bottoms ripped out on the same reef: art may preach equality, but there will never be equality in the preaching, or among the preachers.

CB: *Daniel Martin* clearly relies on certain cinematic techniques, and yet you are suspicious of the deadening power of the cinema itself. Can the novel usefully derive anything from the cinema?

JF: Quite a lot in technical terms, especially since all our conscious, and unconscious, imaging powers as we read—or dream—are now geared to "seeing" narration in cinematic terms. I am sure it is also very useful for a novelist to be clear on what the novel can do that the cinema can't. I read too many writers who seem hell-bent on writing what the cinema can usually do much better . . . and quite as much out of lack of thought as love of money. Deliberately writing a pseudo-scenario to ensure movie rights is bad enough; but writing one out of sheer ignorance of the special capacities of the novel form is absurd.

CB: In *The Collector* you draw a picture of an individual manipulated for selfish ends, in *The Magus* for selfless ends. Is the manipulation of others, then, to be seen as morally neutral, a condition of existence? If so, doesn't that open the door to the self-righteous despot, not to mention the didactic novelist?

JF: The manipulation of others is certainly an almost universal condition of existence, in nature as well as man. I do not see why a necessary condition predicates moral neutrality; of course we must judge each human case for itself. I regard "didactic" as a descriptive term, not necessarily an accusatory one. Speaking for myself, I soon lose interest in novelists who do not show their prejudices and their opinions, who do not try to sell me something beyond entertainment, wit, clever technique, exquisite prose . . . not that those aren't added pleasures.

CB: Like your narrator in *Daniel Martin* you have written stories which avoid happy endings. Is that a fear of endings as such?

JF: The passage where Daniel Martin worries about his fear of the happy ending is strictly autobiographical. Ending fictions has always given me terrible problems, as my editors know. I think this is mainly because I find the actual writing of a novel a deeply rewarding and pleasurable experience—both emotionally and intellectually—and for me the publication is like being locked out of my own self-created paradise. My printed texts are for me dead, cold, detached objects, almost like books by someone else. I analyzed this recently in connection with Thomas Hardy, who I have a strong suspicion was in the same case. Of course one has to kill off the past text, count it as a failure, in order to gain energy and a motive for the next attempt. It is simply that for me the moment of assassination takes place while the victim is still alive, when that last chapter can be put off no longer. Whatever else I might have been, it is not a successful hit man.

An Encounter with John Fowles

Raman K. Singh / 1980

From *Journal of Modern Literature,* 8:21 (1980–81), 181–202. Reprinted by permission of the Foundation for Modern Literature.

Any man who writes *The Magus* cannot be interviewed in the proper sense of the word; he can only be encountered. The distinction is an important one. The usual format of an interview is too rigid for a man who admits that he is not logical, that he is uncomfortable with the restrictions of logical thinking. Not that he is illogical; he simply sees the limits of a purely rational mind.

Our meeting took place in the grounds and rooms of the Fowles residence in Lyme Regis, Dorset. The house is old and spacious; upstairs, if you look out from the room where he works, you see the gray Channel. The house upon the hill is bordered on one side by a garden that appears to be growing wild but is in reality carefully tended. I think of Eden; the author compares writing to gardening and plant-growing. In any case, this is not an ordinary garden.

Most of our conversation was not recorded. The introduction of a recorder, as we walked about, would have been disruptive. Only towards the end of the day, upstairs, did I feel brave enough to switch the recorder on. But even then we tried to maintain a conversational flavor, skipping freely from one topic to another.

What impressed me about your work tremendously—and I think you said in the Afterword to the French novel, The Wanderer [Le Grand Meaulnes], *that each reader gets his own meaning out of it—well, what impressed me were your characters more than anything else. And the complexities of human relationships, mainly between the male and female. I did want to talk to you about this. The way I see it, you seem to culturally unclothe the characters, see them in . . . almost an archetypal situation.*

I don't feel that. I feel I often fail because I don't reach deep enough into them. The trouble is, if you get too deep into a character you're often working against the laws of fiction. . . . A novel takes two to three years to write, and you tend to forget that a reader goes through it in four hours. It's going to be a transient experience, however well you write. Your audience isn't going to pick everything up.

Does that bother you?
   Yes, it does. This is a major technical problem for me, the selective reduc-
tion of things like the one you just mentioned, the analysis of character. I
constantly find that I've really gone too deeply for the sake of the artistic
whole.

*Well, if I can just give you at least the remarks of my students, that's what
they like about it, the fact that the characters are so deeply probed. It may
be that a university audience is somewhat different from the general public.
. . . And also, I think—we were talking about this when we were walking
around—the novels or the characters aren't really dated, [not] even in terms
of time and setting . . . and partly, I suppose, because the characters are
basically human first. They're not really mouthpieces for any ideas.*
   Well, I think consciously about the basic middle-class dilemma throughout
the work.

You do?
   I know this is rather misleading. I mean I don't sit down and think, I'm
going to write a novel about the middle-class dilemma. But . . . I write about
middle-class characters, obviously. This interests me most. The book I've
just finished is all about it.

Your latest book?
   Yes. What is good in the middle classes, what is bad in them. Have they
any surviving function at all in the world except in a few lucky countries like
America?

Do they have any such function?
   It's a threatened class. It's a dying class. This woman who was here yesterday [a university teacher of English from Turkey] kept on asking me: "What
do I tell my students?" They say to her, we live in a country surrounded by
poverty, by appalling social injustice. Who wants to read American novels,
English novels about middle-class characters? It is a problem.

*That factor is something I must have either consciously ignored or maybe I
wasn't interested in it. I'm sure it's there, especially in* The Collector, *perhaps.*
   It does concern me as a private human being. I am very conscious that
people like you and me are highly privileged. My defense is to ask, what is
the great revolution for? The end of the revolution, as Marx himself saw,

must be where all these bourgeois art forms are purified, but in their complexity they must remain the same. You can't imagine mankind living on novels about factories and production rates—or only about social injustice. It's not conceivable.

Do you see the novel as a kind of antidote for certain problems?

Yes. The one principal reason I think the novel is not in any danger as a form is that it is a marvelous changer of social sensibility. In any society on the wrong road, there's always going to be someone who writes a novel saying so; because it's a highly individual form, some writer is always ready to express what thousands of other individuals secretly feel is wrong with their society. There's no art form, actually, that can do this as well as the novel. The novel's in danger in one or two commercial ways because people watch television, they don't read any more, the growing illiteracy . . . although statistically more people can read now, the number who can read novels intelligently is sinking.

Especially poetry, too. I don't know if anybody every buys books of poems.

A high-school teacher here was telling me the other day how she has quite intelligent children who can fully understand semantically, say, a passage from Jane Austen, yet they're totally unable to visualize the leap that you and I don't even have to think about because we've read so many books. These children, there's a blank there. Between lines, they're blind.

What do you think is causing this?

I think mankind is losing the skill of reading books, especially imaginative books. The new culture is conditioned visually by television. This doesn't terribly worry me. I think the novel is going back to the eighteenth century situation, where it's a minority art form for the educated. I'm sure it's going back to that stage . . . which means less read, but not less important. You know, someone like Saul Bellow, in two hundred years' time if you want to know about America today, you will still have to read Saul Bellow.

Or another good novelist—.

Yes. Where else do you go?

I think it was Henry James or somebody who said that really we get a better sense of history out of the novel than you do out of history books.

Absolutely. That's right. So, the novel as far as I can see, is in no danger.

No, I don't think so. You're right.

But for the young novelist it's certainly a tough time. Nobody doubts it.

Then there's the business of the novel being peculiar to maturity. I don't think anyone can write a good novel under the age of thirty. It's very difficult.

I agree with you.

I've lost the reference, but I once read a fascinating statistical article on it. The average age of the greatest novel of twenty great novelists was very late, in the late fifties. Even the average age for the first novels of the same great novelists was, I think, thirty.

That's probably a good sign.

I get these kids from America who write to me—

From creative writing schools?

I have a couple of recent letters here. "I have problems with my novel. And by the way, I'm twenty-two years old." How can you create fictional worlds when you're that age? You can't do it.

I suppose it's the experience and . . . a time of self-analysis

You haven't, in your early twenties, seen enough of the world to be able to imagine other worlds. And you haven't the command of language.

Do you believe in the old theory that a novel gets written whether you want to or not, that one isn't a writer really by choice as much as one is driven by a demon?

Oh, absolutely. Totally. [An] assistant professor of psychiatry at Harvard wrote a very interesting article about *The French Lieutenant's Woman*. He treated it as a patient and analyzed the book. I don't go all the way with his analysis, but I go totally with his theory that novelists are genetically made; and then by circumstances over which you have no control in the first few years of your life.

Not talking specifically about novels, do you think most of our actions are a matter of conditioning, or is there something innate?

I think there's a tiny modicum of free will if you keep yourself very open. I think occasionally you can make a decision which is possibly free. I wouldn't like to argue this on philosophical grounds, but I sense that ninety percent of human life is conditioned. But, you see, that tiny fragment where there's a doubt is vital. All my novels are about how you achieve that possible—possibly nonexistent—freedom. The problem of seeing yourself.

And the price one has to pay—

The price one has to pay. The difficulty in the smallest reward; heaven knows you rarely see yourself clear. It comes as almost a shock.

It's terrifying. Would you say, then, that your work really portrays one or more of what one calls these passions? In other words, the search for knowledge, or whatever?

Search for self-knowledge . . . I'm an optimist in that. I think self-knowledge always does bring you—let's say in the majority of cases—does bring you greater happiness, although it's painful. It's rather like psychoanalysis, I suppose. It can be very painful in process, but I think on the whole one comes out slightly better in the end.

Which of your novels do you like the best; which is your favorite?

I like the worst best.

Which is?

The Magus.

Really?

Yes. I've just written it.

You've rewritten The Magus?

Oh yes.

You mean your next novel will be a variation of it?

No. I haven't changed the general line of the story, but I've rewritten a large, mostly the central, part.

And it will be issued as a separate book, then?

A revised edition. It always disappointed me technically. It was full of mistakes; stylistically irritated me. I missed a number of tricks and means of telling a story. It wasn't quite erotic enough. I always regretted there wasn't more of that. So I've done this very wicked thing.

Rewritten it?

Rewritten it, yes. Not all of it. First and last parts I'll hardly change.

It's a book that's had a profound influence on [young readers]. At least it sets them thinking.

Well, I do notice this a little, because it's provoked far more letters than any other of my books. I know it does, to use that horrid phrase, it does turn them on.

Yes it does. As one of [my] students said, "It blows your mind."

You know it's the first book I wrote. It's a young man's book for young people. I feel a kind of tenderness for it. I told someone the other day it's really where I taught myself to write the novel. We all need a book where we teach ourselves what the novel is.

An apprentice novel, perhaps.

That's exactly it. I can see many of the mistakes I made; I can't correct them all, but I've tried to correct some of them.

I read somewhere that you were perhaps writing a novel about how the Americans view the British or is it how the British view Americans?

No, no. I've only just finished the first draft . . . there'll be rewriting. It's basically about the English, Englishness; what are the English? I regard part of the American experience as an English experience. And so it will be partly set in America. But I'm not going to be writing about Americans, because that's difficult, a very difficult thing for us over here. Simply English people who are living in America. And it will also be about my generation, my middle-class Oxford generation of the English which, I think, is generally rather a sad and failed one.

Before The Magus *did you write a lot?*

Yes, though I began writing quite late; most novelists are at least trying in their teens. I didn't seriously start trying to write until I was in my last year at Oxford. . . . I was twenty-five then. . . . I was very fond of starting stories and dropping them, mainly because you wrote four chapters and then you read back and you realized. . . .

You were embarrassed?

Yes. You know you haven't got the command. I tried to publish one book after I lived in Greece; a travel book . . . it wasn't very good. One section I tried in fiction. That was the first fiction I ever seriously tried to write.

Did you have it published as a short story?

No. What happened, I sent it to an agent who's now become a well-known novelist, Paul Scott. Scott said, This isn't any good as a travel book, but I like the fictional section. And I'm very grateful to him, that really. . . . Well, there are tiny little pushes young writers need. I was very fond of Lawrence, and I saw this travel book about Greece as another *Sea in Sardinia,* or Henry Miller's *The Colossus of Maroussi.* I aimed at that kind of thing. Paul Scott just said, you know, take a harder look at your potentialities in fiction. I did.

I think this may be an absurd sort of question, but who would you say is the great influence or some of the greater influences on your thinking, not necessarily on your novels?

On my thinking? Certainly when I was younger, the French existentialists. I read all of Camus, most of Sartre. This one book by Alain-Fournier, *Le Grand Meaulnes,* has had an extraordinary emotional effect on me all my life. Three years ago I did a pilgrimage, went to all the places where Fournier had lived in France. This in spite of the fact that objectively I can see *Le Grand Meaulnes* is a partial failure as a novel.

Do you work very consciously with your structure? Do you make lots of notes or plans?

No. I make no plans. I'm a total believer in organic growth. I have no idea where I'm going when I start a book. There is for me a marvelous element of pure hazard about writing; you write a tiny passage, perhaps of only one sentence, and yet that somehow has nuclear energy in it. Suddenly you see that you ought to have done more about something earlier on. Or, I have to develop this, this is the way I've got to go. It's rather like gamma-ray mutation in evolutionary biology. I also believe in the old Greek *loxodromia,* the zig-zag principle. You know the Greeks had this theory of the golden mean, the perfect true road in philosophy. And that you reach the golden mean by going too much to one side, then gradually knowing you're going too far. And then you start going the other way. I think when I write I'm always vaguely conscious of this. In simple terms, you're building up too much unnecessary analysis, you'd better introduce a bit of action or something else—and so on.

But you're conscious of this while you're writing, not before?

I'm totally against what I understand is the creative writing approach. You know, planning . . . structure, symbolism. I rely absolutely on . . . it would be an exaggeration to say I write first drafts in a trance-like state. It's not that. Although I'm very sympathetic to that aspect of Indian and Japanese mysticism.

That's another point. When I read The Magus *I was very impressed by what I thought were Indian parallels.*

Well, I'm afraid . . . I'm not an expert on Indian thought.

Well, that's why I use the word parallel *rather than* influence.

I mean it would be largely subconscious.

Because I can even remember, I think it's chapter 36 in The Magus *where Urfe is hypnotized or drugged—*
Yes. Yes. How extraordinary! I was just looking at that this morning.

I think it's chapter 36.
When I was writing *The Magus,* I was enormously . . . the one Indian thing I was deeply hooked on was music.

Ravi Shankar?
Yes. This was a time, the 1950s, when no one in London had yet discovered Indian music. I used to go to the Indian Music Circle with Elizabeth, and very often there would be only four white faces there. The rest would be all the London Indians in exile. There would be me, there would be Elizabeth, perhaps somebody else, and there'd always be that great violinist, Yehudi Menuhin.

Yes. Oh, he's great.
First of all the music hit me. I've never heard music like that. You know the Khans, Ali Akbar Khan? And there was a superb woman *Kathakali* dancer who used to come to London. And the kind of trance depth you get at the end of a long *raga*—I tried to get that into that scene in *The Magus.*

Now I didn't know this about you and Indian music.
I can't pretend I've ever read the *Bhagavad Gita* or anything like that. Zen Buddhism, you know, the Japanese form of it, has always interested me, but—

I found there was, there seemed to be some kind of effort to transcend one's self, or maybe even go beyond the ego, you know, which I immediately thought of as Indian thought or, at least, parallel to Indian thought.
I find Indian culture attractive, like so many Englishmen, but I can't pretend I have any deep knowledge of the Sanskrit classics.

Oh, not many do. Something not related to fiction: what are your opinions of the women's liberation movement, for instance, in America?
I'm totally for the feminine principle, as I hope all my novels prove.

How would you define the feminine principle?
In a Jungian sense, I suppose. I would say I have a feminine mind.

Creative?
Creative, not logical. I'm not a logical person.

Well, that's another thing that made me think of India. This kind of intuitive tendency towards the non-logic, the paradoxical logic.

And the Indian visual arts, the kind of prolixity and fertility you get in some temple art. I do find that very interesting.

There's also another, towards the end of that passage in the park where Urfe says, I think, "Pale men, dark men; but only one kind of woman."

Yes, I think that's true, in a way.

That would be . . . the female principle?

I think the female principle links women, while the male one separates men. There are certain aspects of women's liberation that seem to me rather silly. It always worries me when I see the feminine principle itself being attacked by women. I think there are aspects, for example, the aggressive advocation of lesbianism, that seem to me to deny it. It's not that it's worse than the gay world, but it's simply that this is denying the extraordinary half-maternal, half-mysterious aspect of women. I think they're very foolish to destroy all that.

Oh, I think so too.

I feel a great sympathy for them. They've had such a lousy deal for the last three thousand years.

What made you write The French Lieutenant's Woman *as a Victorian novel from the modern perspective?*

I'm not quite sure, really. I wrote a piece about it for a book called *Afterwords*. . . . One or two books have started on single images. I had this strange image of a woman with her back turned; that haunted me. But when it first came I had no idea of its being in the past.

It was something to do with a woman being rejected and then in some way rejecting a man. This is what I mean by this nuclear energy. And gradually it did become somebody down there where we walked today.

And then I suppose merely the fact that I collect old books—that I have a lot of Victorian books. Although I don't know the Victorian age in the historian's sense very well, I do know the by-ways, the psychological side. I don't collect novels particularly. I'm much more fond of autobiographies. I know that aspect of the Victorian age quite well.

And I also had to, and this is very important, I also had to come to terms with my own hatred of it. Like every English child of my generation, I grew up with Victorian parents and loathed it.

And that helped you overcome it?

Well, I'd long been aware through reading that I'd got the Victorians very wrong. All my generation, I think, has now realized that they had many estimable qualities.

Actually, they're more attractive people than my parents' generation, who were simply copying the real thing.

My parents' generation were, I suppose, like a certain kind of Indian who still wishes the British Raj was there; they were living a doubly phony existence.

Well, I guess you've answered that question. I'm always curious about how one gets, where one gets one's plots. Do you find that a difficult thing?

Yes.

Plotting?

I find it difficult in the sense that you're continually coming to forks.

You don't know which road to take—

And you're not quite sure, very often, which road to take. It's been a great dilemma for me. I don't think this basically matters too much. It's the quality of the chapter-by-chapter writing that's important. And also, I think it's true of life. I'd be suspicious, I'm always suspicious of beautifully automatic plots. You know, that go click, click, click. They're attractive in detective novels and films, but that's not what real life is like. Real life is far more complex and ill-functioning.

And the painful decision—

Yes, yes.

And very often you get it wrong. You write a chapter and you suddenly wake up one morning and you realize you've got to forget it. You go back and take the other fork.

Hazard. I think that's the key thing.

And you always have to look. . . .

Yes. But it doesn't frighten me. I realize I have states, what American writers call "blocks," when I don't know where I'm going, I don't know what I'm doing. I don't know what's going to happen, and I can't see any future. But for me these are fertile periods, although I can't write.

You see, you know things are turning round, they are trying to find an opening somewhere; on the circle they go, round and round. I regard that as an absolutely essential part of writing.

They're not really stumbling blocks as such, anyway.

Well, I loathe this American way of talking about the "block" as some disease that poor writers suffer from. As if it comes from outside.

Yes, right. An obstacle that might get you down—

I was talking to an English writer the other night, and he was saying, the agonies I go through! And he said how is it that you [Fowles] never get worried about your books. And I said to him, when you're worried about a book, it's a good sign. It means you're thinking, you're trying to deal with it. Improve it. You know writers are appalling self-dramatizers. They love to take a sort of movieland view of things: the tragic blocked writer hitting the bottom. Or the bottle. This is where I think the Orient, Japan, India, has it completely over the West.

Well, they think that these blocks, so called, are necessary and aren't really blocks.

I regard them as Western neuroses. I think Zen has a great deal to teach here.

Do you write haikus?

I have. I've got a whole lot I translated once from the *Thousand Leaves*. Have you ever seen the archery ceremony? The Zen archery ceremony?

I don't think so.

You know, all ritual—

On stage?

No. It's a monk's exercise. In a Zen temple. They pick up an arrow and fit it to the bow and draw it. . . .

Invisible?

They have a real bow and arrow. They draw it, and the target's there. And then it's very slow, they draw it back to full stretch, and then the marvelous thing. Where every Westerner would shoot at the target, all the Zen priest does is very, very slowly decontract the pressure and put the bow down. It's a marvelous symbolic way of saying that it's really the—

The process?

The means that matter, not the end.

These men have got to the state where they realize whether you hit the target doesn't matter.

I find that in Indian art too. It's the process you're going through which is important. . . . once the thing has ended, it's not important—
Being published really doesn't worry me any more. This is an old Western literary neurosis: get into print, I must see myself in print. . . . I'm sufficiently Western to want things to be published eventually, but I will not submit to this absurd pressure of keeping in the public eye.

I must have sensed these elements in your work.
I'm very grateful. A lot of people who write about me don't really understand this. What is deeply important for me is to nurture. There seems to be some blindness in literary critics, you know, an inability to think outside certain contexts and set disciplines. They don't think of all the lessons to be learnt from growing plants. That's another metaphor. I think writing is plant-growing; a very, very similar activity.

That's very illustrative.
It's not clock-making. This is for me an American fallacy, that book-writing is clock-making.

Precision work—
Fitting machinery together. You know, I get these extraordinary letters from American academics who obviously think that everything in my books was analyzed before I wrote it.

Pre-planned?
They expect from me a little . . . I don't know what they expect; I mean literally like, How did you put the clock together? It's like asking a plant how it grows. Of course you can tell them all sorts of things, but you can't actually tell them the basic mystery, how it took its final form.

Beyond a certain point, you can't really teach writing.
My opinion is that it's pointless to teach people who haven't got the right genetic make-up; and who haven't had the right infancy experiences—I'm a Freudian—the right kind of separation trauma . . . because I think this really is the heart of all art; you must have had the right experience of the separation of your own identity from other ones. If you have all that, then I think there's something to be said for training. In athletics you accept that unless a child has natural aptitude you don't bother to start teaching him intensively. . . . A boy wrote to me the other day and said, "I want to write a novel." I had to write back and tell him that if you have to say "I want to write a novel"

something is already wrong. The only thing you can really say is, "I cannot help but write a novel."

And then perhaps one can pick up certain rudiments of the craft.

Of course parts can be taught. But again, because the novel is the supreme expression of the individual man, I'm dubious of "creative writing." It must finally be imitative writing.

It is.

Excellent models must be put in front of you by the teacher. But I think it's much better that you should find those models yourself. Obviously, a writer should study literature, but even there. One of our best British novelists, Henry Green, was an engineer. I'm sure one place where good novels don't get written is on the bloody campus.

. . . The good thing creative writing schools do is that it teaches those who want to write novels that they cannot write novels, and they go away disillusioned. . . . Often you have to tell them that you can't really write a good novel, as you said, at the age of twenty.

Another mysterious thing is that young writers will never write about the worlds they know.

The world they know?

I don't get many, but occasionally I see manuscripts. It's extraordinary, but the younger they are the more they insist on writing about somewhere they haven't been.

And universal problems?

Universal problems. I had one last year by an English boy. It was set in Soviet Russia, where he'd never been. Absolutely extraordinary.

Do you read these manuscripts that come to you and criticize them? That's very kind of you.

Well, I get very few. That's a habit that has, thank God, dropped out. I did have one a month or two ago from a young American in Mexico. He had a certain very wild talent. But he couldn't write English! And this is another thing, a madness. I can't get across this argument that if you write, then surely you must respect things like grammar. Grammar is a bore as an academic subject, but it's the basic good manners of writing.

Have you ever recommended one of these people, who have sent you something, to a publisher?

No . . . I'm really very hot on this; I may be wrong, but as soon as I see flagrant punctuation mistakes, grammatical and spelling errors, something seems to me to insult the craft. It's like a would-be furniture maker who can't make a simple joint. Okay, it's not very important; it may be solid even though it's made badly. But somehow it shows a hatred of wood. It's very difficult to convince tyro writers of this. The book starts with love of each separate word.

Are most of your characters people you've met?
No. That's another game I don't play. You obviously draw certain traits from life; occasionally I see something physically about a person which I'll find interesting [and] I'll graft that on some character. However, I suppose, in an archetypal way. . . . Obviously the people you've lived with, and of course, above all, yourself, are the principal sources.

In many of the characters?
Yes.

Would you object to people looking at your manuscripts?
No; but I regard this side of literary research as very unimportant.

How about The Aristos?
The Aristos was largely written when I was a student. . . . I began it at Oxford, and I regard it very much as an undergraduate's book.

Well, it's very impressive.
There are some good ideas in it, but it's the most unreadable book I've written.

I would disagree with that. The form is such that you don't have to go through it [from A to Z] you can pick it up at any page or any section, and then drop it because it's all numbered. It helps the reader; it's very accessible.
Some of it seems outrageously idealistic now; it's a young man's work.

Will you write another one like that sometime?
I have thought about it. I think I'd rather put it into novels now. I have always wanted to do something on America.

American thought?
The whole of the American experiment, using that phrase in the historian's sense. That's always interesting. Where it's gone wrong. I did start five or

six years ago, but then I started reading Daniel Boorstein . . . all those people. I do foresee a novel where I might possibly put something of that in.

Where do you think America has gone wrong?

Putting it in one tiny nutshell, in confusing liberty and equality. It's extraordinary that quite intelligent Americans still assume that liberty and equality are the same. They are *mortal enemies.* They always have been. Once you give a human society liberty, then the more gifted will always start exploiting the weak. The two are not compatible, and therefore America is not an equal society at all.

Don't they perhaps also confuse sameness with equality?

Yes, yes. I would say that is a secondary product of that. I can't understand Americans talking about freedom and liberty, when all around you you see gross inequality. It's a marvelous land, if you're middle class, if you're reasonably gifted with energy and intelligence; a great, great country, no doubt about it. But heaven help you if you're not. If I put it in practical terms, the greatest disgrace of modern America is for me that there's never been a serious socialist party there. And that really is a terrible absence; they've never generated a viable—

Opposition.

The Democrats and Republicans are so similar. I think in a way America's almost too big to—

To manage?

Yes; I'm sure the geographical size is partly responsible.

It's a very romantic country.

America? Yes. I love it. It's a splendid place to visit. I always find it very stimulating; it produces many ideas. But I don't think I'd really like to live there.

You like France?

I adore France. I don't always like the French.

[*End of tape; hence break in topic of conversation*]

People still send you dissertations?

Occasionally you get a . . . I got a very good one on *The Magus* a year or two ago.

What was the general [thesis]?

A drawing of parallels between *The Magus* and *Great Expectations,* which

I had never done myself. When I read this I thought, my God, this girl's on to something. What she didn't know is that—I think I told you down on the beach—when I was writing *The Magus* I was teaching *Great Expectations*. I've never really liked Dickens, but I enjoy teaching him, and I adore *Great Expectations*. Of course I realized that all this had actually been creeping into me.

Without you being totally aware?
    I belatedly realized Conchis [in *The Magus*] is a kind of Miss Havisham figure . . . very interesting.

And, of course, Shakespeare?
    Yes. That was conscious. *The Tempest* has always been my . . . again, it's perhaps not the greatest Shakespeare play, but it's always been the one I felt most emotion for.

The Magus *is a very seminal work. I know you think of it as your first novel and, therefore, not structurally perfect, but there's something in it one cannot quite pinpoint that seems to affect readers.*
    Another thing you realize later in life is that some mistakes you make are fertile ones. This also is in Zen philosophy. . . . Certainly I think the diffuseness of it is bearable.

Were you happy with the filming of it?
    No, no. Dreadful.

You helped with the screenplay, didn't you?
    I wrote the original screenplay, but the director didn't like it and it was changed. And then the producers had a shot at it.

What about the actors?
    Miscast, from top to bottom.

All three of them: [Anthony] Quinn, [Candice] Bergen, and [Michael] Caine?
    Quinn was, I thought, absolutely wrong. . . . Mike Caine is a nice man, but. . . .

What about Candice Bergen as Julie?
    Candy Bergen I thought. . . . She was on television the other night talking about the film, and she rather nicely turned—she was speaking to some-body—she turned to the camera and said, "If John Fowles is watching, I'd like to apologize to him." I think she could have played that part, but she

didn't get the direction she needed. And Karina, the other girl [playing Alison], was a brilliant actress . . . very fine movie actress. But she failed, too.

Did you write the screenplay for The Collector *too?*

In a very incidental way. That was written by two Americans, but I went to Hollywood to put the script back into British English. It had got rather Americanized. That was a better script. It was a better film. It still didn't please me very much.

When you wrote the stories in The Ebony Tower, *you didn't send them to magazines first, did you?*

I don't like doing that. I could do it; I get requests. Some magazine wanted to take one of the stories. . . .

There's a certain consistency—

I tell you what; this is perhaps rather childlike, but I love the idea that when a reader picks up a novel it's—when you buy the book, this is all brand new. It worries me in some way to think that some readers may have already read part of a book in a magazine. So I'm against first serial rights. Second serial rights—selling after publication—I don't argue. I like the virgin feel of a text.

I looked at that book Shipwreck. *That's a marvelous book. The pictures and [your] introduction to it.*

The little girl out there [visiting], her father's my London publisher. I took him down to the Scilly Isles to this photographer's shop . . . [and] like a good publisher. . . .

It was his idea?

In ten seconds he said there's a book here, and twenty seconds later I was going to write it. He has a very shrewd, quick eye. . . . I wrote it in three weeks. Too quick. But it was fun. . . . I had a lovely letter the other day from an old American merchant seaman, somewhere in Virginia, who had somehow got hold of the book and wanted the address of the photographer in the Scillies.

Are there any English authors you know personally?

I've met some. I'm a close friend of one whose new book's going to be a bestseller in America.

Who's that?

It's just been sold for a small fortune. His name is Tom Wiseman; Thomas

Wiseman. He wrote a good novel called *The Quick and the Dead*. But I think a little bit to his amazement he's just written a thriller which could easily go on the [bestseller] list. I hope the American world likes it. It's been a great shock to him. It's no joke, success.

And after it comes, you're still wrestling with it, I suppose.
I can't say I'm fully over it, but I think I have it under control now. It takes a few years. How anyone in America . . . I don't think many people in America can.

The pressures are tremendous there to become a public figure; go on the talk shows, game shows. . . . Do you think some writers think of it [their writing] as therapy?
It is therapy, isn't it? All writers must have a tremendous fix; they're obsessive. This is what's so marvelous about this psychiatrist's . . . analysis of why people write. Why is it that you're never satisfied? Why do you go on trying, trying, trying again? Obviously what you're trying to do is—this is my theory—trying to achieve some primal state of perfection and total happiness, which you're doomed never to experience because you'll never be one year old again.

So you're doomed to failure?
You are doomed to be on an eternal hunt, and therefore obviously it's partly therapy. But I'm dubious about whether it's good therapy unless you're successful at it in critical and commercial terms. Sure, it solves one problem if you write.

If you fail at it, you've got another problem—
I've seen so many other people suffer so bitterly because they haven't had the success they think they deserve. There are not many calm writers about any more.

Calm writers?
That's what I like about Bellow.

He was going to edit—I heard years ago—a journal called Commonsense; *going back to the old values.*
I only met him once. He struck me as being very quick-minded intelligent, slightly nervous on the exterior, but you felt inside he—

At peace?
Precisely.

Do you like Ellison's Invisible Man*?*
    I read that so long ago. . . . I remember it as a good novel but I can't really
remember. . . . I had a great period of reading when I was teaching literature
in the 1950s.

I think it came out in 1954.
    I did read it at the time. I've got it somewhere.

He hasn't published another novel since.
    I thought he'd died.

No; he's still alive. He's teaching somewhere.
    Nelson Algren, is he still writing?

I don't know.
    I read all the modern American classics.

Faulkner—
    Faulkner, Fitzgerald, Dos Passos—

Hemingway—
    Yes. Dreiser, too. I'm a great admirer of Dreiser. Who's that other man
who wrote The Wheat trilogy?

Norris. Frank Norris.
    Norris. Yes, he's good—

I'm sure you like Henry James.
    Yes.

I think of him as an acquired taste.
    He's one of those writers I don't read very much, like Proust. Every two
or three years I'll pick up James.

Do you know Paul Bowles?
The Sheltering Sky?

Yes.
    Fine novel.

And a book of short stories [The Delicate Prey].
    He's [Bowles] a lovely raconteur. . . . Dan Halpern came here a year or
two ago; he'd just come from Tangiers. He brought back recordings he'd
made.

Of Paul Bowles?
Paul Bowles telling various little Arab stories. . . .

I like Bowles because . . . he portrays the shock of two cultures. Americans in the desert or something; everything just collapses.
I suppose he's a sort of failure—after that first novel.

Yes, he didn't get the success he deserves.
I believe his wife's a brilliant writer, too, Sally Bowles.

Yes. . . . How's your collection of natural history?
I don't collect living things. Except plants to grow; I don't collect dead objects. Well, I collect fossils along the beach but only in a very amateur—

It's so peaceful. This view [looking out through the window towards the Channel]. . . .
Yes. It is today. Normally it isn't at all peaceful.

Inspiring, I suppose [Looking at watch]. He [taxi driver] should be here in a few minutes. I'm very grateful for this—
Not at all; not at all.

An Interview with John Fowles

Carol M. Barnum / 1984

From *Modern Fiction Studies*, 31:1 (Spring 1985), 187–203. Reprinted by permission of Purdue Research Foundation.

Barnum: You describe the domain of the novel as "one person's view of life." What is your view of life?

Fowles: One can't answer such a question truthfully in an interview. My sympathies in most public matters are with the Left; my view of the world's future, not very optimistic.

Barnum: Why is your view of the world not very optimistic? Do you mean that we're all going to be destroyed by the bomb or that humanity is not improving?

Fowles: I don't think humanity is improving. I think there's a good chance that we're all going to be destroyed by the bomb. But much more immediately worrying for me is the way we're destroying nature.

Barnum: You have said that the key to your fiction lies in your relationship with nature, particularly because of its being an "experience whose deepest value lies in the fact that it cannot be directly described by any art . . . including that of words." Could you elaborate?

Fowles: My own attitude to nature has changed very considerably during my life, but it has always been important, I would now say vital, to me. I began by hunting and collecting it as a boy and adolescent, and rejected all that; but then fell into another trap—becoming a stock natural historian, obsessed with identifying and the quasi-scientific side. I would now call my relationship one of love, certainly one of need. What most people look for in human friends and contacts, I look for in nonhuman nature. Like nature itself, I regard most of humanity, both private and public, with a good deal of suspicion—as inherently dangerous, though as often through ignorance as malice. The original sin of mankind is for me its age-old contempt for, or indifference to, the other species on this planet. In that, we are as a whole an invasive vermin, or plague.

I don't think any art or science can describe the whole reality of nature, partly because it is its experience *now,* in any given presence and with all the body's senses and the mind's knowledge, that matters. The true experiencing reduces one to feeling. Trying simultaneously to record the feeling is somehow intrusive and diminishing, like talking through great music. I often feel this in writing fiction—that one is trying to describe what one can't and ought not even to be trying; and so is condemned to a sort of vulgar futility, or eternal second best.

Barnum: You have said that your first ambition has always been to alter the society you live in. Is that still true? If so, how do you hope to accomplish that, and what do you want society to become?

Fowles: I said that a long time ago, and would now call it a totally unfulfilled hope. I know I may have helped a little in altering people's view of life—if I can believe their letters. I now think that this is the only practical "political" ambition a novelist can have. I should certainly like our present societies to become much fairer and more equal in economic terms, not so outrageously selfish, aggressive, and stupid in their supposedly Christian principles as America and Britain today. Western society is now in my view far too dominated by the middle-class ethos—anything goes, so long as the bourgeois way of life is preserved. The rise of this subtle tyranny—Gramsci's "cultural hegemony"—over the last forty years seems to me the most striking historical development of the century—and something very similar has happened in Russia also, of course. What fills me with gloom is that in the West people like Reagan and Thatcher are elected *by majorities.* The Russians are not even given that choice; yet I suspect that if they were, they might vote more intelligently.

Barnum: You have said that "every novel since literary time began . . . is a form of quest or adventure." Does this theme underlie your fiction, too?

Fowles: Yes, very much so. Even the dullest narrative is a form of adventure since it deals with a series of events in time. I think that must imply quest, also.

Barnum: In an interview with Richard Boston, you said that "the art of novel writing is being able to put your finger on the archetypal things in people's minds."

Fowles: I don't know if I'd use the word "archetypal" now. But academic critics seem often to me to be blind to a negative side of the novel: what it does not say, what is left out. Leaving out is a major part of the skill of a writer—that is, persuading readers to supply what is not said. This applies all the way down the line, from major ideas to minor description of characters. Most of us learn that too exact notations of human appearance are harmful because they cramp the readers' imagination (though they may not realize it consciously). Hints are better, not exact mimesis; dots, which readers must join up to make the picture. Readers possess a huge stock of latent imagination, both archetypal and in terms of everyday things, and one needs to use this.

Barnum: In "The Ebony Tower" there seems to be too much explanation of David's failure, not enough left out.

Fowles: That was the first story like that I'd ever written. So, in a way, I was teaching myself to write such stories when I wrote it. The too much was because I was angry with the art teaching establishment in this country at that time, and I really wanted to have a go at that. It's very dangerous when you write fiction to want to have a go at something. You almost always say too much. But by leaving out, I always find when I read most other people's fiction that there's always too much in. When you first write, you always put in as much as you can. When you revise, if there is the slightest doubt, you should cut. The most mysterious part of this literary study business is what happens in the reader's mind. We still have no knowledge of how readers' minds work. Theorists have tried to explain it, but I'm still not at all sure how things work, how people do make bridges and can see (I don't know if "see"is the word) concrete things from very few hard details. We don't know what that making up, the very important part the reader contributes, is about. That's why I suspect that leaving out is the thing you learn last in the novel. What you don't need to say, what the reader will do for you.

Barnum: Whereas I think you put too much into "The Ebony Tower," I think you leave out so much in "The Cloud" that the reader isn't left with enough to hold on to. And yet you say that it's your favorite story.

Fowles: As I say, I'd never written a nouvelle before. And I printed the stories in the order in which they were written; so that, in a way, for me marks a progression in this leaving out sense. I think that why I like "The Cloud" is that I feel it's about right; but lots of people haven't really understood it, so perhaps I did leave out too much. It feels all right for me, if I'm allowed an opinion.

Barnum: You made a comment several years ago about the problem of cinema: how it's an inactive medium because you participate by observing rather than by getting involved in it.

Fowles: I don't think I quite said that. I said it takes the business of imagining for yourself and puts it in someone else's hands. It is my quarrel with the cinema that it must destroy this audience imagination to a great degree. I sincerely admired Meryl Streep's performance in *The French Lieutenant's Woman,* but I am not so happy that she—or anyone who might have played the part—must present a fixed image for the subsequent reader. This mobility or fluidity of image, in terms of how readers "see" the text, is a very important asset of the novel. No reader has ever read the same book in the same way.

Barnum: When did you first know that you wanted to be a writer?

Fowles: When I was at Oxford I began to think about it. I didn't really consider it seriously until I was in Greece. I made my first serious attempt in Greece.

Barnum: Was it *The Magus?*

Fowles: No, the first book I tried to get published, the first one I submitted, was a travel book. And I sent it to an unknown agent at the time, Paul Scott, now one of our best known novelists (he's dead). And he said, "It's no good as a travel book, but I think you're a novelist." This was because one small section of the book was written in a more-or-less fictional vein. He said some of it reminded him of Hemingway, by chance not a novelist I greatly admired, but he wasn't to know that. And it sounded very high praise at the time. I'm very grateful to him because that one sentence in the letter really kept me going.

Barnum: Do you find being a writer difficult?

Fowles: I sometimes get very depressed, but I think all writers do. It's the classic manic-depressive trade, largely caused by the amount of time it takes. I mean, if a photographer shoots a couple of bad films, he's over it in a week. You can't do that with the novel, living with it for a year or two years or longer. You have to acquire a certain sort of brave vulgarity over it.

Barnum: What do you mean by vulgarity?

Fowles: Perhaps "vulgarity" isn't the word. A plebeian toughness. An ability to plod on, regardless. I suspect countless writers don't really have it. They live on their nerves, on the edge of things. I guess in America, too, this awful value put on contemporary fame must be especially trying. I know one or two young American writers who have gone badly wrong because they have had successful first books.

Barnum: Do you consider writing a pleasure or hard work or both?

Fowles: Both, but not at the same time. The revising or editing is the hard work, but there's a certain enjoyment in that. It reminds me of when I was a teacher: doing a really good correction on a bad essay. You derive that sort of feeling; you've done a thorough job. It needs very different kinds of mind. But the pleasure, yes, is in the first writing. And in the way you work it up. Then you have a period of agony, when you know you have corrected the galleys and the public book is out. That's always an awful time. And you wonder if you got it right or very wrong.

Barnum: Do you place a lot of stock in its critical reception in terms of judging whether you got it right?

Fowles: No.

Barnum: What, then, does tell you if you got it right?

Fowles: I haven't really thought about it. Oh, you get enough praise—I always have somewhere—to keep you going in terms of your own ego. But I think the main personal reaction is that it's dead, irrespective of praise or damnation. Once the text is published, it's dead. And you know you can't do anything about it.

I dislike so much the general literary climate in Britain that criticism here doesn't bother me very much. I know I'm going to get bad reviews because I know certain critics are against me. That doesn't worry me. I might be worried if I got bad reviews all the way down the line. Readers' letters I do regard. You can tell from them far more accurately than you can from the critics whether there is something there.

Barnum: Does your desire for a response from your readers contradict the statement you once made about being able to write for a party of one, yourself?

Fowles: Not at all. I did not say I *wanted* to write in total isolation. A rather unfair extra privilege that best sellers receive is this contact with their readers. Some such letters are plain stupid (not least in their praise), some are from celebrity-seekers, others from cranks of one kind or another; but a majority are very revealing for the writer and give him or her that most difficult of all information to obtain: how the book is actually seen and read by a wide range of people, from university professors to lonely housewives. Quite frequently they are not really about the book or me at all, but about the letter-writers—that is, they have to explain themselves to explain why they

have been affected by what I write. I cherish these especially. I got a letter
from an exmonk the other day, who claimed that *The Magus* had got him out
of the monastery. I told him, not really. It had just given him a nudge along
the way. I think that's all one can ask of the novel. It can't change society,
but it can push people a little bit or show them the way. Such reader response
is to my mind a good deal more valuable than any but the best professional
reviews and academic studies.

Barnum: When you write, do you have a specific reader in mind?

Fowles: I would say it is someone who is made up of all the readers who
have written to me, which must be many thousands now. You form a kind of
"compound familiar ghost," to quote Eliot, out of that. If you asked me to
describe it in words, I should be rather hard-put to say much; it's just that I
have a rough notion of the kinds of people who like my books, both here and
in America. And in a way, I do write for them. You see, I think your question
is important, a key thing. Many young writers don't really know who they're
writing for. Or they're much too obviously writing for their university teachers, or critics, and so on, and that's not good enough for me. That's incestuous. I think a good sign for a young writer is when he seems to be writing
for the educated general public that he hasn't yet acquired in reality; or,
alternatively, he's writing for himself. In a sense you yourself constitute your
most important reader; if it doesn't please you, then sure as hell it's not going
to please anybody else. You have always first to write for yourself; then, if
you're lucky enough, as I have been, to have lots of feedback, you write also
for this acquired constant reader, the compound familiar ghost.

Barnum: Do you aspire to be considered a great writer, one whose works
will stand the test of time?

Fowles: Yes, and so does every serious writer. But history is harsh with
such hubris. Today's "great" writers are very often forgotten tomorrow, and
the forgotten today not uncommonly become tomorrow's great writers. The
egocentric vanity of some contemporary writers seems to me absurd and
childish, and betrays a deep insecurity. I do not share it. I don't know what I
am or shall be in these terms, and think it a blessed ignorance.

Barnum: Do the ideas for your novels come to you the way you might
want poetry to come to you?

Fowles: No, because I think a poem comes at once. I used to get a line, it
was always a line, but the complete poem was very close behind. Whereas

with the novel, what happens, so far as I'm concerned, is that you have an idea, but it's just one of many ideas. It may stay latent, a dry seed, for years. Then gradually it stirs, begins to obsess you slightly. One day it really obsesses you, and you're in business. It's a much slower germination than with the poem, I find, but all writers vary so much. I don't really know if the novel idea or image which slowly grows doesn't actually come into being, of course, because of some attitude in it. Or maybe it's a certain interest in a particular field which then gives birth to a specific image, the thing that actually obsesses you. Which comes first, I really don't know.

Barnum: What do you believe to be your best novel?

Fowles: Let me just say in general that I'm absolutely against this word "best." I don't like anywhere in literature such phrases as "the best ten writers in America" or "the best poets in the South." I dislike the word because I think of other writers in a natural history way, like the plants out there in the garden. Some plants do interest me more than others, but I wouldn't use this "best/worst" notion of them. I don't like it at all.

I suppose *The French Lieutenant's Woman* is technically the best written. I have a great affection for *Daniel Martin.* In many ways, I feel that book is a good friend. *The Magus,* which is the first one I wrote, still, I think, excites me more than the others. It still slightly puzzles me how I could have written it. I know that I've had a whole series of different relationships toward what it meant. And so my feelings are rather like that. I couldn't really say which is the best. It depends on what you're looking for.

Barnum: Did rewriting *The Magus* give it favored-child status?

Fowles: It may have increased that feeling a bit. It was really very badly reviewed at the start, not so much in America but in England. And so I felt defensive toward it. I could never feel defensive over *The French Lieutenant's Woman* because it was received right across the board; I think it had only two bad reviews out of a hundred. So, yes, it's always been for me a slightly crippled child—I watch over it a bit more carefully.

Barnum: Do you think both versions of *The Magus* will remain in print?

Fowles: The second version is the one I want to see reprinted. I can't imagine anyone ever reprinting the first.

Barnum: Do you publish translations, reviews, and other nonfictional pieces to avoid the "cage of novelist," as you call it?

Fowles: I do very little reviewing, mainly because I think novelists have quite enough against them without stabbing each other in the back. I enjoy brief sorties into nonfiction, such as translating for the National Theatre in London, introducing photographic books, and the rest. Part of me always had a love-hate relationship with the artifice of fiction—a pagan in me loves the invention, the tricks, the skills, and a puritan in me has a kind of nausea, or boredom, with it. This manifests itself mainly in terms of being a very slow producer. I don't mean I spend months agonizing over every sentence; but much more that I put books away and forget all about them for long periods, sometimes for years on end. Nine-tenths of the pleasure lies for me in the writing, not the written or published. I adore unfinished books, in the sense that they feel still alive. Publishing is death, the skeleton in the desert, to the writer—or to this writer—the cage, or *gabbia,* he has to live in.

Barnum: You've said that the process of writing is something that should be studied.

Fowles: Yes, I have thought of doing this. It's difficult because if you're doing it seriously, you have to keep notes on yourself, and you have to do it from the very beginning of a text.

Barnum: But it has to be very conscious, then, so wouldn't you be creating your own view of the process?

Fowles: Well, the reason I haven't done it, although I've thought of doing it, is that I feel it would disturb the text if you were to stop and say, "I'm doing this because. . . ." You would gravely distort the end-product then. That's why I don't do it. To write the text you have to live in the myth of it, and you can't be a cold-blooded anthropologist, actually waiting and watching the myth come into being. But there's very often enough evidence in the text itself, to a sensitive reader, to get somewhere toward it.

Barnum: On several occasions you've said that we need more understanding of the psychopathology of the novel, and you cite Freudian and Jungian psychology as the two best instruments of analysis. Could you elaborate on this point?

Fowles: I am much more interested in how writers work and function, what I have called the ethology of the writer—on the analogy of biology, where ethology (how the living animal behaves) is now a central study, compared to the endless classifying and anatomizing of Victorian biology— pigeonholing and cutting the (dead) subject to pieces. I take the view that Freud and Jung were both very close to novelists themselves, or myth creators (as was Darwin, by the way); but they provide very useful scales or maps. I have often found psychoanalytic and psychiatric investigations of books a great deal more fertile than purely literary (or classifying) ones.

Barnum: About *The Magus* you've said, "I only knew the basic idea of a secret world, whose penetration involved ordeal and whose final reward was self-knowledge, obsessed me. In a way the book was a metaphor of my own personal experience . . . an allegory." Are all of your books this sort of experience . . . an allegory or metaphor of some aspect of your life?

Fowles: Yes, I think so, but often in an indirect—that is, not autobiographical—way. I think I'd rather use the word obsession. Some aspect of your experience begins to obsess you, and you have to seek some metaphor to express and to objectify it—a mood, a story, a character, a place. This process also finally kills the obsession, incidentally. Self-therapy is a very strong drive behind all artistic creation. Fraser's *The Death of Narcissus,* a study of paedophilia in writers like Lewis Carroll and J. M. Barrie, more or less suggested this: that writing was the best known cure for this particular perversion. We writers are all, I believe, highly unbalanced people who just happen to have the means at hand to cure ourselves—or at least until the fall off the tightrope threatens.

Barnum: Turning more specifically to your fiction, in *The French Lieutenant's Woman* you say that it's debatable whether Sarah is a deceiving woman. You left it open. Yet in several places in the novel we are told that she is acting for Charles's good, which would seem to place her actions in a positive light. Do you think this a false reading of her character?

Fowles: I deliberately left her character and motives very open, and I am not going to encourage one interpretation over another. I would not blame her—as symbol of a certain class of then much-exploited womankind—for using Charles to find her own freedom, nor would I blame anyone for supposing that "use" was finally also for the good of the person used. This remains for me the problem of feminism—indeed of all revolution . . . its unhappy habit of beginning for just and good reasons but ending as one more tyranny, not very different from the one it started by destroying. France is the classic case, between 1789 and Robespierre.

Barnum: In the "The Ebony Tower," if David were to choose Diana, you have said he might become a better person, but he would have betrayed his moral being. In *The Aristos* you write that "sexual attraction and the sexual act are in themselves innocent, neither intrinsically moral or immoral" and that "adultery is the disproof of a marriage rather than its betrayal." Are you trying to put David in a double bind here—damned if he does, damned if he doesn't?

Fowles: A double bind of a kind. I meant to suggest that if he ran off with Diana he would be a better artist—not necessarily a better person. One central truth the story was meant to air was that good moral behavior and good art have no relation at all. I was taken round Thomas Hardy's house recently. On one floor is his study, where he wrote *Tess, Jude,* and countless other fine works; directly above the study are the two miserable attic rooms where his first wife lived and died. He treated her with a cruel lack of understanding in her last years. You stand there and feel the pain, their separate isolation, in those tiny upper rooms still. But how does one judge? What is the cost of a caring marriage? What is the cost of a masterpiece? Every writer lives with this, in one way or another. So, yes, David is damned if he does and damned if he doesn't but damned in different ways.

I wish someone would study novelists' wives—and/or husbands now. I wrote a poem about this once, based on a Greek folk-legend. A mason of Arta had to build a bridge, but it always fell down. One day he was told it would stand only if he buried his wife alive in its foundations. So he buried her alive, and it stood. The world at large has always been on the mason's side. I doubt if he himself is so sure of his justification.

Barnum: Elizabeth plays a very important role in your life as wife and critic, doesn't she?

Fowles: A writer's wife is vital. Always, without exception.

Barnum: Does she read everything while you're writing it, or afterward?

Fowles: The one novel she didn't read until the very end was *Daniel Martin.* She's read everything else. And she hates some of them. But, you see, you have to live with that as a writer.

Barnum: Does that bother you that she hates some of your writing?

Fowles: Yes, it hurts, but on the other hand, I give her a terrible life. Well, not me in particular, but every writer gives his wife an appalling life. If you're any writer's wife, you're condemned to a lot of loneliness. The person you are married to and live with—I suppose it works the other way around as well—is deeply involved with other people, even though they're only fictional.

Barnum: In love with someone else?

Fowles: Yes, with a female character you can be in something very like actual love. When you're writing hard you really are locked up in another world, and I think that goes against everything our culture requires of a decent marriage.

Barnum: Concerning models for your characters, you've said that "in an archetypal way" characters are "obviously the people you've lived with and . . . yourself." Is Elizabeth the model for Miranda, Alison, Sarah, and Jane?

Fowles: I have a very strong feeling against copying characters straight from the life. If I do that in a psychological way I usually feel driven to change the physical appearance or life circumstances of the character beyond normal recognition. (British libel laws are also much nastier than American ones.) I think of all my main female characters (including the muse Erato in *Mantissa*) as aspects of the one person, and to that extent they are drawn on the person I have shared my life with and from whom I mostly derive my notions of Eve. But this is remote from (say) a painter's "use" of a favorite model, like Rossetti with Lizzie Siddal. Much more at an almost archetypal level.

Barnum: In writing "The Cloud," you said that you had James Joyce and also T. S. Eliot in mind. In what way?

Fowles: I did have *The Waste Land* in mind, particularly. I don't much like Eliot as a thinker or human being (he was another classic wife-destroyer, of course), but his language and symbolism remain potent with my generation. I'm not quite sure now why I mentioned Joyce; perhaps because of the use of the stream-of-consciousness technique.

Barnum: You have called Eliot a "slogan maker," a "phrasemaker," and a "word man." Those terms seem to demean his stature or importance.

Fowles: Well, again, I don't really like much of his philosophy of life. But "slogan" was unkind—he did write some very memorable lines. I've got a particularly bad memory for that sort of thing, but some of his lines in *The Waste Land* and so on have stayed with me all my life.

I think our best poet now is another person whose philosophy of life I find pretty awful, Philip Larkin. He is undoubtedly the best contemporary English poet, a magician with words. But again he's a Tory; he hates things like children; he hates everything foreign. But he can write poetry better than anyone else.

Barnum: Well, it's interesting you should say this about Larkin because, to get back to Eliot, every time I've asked you about the influence of Eliot in your work, you've always downplayed his importance, and yet you often cite him in your works.

Fowles: I once said that Eliot was to me, in fact to my generation, like Horace was to the eighteenth century. You could hardly write then without including a snatch of Horace somewhere, and I think now that's rather the same with Eliot. I don't know what young people think of him.

Barnum: I read an interesting article about "The Cloud" in which the critic compared certain parts of your story to *The Waste Land,* showing a line-by-line similarity. Did you have this work in mind with that story?

Fowles: Yes, certainly with Eliot in mind. That one I'd confess to at once. But there's another academic article comparing *The Magus* to a Chaucer tale—was it "The Miller's Tale"?—I'm not very good with Chaucer. The one with Nicholas and Alison. Somebody wrote a paper on that and sent it to me. He must have been terribly disappointed, for I'd never read Chaucer when I wrote *The Magus.* He made a good case, nonetheless. In general I find the academic mania for influence-tracing rather tiresome, and dangerous for the hunter, also.

Barnum: You have said that you read virtually no books on theory, and yet you seem very comfortable with such terms as deconstruction, structuralism, and so forth.

Fowles: Well, my goodness, put me in front of a class and ask me to teach deconstruction and I would be very hard-put to do it, I can assure you. I've read one book on deconstruction, another on structuralism, and so on. Occasionally, I've had a shot at the French gurus like Barthes and Derrida, but I find them very difficult to understand.

Barnum: You seem to make fun of them in *Mantissa.*

Fowles: Well, I did in *Mantissa* because I think they've been granted altogether too powerful a position on the intellectual side.

Barnum: Have you also moved away from existentialism, which you have described as "a kind of literary metaphor, a wish fulfillment"?

Fowles: I now view many cultural movements in the same way. Existentialism did seem to my generation, immediately after the end of World War II, like a breath of fresh air. We all took it a lot too literally, mainly because we were ignorant of French intellectual tradition and their rules of rhetoric.

The Anglo-Saxons have never been very good at playing with ideas at a wicked remove from reality or practicality.

Barnum: To return to the novels, did you know that *Daniel Martin* would end happily, or did you wrestle with the notion, as does Daniel Martin?

Fowles: I don't plan books in advance, and it wasn't until *Daniel Martin* was half written that I began to feel clearly that it must end "happily." I remember it first seemed an odd, even strange idea—almost an eccentricity, a gratuitous act. There was no problem, bar the usual line-by-line writing ones, after the decision was taken. I have long disliked mere voguish pessimism or absurdism—the chic café society "cult of the black." The genuine article is perfectly legitimate, of course, but various pseudo-intellectual equations, such as serious equals black (or leftwing equals experimentalist), do not impress me. I am not against the avant-garde in itself, but I think it should be judged by the standards of any other kind of art, not treated as automatically more significant and interesting.

Barnum: In *Daniel Martin,* Jane seems a flat character to me and not my favorite. I have a hard time relating to her as a person. But a friend of mine who is older than I told me that when I am a bit older I will understand and like Jane better.

Fowles: She was meant to be—I wouldn't exactly say flat, but difficult. Not very attractive sexually. An awkward woman. And your view was quite widely held. In fact my American editor Ned Bradford wanted me to change the book. He wanted Daniel to end with the girl Jenny. And I told him he was being extremely wicked. He was a very great editor, and I was deeply fond of him, but I wouldn't have changed the ending under any circumstances. I got quite a lot of mail over it, but I regard preferring Jenny to Jane as another American myth—the passion for eternal youth. It was partly because I've seen so many women of my generation dropped, slaughtered, for some twenty-year old.

Barnum: You have said that the happy ending provides "a somewhat false sense of having solved life's problems," which means that it threatens creativity. After writing *Daniel Martin,* did you feel threatened by the loss of creativity or less inclined to write?

Fowles: *Daniel Martin* did exhaust me, but I don't mean in an unpleasant way. It said quite a lot about me, and it said quite a lot about what I feel about my generation and class in this country. So, in a way, it was a good voiding novel. Novels always leave you feeling empty in the end, but that one particularly so. I wouldn't describe it so much as a loss of creativity as a feeling of being less obsessed by the novel.

Barnum: You say that the skeleton of a novel must be the narrative and that you're good at writing narrative. Yet there doesn't appear to be a narrative skeleton in *Mantissa.* Why not?

Fowles: I don't in fact agree that it has no narrative. But it is a work about the *process* of writing, at a remove from the usual functions of fiction-writing, so narrative is a lesser consideration.

Barnum: Was *Mantissa* intended as a playful interlude—to pass the time until the muse came again of her own volition?

Fowles: A playful interlude in a way. But then I regard a great deal of the daily reality of writing fiction as akin to play. It certainly wasn't written because the muse had gone away, as you imply. The awkwardness and argumentativeness of characters, their refusal to fit preconceptions, is for me a prime sign that the muse is at work. She—or the nature of inspiration—has always been intensely polymorphic—and often "maliciously" contrary—to me. When I was working with other people on the script of *The Collector* in Hollywood, we used quite often to slip into comic versions of it, pure send-ups. I noticed at the time how muselike this was, how we seemed forced to imagine the very opposite of what we were "officially" there to do. Neither the writer nor the muse in *Mantissa* is meant to be consistent—their forte is in aiding and abetting each other to put on mask after mask, teasing each other out of set attitudes. It is not so much that nothing is serious as that nothing is stable. Literary students know the text as a printed, immutable thing. It is very different in the writing, when it is as much in the head as on the page. All situations are haunted by their opposite, and all characters, the same. Only writers can know all that their fictions might have been but are not, and the countless quarrels that lie behind even the easiest, smoothest final text. Narrative in *Mantissa* was never important, nor was character consistency; the duplicity, cussedness, absurdity, anger, fun, love-hate of the relation of the would-be serious writer and his own imagination (or unconscious) dictated events.

Barnum: In an old *Life* interview, you said that "doing fiction well is like eating or making love." Did you have this concept in mind with *Mantissa?*

Fowles: I meant that it should come as a natural activity, take place so, or at least during the first draft. Another necessary ability of the novelist is to write almost unconsciously in this first phase, and yet to become his own and very conscious teacher—or corrector—in the final one. I think this is beyond learning; one has it from birth, or nature. The two processes need profoundly different qualities, almost a beneficent schizophrenia: an ability to be young and green, and another to be old and wise. That is, as in eating and love-making, to be both natural and learned—both hungry and a gastronome.

Barnum: You've said that you "deplore the stress on purely clever writing . . . which says nothing about the human condition." Could you possibly be accused of writing in this vein in *Mantissa?*

Fowles: Yes, perhaps. It depends whether you think writing is a part of the human condition. I did mean the title *Mantissa* (a minor addition) quite liter-ally. I confess I despise the American notion that "important" writers must eternally mount to greater length, greater depth, greater seriousness; I think this very often produces huge and over-inflated balloons. The writer is burst because he has swallowed the public myth of himself. I regard the public image of myself as an enemy, a stranger called "John Fowles," who bears little relation to the reality, and so I try to escape him or at least not to encourage him too much.

Barnum: Is the cuckoo clock in *Mantissa* a mechanical extension of the bird imagery that appears so often in your fiction?

Fowles: The ghost behind *Mantissa* is very much Flann O'Brien's *At-Swim-Two-Birds.* He is for me one of the finest Irish writers of this century and a major figure in the development of the self-conscious novel since the death of Joyce. The cuckoo clock seemed to suit him, as it does all the obses-sive aspects of being a writer (or a critic, perhaps)—the not being free to do anything but this. Absolutely nothing to do with my love of birds, outside literature. The cuckoo for me represents "absurd and monotonous obses-sion." It is also the traditional sign of the cuckold—the man made a fool of.

Barnum: You say that all your books are about freedom. Do you think that the fiction through *Daniel Martin* was about freedom for your characters as representative figures and that *Mantissa* is about the artist's freedom—your freedom?

Fowles: I'd rather say they are about the difficulties of attaining personal freedom, especially in terms of discovering what one is. As I grow older I doubt whether we have very much freedom to change basic and major behavioral patterns; that is, I think we are all very considerably conditioned. Nevertheless, I cannot believe we are totally so. The writer's own position in this is of course highly ironic, since nobody could be less free in terms of being under the power of a major obsession—the very need to write. *Mantissa* was much more about the conditioning than the freedom; *Daniel Martin* certainly attempted to show characters escaping from all that has determined them, as did *The Magus* and *The French Lieutenant's Woman,* in differing ways.

Barnum: What lies beyond *Mantissa?* What projects are you working on? You've mentioned the draft of a thriller. Also something about European attitudes toward nature and conservation cast in the frame of an orgy on the Mediterranean coast. Also something about the problems of a writer who hasn't been published and another about the innocence and greenness of young Englishmen. Do you have plans to publish any of these?

Fowles: The thriller was a mistake, and nothing will ever come of it. The other ideas are all lying fallow. The two last you mention were both novels I wrote in the 1950s, and which I might publish one day, though it would have to be a little under the rubric of juvenilia. I am near having another novel ready, to be published, I hope, in 1985. I once said very firmly that in no circumstances would I ever write another historical novel after *The French Lieutenant's Woman;* so naturally this is a historical novel. (I have learnt to fear my own announcements about what I shall or shall not write. They provide too tempting a challenge to the wicked muse to show you up for an idiot.) I am currently introducing a photographic book on British landscape, a retrospective of work done in that field by a photographer I much admire, Fay Godwin. I like her because she sees in a very peculiar way which I approve of. Something in her is aware of the dangers in photography. I'm also doing a book on Hardy, a photographic piece. It should be quite interesting.

Barnum: Can you tell me about the new novel?

Fowles: This next novel is intended to be readable. I don't think I'm going to play any tricks in it. It's just going to be a straightforward account. I've always liked Daniel Defoe. It will be kind of Defoe-like, I hope. In another way it will be about an aspect of the Anglo-American character that has always fascinated me: the movement of Dissent. I began writing it fairly soon after—a year or two after—*Daniel Martin. Mantissa* was really written as *The Ebony Tower* was—as a break. I knew I wanted this novel to last several years, and *Mantissa* was just thrown in.

Barnum: Is the way you describe writing *The French Lieutenant's Woman* in "Notes on Writing a Novel" typical of the way the creative process works for you?

Fowles: Yes, practically always with me. This next novel came from the image of a group of people riding across a skyline. Just figures on horseback going across a skyline, rather as in a wild western. I've had this image for ten or fifteen years. These people are going on a journey. As they're on horseback, it must be historical; obviously it's in the past. But it's the image that is the seed. Like the woman in black with her back turned in *The French Lieutenant's Woman.* She might have been in an airport or anything, but she became associated with The Cobb, the harbor at Lyme Regis, and that's how it started. The new novel is now three-quarters done, but there's always the end.

Barnum: You don't know how it's going to end?

Fowles: Yes, I know how it's going to end, but I don't know quite how to write it. This is a familiar problem with me: how to end novels. When I approach the end of a novel, I grow anxious that it won't end as it should, the characters won't behave correctly for the situation, and so forth.

The truth is, I don't want them to end. I've noticed that toward the end of a novel I keep on getting new ideas, which I don't really need. Things are usually quite complicated enough already. I know this is because I'm really in the game for the writing, not the being published. I've sat with this one for many years, not wanting it to end. Which is not good.

Barnum: You once described *Mantissa* as "a fairground at night on a distant hillside." What does this mean?

Fowles: Well, I do rather think of everything I've written, including some things that haven't been published and may never be, as a landscape around me, and I was trying to express that *Mantissa* was fun to write for me, but I wouldn't stress its importance in this general landscape. A jangle of sound and light, but a long way off. On a distant hillside, not a major or closer place.

Barnum: I see your fiction as a kind of landscape, too, but in a different sense, one that allows the reader to enter and to learn something about life.

Fowles: Well, one hopes for that. One hopes for that.

An Interview with John Fowles

Jan Relf / 1985

Reprinted by permission of Jan Relf and the Harry Ransom Humanities Research Center, The University of Texas at Austin.

Q: If your novels are, as you've said, about the difficulties of attaining personal freedom, can you define what that personal freedom means to you?

A: Well, I used personal in that sense so as not to suggest political freedom,
or really only any one condition of freedom. Partly it'll come from your own
tastes and instincts. I really mean being able to live as you think you ought
to live—yes, there is a moral touch to freedom. I'm hostile in general to all
conventions, I think, literally without exception. Freedom can mean such
different things to so many people, but for me an essential definition of it is
that it's always between two people. It can never apply to just one person—as
it does in café society, say. It must always be between two, or of course
between one and many people.

Q: How close in your mind are the concepts of freedom and authenticity?

A: Very close indeed, yes. I don't think this is quite how the existentialists
saw it. Authenticity was for them a sort of external moral ideal, but for me
it's being as honest as you can in what you do—with yourself, and, of course,
with these mysterious others who constitute the other side of the equation—
you must consider them. Which is certainly why I remain on the Left politically—but probably not in the sense that a good contemporary socialist
would think of it.

Q: *The Magus,* like the other novels, seems to assert the existential concept
of the necessity to choose, and to *go on* choosing. This could be construed as
a kind of moral expediency, or refusal to make permanent commitments. Do
you see it this way?

A: Yes, well, that was a criticism of existentialism at the time. I think I'd
say about existentialism that it was the great movement of my youth, but
many years have passed since then, and it's indeed many years since I've
read Sartre. Now, I don't quite know. I find you still have vaguely existentialist moments, but it can be rather limiting—you feel as if you must behave as
you've behaved in previous similar circumstances. You take decisions which

119

perhaps are against your own natural instincts. There was always for me something in it of doing what you didn't really feel like doing, of going against where reason or convention might lead you. It was really a pressure *not* to conform to what most people would do.

Q: The Gramsci epigraph to *Daniel Martin*—("The crisis consists precisely in the fact that the old is dying and the new cannot be born; in this interregnum a great variety of morbid symptoms appears")—sounds a little like a case of evolutionary constipation. How do you perceive this "crisis"?

A: The present crisis? Oh my God, that's a difficult one. Well, certainly in political terms, it's the need for a much fairer and much more socially egalitarian society, and I see very little sign of that. That's one desideratum—and we're a long way off. You see, the only way you can answer this is by picking on various things in society—the "morbid symptoms." I particularly dislike the selfishness of a lot of bourgeois society. Its real drive is simply "I"— things like the political apathy in American universities, consumerism, capitalism in general.

Q: Do you see that same crisis as applicable to *The Magus* and *The French Lieutenant's Woman?*

A: The morbid symptoms? Nicholas was certainly meant to be an exemplar—an example of what was wrong with that immediately post-war generation—my own. Charles is a more difficult problem. There really isn't much link between those two. Nicholas was set up by me to be a gallows example in a way. One thing about him—he *is* writing his own story—and no critic has ever taken that into account. All these terrible things they say about him—that he's a typical, totally selfish, modern man—they've never noticed that he's saying these things about himself. He's talking about "as he was" from a present (of which you know nothing) to a past.

Q: There seems to be a conflict between existentialism and the strong evolutionary theme in the novels, in that evolution assumes an ordered, purposeful universe, and existentialism denies it. Is this a conflict, or is there a reconciliation between the two ideas?

A: Yes, I'm aware of this. It's partly that what is very important for me in my ordinary life—in my metaphysical life also—is nature. And nature does appear to be highly ordered. Of course, it's been made highly ordered partly by science. And to an extent I think existentialism was always a slightly artificial thing. Do you know the French expression, *mise en ordre?* Putting in order. It's from Lévi-Strauss. There was a putting in order in existentialism which is very different from the putting in order which comes through nature. Yes, I think there's a conflict, but for me it's nature that's won, in my own terms. That is, I tend more and more to take a natural scientist's view of life, that we are very largely determined.

Q: Can I ask you about the "lost domaine"? If I remember rightly, Fournier's hero in *Le Grand Meaulnes* rediscovers his domaine only to find that it no longer has the same meaning for him—rather as Daniel does when he returns to Thorncombe in adult life. Do you see the renunciation of the domaine as a prerequisite for mature, authentic self-hood?

A: Well, we must be careful here. If you mean renunciation of a series of domaines—places or situations that have fascinated you—you'll not be mature until you go from one to another. But the concept of the lost domaine, although with constantly changing circumstances and faces, is, I think, very important, especially for novelists. If we're writing a novel, we're writing about a lost domaine. And any novelist will tell you as soon as you've done something in a novel, *it* loses a lot of interest for you but not the general concept. What I can't understand about really good scientists is that they do stick through all their lives to one small specialized area—yes, which is their domaine. And I think that's marvelous. I suppose some novelists have it in a sense that they always use the same kind of basic situation, or tone, towards you—Graham Greene is an example. And they get virtue through that of course—they become very expert in their limited domaine. But for me, in terms of narrative, you do have to move on to something quite new. But even then, many of the situations inherent in the last "lost domaine" situation do carry forward, as a rule.

I mean, I've always said that all my heroines are the same woman in fact. They're not nearly as distinct for me as I'm sure they are for most readers. Going back to my Jungian days, I'd say they are all the *anima,* one in *anima.* *The Magus* was very, very much—no critic's ever realised this—on the model of *Le Grand Meaulnes.* That book has haunted me all my life. I can see it has many faults—I would write a very critical essay on it—but . . . it's not only me. My favourite French writer, Julien Gracq, is equally hooked by it; you can tell he can't get the image of this book out of his mind.

Q: Can I ask you a couple of questions on *The Aristos?* About the Nemo—I think I understand the concept, but I'm not sure of its relationship to authenticity. It seems to be an inimical one. But you say that "it is an evolutionary force, as necessary as the ego." What role does the Nemo play in the quest for authenticity?

A: Well, I wouldn't take *The Aristos* too seriously. That book was begun when I was still at Oxford. For me, it's something that's a long way past. I think I meant by the Nemo the dread of being or becoming a nobody. It's like electricity—it can be good or bad—you can't define it in moral terms. It haunts all of us at some period of our lives—that existence is nothing, all a waste of time. But on the other hand, on the principle of the opposite poles I was writing about, it's also a source of energy in a way.

This may seem irrelevant, but the other day I asked a well-known editor to define the general fault in all the books she'd rejected, and she said, "Too much imagination, not enough technique." But this is the prime source of why people write novels, I think; it's trying to make the one behind, the technique, catch up. It sounds a negative thing as she put it, but I don't think it is really. All of us know that our technique is never good enough for our imagination. We can always imagine more beautifully, more precisely, more cleverly, more romantically—more than we can ever get it down on paper. This lack haunts all novel writing. And so with the Nemo.

Q: The concept of the Few and the Many in *The Aristos*—I know you've been challenged on this potentially offensive distinction . . .

A: Yes, well, it was a provoking way to put it, but I'm not an egalitarian in that sense. I mean, all that nonsense in education a few years ago, where all children were supposed to be equal, and it was the education that failed them—not their natural aptitude. I thought that was awful, pure wishful thinking.

Q: How do you see the responsibility of the Few?

A: Well, I think it's going back to the question of authenticity. It's being a little more honest than convention or social circumstance will usually allow. It's *not* playing social games.

Q: Do you see the Few as having a responsibility towards the Many?

A: I think they obviously have. If you are well-educated, and intelligent, or even reasonably well-off in economic terms, then you do have a responsibility to share some of that. That's all I meant by it.

Q: In writing on marriage in *The Aristos,* you say that passion and harmony are antipathetic, although "we tend to think of them as the twin gauges of a Perfect Marriage." Your views here seem to have a lot in common with those of Denis de Rougemont. Was he an influence at that time?

A: Yes, that was a very important book for my generation, at university. We all read *Passion and Society*. It's partly a question of time. I mean, passion is marvelous when you're young, but I think you want to be extremely dubious about it when you're middle-aged and older. It's trying to have passion and harmony together which is impossible.

Q: In your novels, women seem to have a greater ease and success than men in attaining personal freedom and authenticity. Do you see men as being more imprisoned by their gender than women?

A: Well, it appears that they are, but I think we're imprisoned much more by the role that gender has played in cultural history. Men haven't shaken off the past as well as women. Yes, I find that. It's talking in very broad terms, and one can always think of hundreds of exceptions, but I've always said that women live in the now, whereas men live half in the past and half in the future—the one place we're not happy is where we actually are. Again, I think this is a historical condition. It's a sort of biological difference in the feeling about time. There's a vital difference between the two sexes in this business of the apprehension of time.

Q: I have a question here about Bruce Woodcock's somewhat hostile criticism. He argues that your stance as a feminist writer is a posture, and that what you're really doing is to promote, by a process of realignment, the very myths of masculinity which you are purporting to expose. How would you answer such a charge?

A: I don't feel that I am doing that. His viewpoint was fairly extreme in feminist terms, wasn't it. I daresay by that standard I do fail.

Q: But do you regard yourself as a feminist writer—it seems so to me?

A: This business of feminism . . . you see, liking women, quite apart from sexual things—liking the womanly way of seeing life, came to me when I was still at Oxford, long before modern feminism came into being. *The French Lieutenant's Woman* was so successful in America largely because the American feminists took it up—it was their bible for a short time. But now they've swept on really past where I am. I know some women writers don't like me very much. I have been called the greatest block to intelligent feminism in the British novel. All I can say is that I don't agree.

Q: Can you encapsulate your position on the "woman question"? Or is it something that's too complex to be encapsulated?

God knows, I have sympathy with the whole domestic side of feminism—the outrageous responsibilities that are put on young mothers, for instance—I know that only too well from my own life. And I'm all for equality of pay, equality of opportunity and things like that. The whole lesbian side of feminism I haven't really gone for—the "lesbianism is your duty" line—I think that was a fad and it's on its way out. And there's a certain kind of militant feminism (which too often turns women into pseudomen) I can't really make up my mind about. But Greenham—that's fine. The general principle is fine.

Q: I did manage to get hold of the spring issue of *Modern Fiction Studies*. You said that there were some articles there with which you disagreed, and it struck me that Frank Novak's article—"The Dialectics of Debasement in *The Magus*—might be one area of disagreement.

A: Was that the one where he makes Nicholas a figure of modern nihilism?

Q: Yes. He says that it advances a "view of life that is both empty and terrifying;" he questions the "motives and morality of those who conduct the godgame," and suggests that the "godgame advances the nihilistic doctrine that there is no meaning"—and that Nicholas's response is an "incapacity to learn, to change, to wrest any meaning from the experience."

A: Yes, I did think that was off-beam. I have a suspicion that Mr. Novak is born again, and that I was offending him in some religious sense.

Q: One thing I did agree on was that *The Magus* does induce agitation and anxiety in the reader—at least on first reading. I wondered if that was part of the intention of the novel?

A: Students do get very worried about what it all means—about the meaning of life. But you see, I think a very important element in the novel is an area that you cannot know, a kind of area of mystery. And when I wrote that novel, it did really reflect my own not knowing what life was about—not that I understand it much better now! That's why the book is a failure for me. It's vague in places where it could have been clearer. But I think that missing area of certain knowledge is important. I've just written another novel which I'm sure is going to enrage people, for rather similar reasons.

Q: Is that *A Maggot?*

A: *A Maggot,* yes. The most obvious questions, that any decent American novelist would answer very carefully, are left sitting there. They're raised, and then the wretched author attempts no answer to them. But that for me is an important function of the novel. I rather like novels that aren't connected

and carefully linked—where you get the equivalent of a blur in impression-
ism. You're not quite sure what the author means you to think. That can be
disturbing, yes, but another awful myth of the novel is that the reader just sits
and reads, and the writer does all the work. Actually, we know the reader
contributes an enormous amount, but we don't really know what it is. We
don't know how most readers see even a fairly graphic passage.

Q: I think what worries Novak, more than the unexplained mystery, is the
seeming gratuitous cruelty of the godgame, and how it's justified. Is it meant
to be justified?

A: The whole book is based on a notion of reality. It's a long metaphor
about reality, although I did, perhaps rather foolishly, write it in realist terms.
But I think ordinary life is cruel . . . there's an appalling amount of gratuitous
cruelty in it. That's one of the reasons I have no belief in a God. Life is full
of cruelty and of not knowing why things are happening, or have happened.
You can blame the godgame on Conchis—you can say "that man is really a
sadist," as quite a number of people have; I blame God, or the system that is
the case.

Q: But it's not only Conchis, is it? The ethos of the godgame could be
construed as a kind of fascism. I mean, the justification that Lily de Seitas
offers for it, that "All that we did was to us a necessity," is disturbingly
similar to Wimmel's justification for the Nazi atrocities—"the German historical purpose."

A: Yes, that is a weak part of the book. I've never been happy about that.
When I rewrote it, I thought of leaving it out. I did toy for many years with
the idea of making Conchis a woman too, but I realised some of his acts were
male (because the writer's male) and so I couldn't do that.

Q: Novak's criticism takes the trial scene seriously, and the analysis of
Nicholas does seem to be an accurate one, but a serious purpose seems to be
undercut by the contrived jargon and the masque-like presentation. How seriously did you intend this scene to be taken?

A: Well, the jargon is not meant to be taken seriously, but I wouldn't like
to say that some of the conclusions Nicholas drew from it (because you must
remember that *he* takes it seriously too) are not to be taken seriously. But I
meant more to suggest that the game was proceeding into an artificial level
now, and that it's not quite like the other things, which are played straight. It
is becoming theatrical in the bad sense—too much dressing up—yes, going
over the top.

Q: If there's a problem for me with *The Magus,* it's that the ending appears to be very pessimistic, in that I see Nicholas as still unredeemed, inauthentic.

A: That's because of this business of nobody remembering that *he* is describing everything, writing about everything, at a period presumably many years later. I thought this would be recognised, but obviously I've made a mistake, because nobody has seen it that way—you know, rather like St. Augustine's *Confessions,* a reformed man, writing about his past errors. I meant to suggest he *must* be reformed *if* he wrote the novel—though I'm not saying he's perfect. But even on a much simpler level, I meant it to be assumed that Nicholas and Alison would get together. That last bit of Latin—you can't read it in any other way. I certainly didn't mean to give an extremely pessimistic tone to the ending.

Q: It was suggested to me that perhaps if the reader perceives Nicholas as inauthentic at the end, it means that the reader has taken the lesson or message of the book.

A: Nicholas as he was *was* inauthentic. There's a well-known story . . . I had two letters from America; one from a woman who was terribly rude about the book, especially about my using bits of French and Latin, and said "I just want one straight answer out of you—did Nicholas and Alison get together in the end?", and of course I wrote back and said "No." And the other was from an old New York lawyer who was in hospital, dying of cancer, and his letter said, "I've just got one request—please tell me if those two did get together and managed to make it"; and of course to him I wrote back "Yes." Certainly there was that slight litmus paper feeling—you know, if it reacts blue, then the answer's "no," and if it reacts the other color. . . . The same thing is in *The French Lieutenant's Woman* in a way . . . the double ending.

Q: I'm reading Simon Loveday's criticism at the moment, and he makes quite a convincing case for seeing the patterning of the novels as that of the romance. He does say, however, that this is a view which you've consistently rejected. Is this because you see any kind of generic classification as a limitation?

A: Yes, I do. I mean, I didn't disagree with his general thesis, as I recall it, about romance, but I dislike the schoolmaster syndrome in modern Eng. Lit. criticism. You know, this boy has talent only for this, and therefore he must jolly well do this. I dislike all that classifying aspect in Eng. Lit. study very much.

Q: Do you see the text and conventions as constraints on a writer's authenticity?

A: Yes, I hate being caged in one type or genre of novel, so that means I'm really against the classic English novel, Jane Austen, Richardson, all that line. At the moment, I'm paying tribute, a *festschrift,* to Golding, who for me is the ideal type of novelist. He is determined to be his own man, come hell or high water. Sometimes it leads him into error—but he's not going to be anyone else but William Golding.

Q: Frederick Smith's article on the style of revision in *The French Lieutenant's Woman* (in *Modern Fiction Studies*) suggests that the novel is "trying awfully hard to *be* a Victorian novel." This seemed like another possible area of disagreement?

A: Well, only in a pastiche sense is it trying. Curiously, only two hours before you came, I had a new novel from America. It looks like a very skilled attempt to rewrite *Tom Jones,* and purports to be a second part of Fielding's novel. It's like a very clever modern version of something Fielding *might* have written. But if I'd wanted to make *The French Lieutenant's Woman* something that might have been written by Dickens or Thackeray, then I'd have done that. So I'm not sure what he means by "trying to be." It suggests that a book has a will of its own, doesn't it?

Q: From the same criticism, I learnt that *The French Lieutenant's Woman* in the original draft had a single resolved ending, and that it was your wife's commentary which urged revision to the present, irresolute endings.

A: No, it wasn't quite so. There was a whole passage more, which I did cut because it was meant to be humorous and comic. In that, the author figure, who I just show sitting in the train, was in fact an escaped lunatic. It was quite funny, but it was out of the tone of the book; and Elizabeth pounced on that with the proper savagery of good writers' wives, so it went. When I first wrote the book, I handed it in with the "happy" ending last—perhaps that's what Smith's talking about. I wrote to Tom Maschler, my editor in London, and said I wasn't quite sure whether this was right. He came down absolutely against having the happy ending last, and so did Elizabeth, and that was that. Tom's a very good editor, you can't beat his nose on things like that. He did a brilliant job on *The Collector.*

Q: Do you mean he suggested revisions?

A: No, not revisions. He just suggested that I told the story in a different order. And so the order—you know, his story, then her story, and his little bits at the end, are purely Tom, all his idea.

Q: So that Clegg's narrative frames Miranda's?

A: Yes. Originally, Clegg's going off after another girl, and getting rid of Miranda's body, came immediately after his own confession; which took all the tension out of the book.

Q: In the first half of *Daniel Martin,* there's no attempt at what Northrop Frye calls "persuasion of continuity." Some readers have found this a problem, in that they find it difficult to enter the novel satisfactorily. What was your reason for the forward-backward movement in time here?

A: Because I was thinking of a different concept of the novel, telling it more or less without narrative. I know I have a gift for narrative, and I decided I would throw that away, for the first half of the book anyway. My idea was much more of views of various past events all regarded as being equidistant on the horizon, so that it wasn't in a narrative, chronological framework. Like bits of coloured glass. You know, when you get very close to stained glass you can't think what on earth the whole window looks like. I meant that sort of thing, whereby a framework comes retrospectively.

Q: So that the "whole sight" comes by standing back?

A: By standing back, yes . . . I wanted to treat the various incidents in Daniel's past much more emotionally than rationally or chronologically, so that something that had affected him deeply was prominent in the way you wrote it, not because you built up to it coherently, like a prepared climax.

Q: There seems to be a shift in *Daniel Martin* to me—in that the existential concept of time (at least according to my understanding of Sartrean notions) denies causality and the relatedness of past to present to future, whereas *Daniel Martin,* with its emphasis on "whole sight," seems to be insisting on a kind of panoramic and related overview?

A: Well, I did have slightly the Sartrean view in mind when I wrote the beginning like that, with those apparently unconnected fragments, but I would certainly disagree now on the Sartrean view. I think one is what one has been, what one *was.* To say that there's no moral or cultural connection with what one is seems to me to be absolute nonsense.

Q: *Daniel Martin* does make an explicit reference to Forster and "only connect." Is this novel asking one to make those Forsterian connections?

A: The connecting that takes place in that book is between Daniel Martin and his past. He's got himself into a world where you can keep the past very safely at arm's length and not really have anything much to do with it. The course of that book shows him trying to get in contact with it again. And connect with it in that sense.

Q: What about Jane's past—she symbolically buries it, doesn't she, but has to come to terms with it as well?

A: That's another form of connecting. She connects when she buries that ring. That for her is the connecting symbol. Do you like her? A lot of women don't like Jane.

Q: Yes I do. I know Carol Barnum didn't, but she said that was probably because she was so much younger than Jane. I suppose I'm about the same age as Jane, and I can identify with her and find her credible and appealing. But I did have a bit of a problem with Jenny, not so much as a person, but with her dismissal. I wondered if that was a problem in the writing of the novel?

A: The way he dismisses her?

Q: No, the way you dismiss her.

A: It didn't come as a problem. Curiously enough, it was one of the first things I knew, when writing, that she would be sent on her way, on Hampstead Heath. It's the way a little image about some scene often hangs through from the beginning to the end. No, it wasn't a problem. I did explain in "Hardy and the Hag", in a slightly naughty paragraph, that slaughtering a charming heroine, or hero, is really no problem for the novelist, because the novelist is usually thinking that there are plenty more where that one came from. In that sense, we might be a little cynical. But I'm quite clear that the general intention of the story required her to walk out.

Q: The only problem I had with Jane was her affair with Peter. I wondered why you introduced him, because it didn't seem entirely credible to me that she would have had an affair at that particular time in her life. He seemed a bit gratuitous.

A: He didn't come in with any reality, did he? I think that might have been wrong. When you're writing novels, you tend to be gratuitous if you're not very careful. You think, "I need her to have another lover," and you don't really think it through, that perhaps she doesn't need another lover. Perhaps she needs something else. And I must confess also to a thing that does influ-

ence us all, and that's personal dislikes. I've never liked the atmosphere of
north Oxford—the one that Iris Murdoch's portrayed so well, you know.
Fortuitous sex, casual adultery and all of that . . .

Q: One reference to the "Hardy and the Hag" article mentioned your
desire to reward the "surrogate self"—and I wondered if the ending of *Daniel
Martin* represented a desire to do that?

A: That mattered very much in *The French Lieutenant's Woman*—I wanted
(in the way you are always a reader of what you're writing, which is very
onanistic of course) Charles and Sarah to get together in the end. But I don't
think it's affected me since. In the case of Daniel Martin, I thought he'd
earned what he got from Jane. And then, there's all this business about the
dictatorship of the black in modern art, which I'm not very fond of—you
know, that serious, intelligent art must be black and pessimistic.

Q: Yes, there's a work-out over that *Daniel Martin,* isn't there, in the
orchard?

A: That's right, in the orchard. So in that sense, he had to be rewarded.

Q: But the ending does seem to have a sense of closure, which an unresolved ending doesn't have—as though questions have been answered. You
know, in *The Magus,* you talk about questions as life and answers as death,
so when a novel ends with what appear to be answers, one wonders what the
writer's stance is—whether it represents a change of viewpoint?

A: I think that meant a change of viewpoint.

Q: Was it a decision you took early on in the novel?

A: That it should end happily? Yes. But I point out in the Hardy piece also
that this is a very special problem for the writer. Leaving your heroine happily married, or in a resolved situation—well, it's like ending a piece of music
on the tonic chord—there's a kind of completion and it's dead now. This is
why Hardy quite happily kills off Tess of the D'Urbervilles. And why unresolved endings are easier to write, because in fact this leaves you with an
unresolved gap in your life, which you need to fill—by writing another novel.

Q: On *Mantissa*—there seems to be very little criticism available. Do you
think the critics are shy of it?

A: Well, the idea of that book really came from a commission for a private
press in America, and it was going to be one of those little things one "did
on the side." Unfortunately, my two main publishers insisted on doing it—
but no one has really tackled it.

Q: I did read it as a very funny book—ironically humorous that is.

A: Well, it certainly was meant to be. Not taken with the appalling heavy seriousness of some of its critics.

Q: Yes—at one point Miles says "There may be a place for humor in ordinary life, but there is none whatever for it in serious modern fiction." I wondered if *Mantissa* was your answer to this charge? To write a serious reflexive novel which is also very humorous?

A: A little. I mean, I'm rather split on things like deconstruction. It does have interesting ideas, but the dreaded seriousness with which all that was taken at one time I thought did need—yes, debunking.

Q: It's very much about the process of writing, isn't it?

A: About the process of writing, yes, and of being a writer; and I threw everyone by not producing stable characters—because the Muse and Miles change masks continually all the way through. It makes it difficult to review, I suppose.

Q: I wondered if it were also an answer to those literary theorists who insist on dissociating the writer and the text?

A: It was a little bit that, yes. There's so much in deconstruction—this notion that all novels have been written before, that they're only regurgitated past texts, all that sort of thing. Even if it were demonstrable, I don't think it really tells you very much. The fact that we're all reproducing past texts, in a way, is so obvious that it's cliché.

Q: You have said that irony is a problem for the modern writer, in that it "needs the assumption of superiority in the ironist." It seems to me that there is a dual author-persona here in *Mantissa*—one who is being ironic at his own expense (the writer plagued with the tormenting muse, the feminist plagued with chauvinistic fantasies), and the one who floats "godlike, alpha and omega," detached above it all. Is that right?

A: I think it's fair to say that, yes. There *are* two kinds of irony—one's almost slapstick.

Q: Do you see yourself primarily as a didactic writer? As a writer with a message, or an insight which you hope the reader might find helpful or educational in the philosophical sense?

A: All through my literary life, "didactic" has been a curse word, and usually when it's used about me, it's used in a cursing way. I'd have to go back to why I like Golding. You know, we're not a school, but if there were such a school, we might be together in it. It's simply that I think one's duty is to be oneself, and if one's being oneself, then a fairly clear expression of opinion, of likes and dislikes, must follow from it. I suppose the actual stylistic way I write must sound didactic on occasion.

But I think bits of dull old bread, among all the other dishes, make sense. I have a theory about Jane Austen—that she's a very up and down writer. Many of her passages seem to me boring, flat; and then you come upon those absolutely dazzling pages; where every line of dialogue is perfect in every syllable, and she's observing with her usual shrewdness. This is her trick, in a way—that she can be dull for a few pages, and then come those flawless scenes and pages.

I think that aspect of the novel, the dull, the pale brown passages, is in fact very useful. Modern thriller writers try to keep it all bright red, or bright blue, but I think if you're trying to do something rather more serious, then you have to accept that part of what you do *will* be boring, and not so good. It's this sort of up and downness which actually makes the novel. George Eliot, I feel, overdoes it—she's too dull for too long, but again, when she gets a good scene, or when she gets the general balance right, as in *Middlemarch,* then the effect is really very desirable.

Q: I wondered whether, in leaving your reader to make his own choices, especially in the choice of endings, you're offering the reader a kind of existentialist lesson in the making of responsible choices?

A: Yes, a bit. Do you remember the Rorschach test, where you had to say what some inkblot shape most seemed to resemble? I quite like that kind of image of what the novel can do to give a sort of freedom to the reader. It's extremely difficult to give the reader any freedom (except in the natural way he or she reads), but that's an ambition I have.

Q: I do sense a pessimism in your writing, about things like the "state of the nation" of the "future of the cosmos"—and yet there is also an optimism I think, in the love of nature which is so strong, especially in *Daniel Martin,* and in the assertion of man's potential for growth, authenticity, evolution . . . Does this reflect oscillations of mood—or does one predominate in your world view?

A: But we all feel this, don't we—depressed by the world? Yes, I do think the world's in a very bad, nasty state. Yes, I do think it's getting worse. Among other things, there's a growing debility caused by the diffuseness of language itself. I think contemporary language is so diffuse, so second-hand, now, that it's losing a lot of its ancient power. I'm very fond of all the old dialects, which have disappeared, even round here, and that's only one tiny symptom. Selfishness worries me too. The world's becoming more selfish, more egocentric. I've given up ideas of changing the world. I think all the novel can do is to change people's sensibilities—if you're very lucky. It's not so much that I think you can make them change their minds about any specific thing, but perhaps you can change the way they see certain things. Whenever I say this, people say things like "what about Sinclair Lewis and the American socialist novelists—they did change the Chicago slaughter houses," and so on, but I'm not really very sanguine.

Q: The new novel—*A Maggot*—is it going to be the Defoe-like historical novel which you mentioned to Carol Barnum?

A: Yes. I first mentioned it in Exeter, years ago. I was addressing some group, and I was explaining how such things came into one's mind . . .

Q: Do you mean that image which starts a novel for you?

A: Yes. This was simply of people riding on a hillside, for no apparent purpose at all.

Q: Is it concerned with similar themes—of authenticity and freedom?

A: Yes, it is in a way, but it's mainly concerned—in my mind that is, not in textual terms—with the rise of an extraordinary sect called the Shakers. The woman who founded it was a working class woman in Manchester called Ann Lee—I don't say anything directly about her, but the novel ends with her birth. It's really about the rise of primitive Dissent in the 1730's.

Q: Is it a reflexive novel, in the way that *The French Lieutenant's Woman* is?

A: Only in the sense that I do break in here and there, and comment on what's happening. But much less than in *The French Lieutenant's Woman*. Like everything I write, it's a kind of exploration. That period has always interested me, because it was a very dull period in intellectual terms, the early eighteenth century. And because of the rise of these very primitive types of dissenting religion that arose then. But I shall be cursed there, that's for sure. Didactic again, and all the rest of it.

A Conversation with John Fowles

Carlin Romano / 1986

From *Boulevard,* 2 (Spring 1987), 38–52. Reprinted by permission of
Carlin Romano and *Boulevard Magazine.*

In September, 1985, Fowles came to the U.S. for the first time in eight years
for the publication of his latest novel, *A Maggot.* An 18th-century detective
novel of sorts, it is, like many of Fowles's works, open-ended, forcing the
reader to decide what occurs in it. At a certain point in the novel, the narrative
stops and the remainder of the book becomes, in large part, the transcript of
an investigation into earlier events. A key character in the book is a young
prostitute whose reputation as the Quaker Maid in a London brothel has made
her an especially prized companion.

This interview took place September 9, 1986, in the Manhattan offices of
Fowles's publisher, Little, Brown.

Carlin Romano: Do they have author tours of this sort in England? You
know, a day in Manchester, a day in York?

John Fowles: Yes. There are quite a lot. They're usually sort of semi-
official, you know, it's "the arts council tours writers in the Northeast," or
things like that. I don't take part in any of that, but many writers feel they
have to do it just for the sake of literature.

Romano: In reading about you, I came across a new book, *The Romances
of John Fowles* by Simon Loveday. Do you know that book?

Fowles: Yes, I read it in proof and didn't much like it. It belongs to a
school in England I call the fishmonger school. They put you on a cold slab
and then filet you and dissect you. It's sort of fashionable in England, you
know, to cut the writer down to size. I don't disapprove of that, but it's the
coldness with which it's done. I don't think this has happened to living writers before. This incredibly detailed study of their work, as if they're dead.
You feel dead at the end of it, you see.

Romano: It is a strange mentality at work in Loveday's book, this business
of making your work fit the "romance" in this respect and that respect.

Fowles: Yes. Pursuing a thesis. I had an even worse one recently, which

134

proved I wasn't a socialist, I wasn't a feminist—everything about which I do have convictions, you know.

Romano: One quote, though, sticks in my mind from that book. I don't know if it's something you did say, or that you renounce now, but Loveday put a lot of weight on it. It was your saying at one time that you would rather be a sound philosopher than a good novelist.

Fowles: Yes. I've always had a hankering towards that, and I'd rather be a good poet than a novelist, if I'm honest. But I'm afraid I realize at my age, none of it is to be. It's just that I think you have to have ideas if you're going to be a novelist. I know that's not philosophy, of course, in the modern sense of the word. But the notion that novelists shouldn't have ideas, I think, is rubbish.

Romano: Suppose you could state, in *The Aristos* or somewhere, all the beliefs you actually hold in straightforward philosophical language. What would be the reason then for expressing them in a novelistic form?

Fowles: There's a quick answer to that—which is just to get them consumed. The nice thing about the novel is that it usually has a sugar coating. I mean, nobody really swallows pills with only pleasure. For example, I had a problem in this new book, this extraordinary Shaker philosophy, or rather theology, which I have some sympathy for.

Romano: What about the common response of the literary critic toward many writers who do have ideas, and want them to come across in fiction— that starting with ideas, and building characters to express them, is *prima facie* wrong. That if your ideas come first, in any regard you're doing something improper as a novelist.

Fowles: I certainly don't agree with that. I'm not really into anything—a believer in compartments, you know. I feel that I'm a tiny bit of a scientist, I suppose. I dislike intensely the parochialism of "goods" in modern science, where you get somebody who knows everything about some tiny subject, and never ventures an opinion on anything else. The scientists I know, they're very often rather awkward customers. Who is it in America, that paleontologist Jay Gould, who doesn't really hide his Marxism? I like that—that's nice. The excessive specialization in science, I think, is nightmarish.

Romano: I was trying to think of an analogous figure to you in American literary culture, someone who rejected the idea that strong moral judgments

136   Conversations with John Fowles

and philosophical beliefs undermine the rights of fiction. The closest I came was the late John Gardner.

Fowles: I hadn't read him. He was kind to me, I believe, in one of his books. But I hadn't really read him. I read *October Light*—I quite liked that. And somebody sent me recently an extraordinary piece on whether he killed himself or not in that motorcycle crash. I found that rather attractive, this mystery about his death. I think the article came to the conclusion that he didn't do it on purpose. But it did raise various problems about the ways it had been handled officially, police evidence and so on. Very sad that he did go like that. He was an original, I felt.

Romano: He was, to say the least, unembarrassed by ideas. Most American literary types are embarrassed by ideas. They know you're not supposed to have them and certainly you're not supposed to flaunt them. It's one reason I get bored a lot by fiction I have to read.

Fowles: Don't worry. So do I. So do I. I find a very little fiction goes a long way. And as you grow older, it's the older fiction you like. When I was flying over here, I was looking in a bookstore with every book you could want. God knows why, suddenly I bought a Hardy I'd read a dozen times before. It somehow represents sanity, reading all that.

Romano: I wanted to ask you a few general things about your career. Has there been a conscious wish on your part to be seen, as a novelist, in the way you are seen?

Fowles: If you'll forgive me, I think that this is suggesting a power of free will in the novelist that doesn't exist. I mean, the notion that we make ourselves what we want to be is, I think, very fallacious. I think we're largely—all human beings—conditioned. The degree in writing to which you can make sort of conscious existential choices—"I choose to do this"—I'm highly dubious of that. In a strange way, the actual act of writing can give you this strong feeling of free will on paper. You know, it can be constant, even rather frightening, because you write every word, you have a hundred—or at least three—choices, anyway. And I also think, you see, it's very important to know what you're leaving out in a novel. I don't think this is taught in creative writing. It's what a novelist doesn't say that is almost as important as what he does say. What he refuses to explain. In this latest novel *(A Maggot)* I'm refusing to explain. It's risky obviously, but you have to make sort of a fairly deliberate choice about that. Am I going to try and explain what really happened, or am I not?

Romano: That's a risk you've taken before.
Fowles: I've taken it before.

Romano: One observation about your work is that you provide options on a regular basis—you did in some of the other novels. How much of this is a request for what might be called audience participation?
Fowles: Well, I'm a great believer in the importance of the reader. For me, no academic literary inquiry has really begun to touch this. We don't know what happens in a person's mind when he's reading. But certainly it can be a very creative or a very misguided process you know. But I think because I don't know what readers are thinking—no one knows what they're really thinking—there is for me a place for giving them clear options they can take so they *have* to intervene in the book. I partly like this because I'm a great believer in the "I-Thou" theory about writing. You know, however many times a book is read, it takes place, it becomes real, between two people always. And I feel that some novelists don't really realize that, that they're sort of addressing an audience of thousands.

Romano: Do you face what perhaps the moviemaker faces, that the people commercially receiving your book want the clear ending, the happy ending?
Fowles: Yes. I'm well aware of that, especially in this country. I hope I do it when there is for me a clear reason for giving the alternative ending, sort of allowing two possibilities to coexist in a book. I think that could be dangerous if it became your gimmick, as it were.

Romano: For instance, with *The French Lieutenant's Woman,* did you encounter any actual opposition to the way you ended that?
Fowles: Yes. I've told this story many times. I had two extraordinary letters from America, one day. One lady wrote and said, "Your book drove me wild with rage. Why can't you say what you mean, etc. etc. I just want you to answer one plain question"—this is over *The Magus*—"Did the boy and girl at the end get together? Did they make it?" I wrote back and of course said, "No."
The other letter was from a New York lawyer dying of cancer in a hospital there. And he said, "I enjoyed your book and I just would like to know what you feel happened to those two at the end." And I said, of course, they made it—they got together. But I tell that story because that's how I feel—I don't know the answer. And I tend to react as people want, or don't want it—if they've annoyed me—to end.

Romano: Many major writers become prisoners of certain clichés about them. There are little encyclopedia articles about them already, there are clips that people like me can look at . . .

Fowles: Yes, awful . . .

Romano: So your reputation does preceed you. What do you think of the cliché of John Fowles at this point?

Fowles: He's an enemy, an enemy! I think of him as "Fowles." I'm John and he's "Fowles." I mean, it's the language of all these doctoral theses: "Fowles does so and so." I just had to write a piece about [William] Golding. I really based it on the notion of "Golding" in quotes, and Golding the real human being. I don't think any of us live with it happily.

Romano: Are there particular parts of it you'd like to reject while we're here? "Philosophical novelist," for instance, appears in almost everything I've read about you.

Fowles: Well, I wouldn't call myself a philosophical novelist. But it's really a matter of ideas. I have criticized the feminist movement in some ways, but I know at heart I'm a feminist—I'm very much pro womankind. But when people write books proving I'm not—yes, that annoys you. But you can't do anything about it. And I think, in literature, it all comes out in the wash in the end. You know, your number is God's after you're dead, probably.

Romano: Still, novelists in the English language who are not afraid of philosophy are rare.

Fowles: I'm not a philosopher, as you must realize. My father was very keen on it. Very strange habit in a businessman, but his hobby was philosophy.

Romano: Generally speaking, there's little connection here between academic philosophy and the rest of the media culture, including the literary world. Most of the top philosophers are hardly known to literary people here.

Fowles: Well, some of them are difficult, aren't they? I mean, you know, the French literary theorists. Heaven help you if you're really determined to understand them. Have you tried to read Derrida?

Romano: I've tried. The only full moment of communication that ever took place was when I physically ran into him at the door of a pizzeria in New Haven. He has a very bad reputation for only speaking French, even in this country. He was sort of forced to say "Excuse me."

Fowles: That was a very meaningful statement by his standards. I've tried to read him and Lacan. You know, when you have to read a page three times even to begin to understand what it means. . . . It's sad in a way, being so obscure. Ayer is comparatively plainspeaking, isn't he? But philosophy has lapsed very badly, I think, recently. The whole linguistic school, Oxbridge, really killed it.

Romano: Did you read much philosophy at university?

Fowles: Well, we had to, you know, as part of the French course. One had a philosophical part, Descartes and all that.

Romano: Are there philosophers you find yourself unusually in accord with?

Fowles: I think an honest answer would be that it's some years since I've read very much philosophy, and I couldn't give an honest answer. I used to adore Plato, but that was for literary reasons, I think, more than what he was saying. Heraclitus did deeply appeal to me, but I suspect now that that was more literary, the extraordinary brevity of those tiny fragments that have survived, and some of the other preSocratic philosophers. But Kant I could never really get on with very much. Descartes, I couldn't. Lacan, I think, was the last philosopher I read, about a year ago. I really gave up. It's all these neologisms. I wouldn't mind if they published a long explanatory glossary in the back.

Romano: Let me go back to some of those clichés about your work. How about Loveday's idea, which he describes in his book, about your wanting to distinguish between the aristocracy and the rest of the world, "the one and the many"?

Fowles: Well, curse the day I ever stated that idea as baldly as I did. For me, it was a biological idea, basically, but, of course, it has been seized on by left-wing England as a quasi-fascist idea. But I tried to answer that when I rewrote *The Aristos.*

Romano: Does that idea persist in English literary circles that you're somehow elitist?

Fowles: I don't really think so anymore. It's just that I said all that in a period in England when you couldn't say that many human beings are rather stupid and rather dull, and you know, all the ordinary things that are sort of obvious, final common sense. I would call myself a democratic socialist, of all political terms. You know, I support the Labor Party, which is very difficult in England (Laughs).

Romano: Even with Jeffrey Archer getting prominent on the other side?

Fowles: Yes. I have an awful feeling he's a shyster, really. Still, in their party, they're all shysters.

Romano: How about such remarks about your work as its "reverence for nature," its "feeling of nature as sacred in some way"?

Fowles: That's very true. I have a deep love of nature, a need of it, which I'm deprived of at the moment. I mean I hate big cities, I must confess. This is partly an aesthetic thing if I must say so. But I also have really more philosophical views. I think the deprivation of nature in the average city in regard to the average man or woman is reaching appalling standards here and in London. This, for me, is the great cancer of this century. And also the way that all the media now really present nature as an entertainment. You know, you have these marvelous Attenborough films, and all the rest of it. And I think this harms local real nature around you. You only want exotic birds or fish off the barrier reef. I object to this very strongly.

Romano: You once talked about the desire to exile yourself from the England of London without leaving England.

Fowles: Well, first of all, I'm against writers leaving their own country. I know Durrell's done it and D. H. Lawrence, there are countless famous examples. And I can understand it when the psychological situation is so awful that they've got to go abroad. But I think it's dangerous. I think the one thing you mustn't exile yourself from is your language, your mother tongue, the tongue you write in. But I'm in exile really from Britain, the notion of Britain, the monarchy. I'm that rare thing—an English Republican. I have no time at all for the British monarchy. And Americans constantly embarrass me by saying "how beautiful and charming your Queen is."

Romano: Do they say that really?

Fowles: Yes. Yes. You know, "She's such a lovely woman." They imagine because you're English, you must care. We English Republicans are a tiny percentage, between 5 and 10 per cent of the whole country. It is *the* lost cause of all lost causes.

Romano: It always seems to me that there's a thin veneer of upper American newspaper and magazine editors who assign stories on Princess Diana, and nobody else really cares. But they keep putting those stories out, so people have to read them.

Fowles: A lot of those upper class kind of Americans have never been republicans in the small "r" sense. They still long for an aristocracy and a supporting monarchy.

Romano: Do you feel that after living in Lyme Regis as long as you have, you would be comfortable writing a contemporary novel about contemporary London?

Fowles: Would I be happy to do it? Oh, yes. The generation I feel I'm beginning to have trouble with—but I think all people my age feel that—are the young people. I don't know if I have their language or preoccupations. I should be troubled creating a young contemporary hero or heroine.

Romano: In the U.S., some people think that in the media age, it's possible for small-town Kentuckians to know how New Yorkers talk.

Fowles: I feel that a little. I could have a shot at it. But I wouldn't go to that kind of subject, just as I wouldn't go towards doing a full-scale American character, because, as I'm sure you know, the most difficult two cultures are Americans writing about Britain, or the English trying to write about America. I mean, the mistakes in dialogue that crop up are legion.

Romano: Is there a simple answer to why you choose to write about the 18th century in your new book, *A Maggot?*

Fowles: Well, the Shakers had to come into it from the beginning, so, in a sense, I put it in the 18th century because I think it's the early years of the Shakers that interest me much. It's partly out of always loving Defoe's work too. People often say, "Who has influenced you most, you know, who is still alive in England?" and I usually answer "Daniel Defoe," which is quibbling about what you mean by alive. But I belong to that stream in the English novel, as opposed to the Richardson, Austen, classical stream.

Romano: How do you feel when critics find all of these archetypes of literary criticism in your work, such as when Loveday and others say that you're always writing a "quest" novel? Do you sit down and think, "I'm going to write a quest novel?"

Fowles: No, I don't. But to that I would plead guilty at once. The notion of the quest has always attracted me very deeply, especially in the early Celtic novels, you know, the 12th-century novel. Another person who's influenced me in a bizarre way is a lady called Marie de France. I don't know if you've ever read her. She wrote things she called "Lais," which were really short stories in verse. And for me the whole essence of good fiction writing really is in those very short stories.

Romano: Given that you have a great appreciation for this "I-Thou" relationship in reading, do you nonetheless have any preferred response from your readers, a sense of what your ideal reader should think?

Fowles: Well, this book, I approached, I suppose, vaguely with the notion of South American magic realism in mind. I derived that, actually, not from Garcia Marquez, though I admire people like that, but from one of the very great influences on my life, the French writer Henri Alain-Fournier who once said, "I only like the marvelous when it is enveloped in strict reality."

I remember when I first read that, I seized on it as you do when you hear somebody say exactly what you think. This book was a bit of an exercise in wrapping the marvelous in strict reality. I wished also to give one person's undoubtedly quirky view of what life had been like in the 18th century. I think this is something the novel can do. I do a certain amount of proper real history, at home, you know, because I run the local museum. And I like that, too, but that's a strict discipline, where you mustn't cheat, you must quote from documents, give references. But I would hate if that became the only way of approaching history. So, in a way, this book is Mr. Fowles's magic-guided tour of a curious period in English history, the early 18th century.

Romano: Is there any mockery of the investigatory process intended, and what it can give you?

Fowles: Well, I've always liked that as a technique, because I'm a collector of books, and I've always loved 18th-century trials. And this is where the business of what you don't write comes in. A lovely thing about the Q & A form is that you're cutting off an arm, in fact. Because in most novels, you can say, "She smiled," or "She looked sad," or "She went to the window," or whatever. And, of course, you forbid that once you enter this form. So you have to make your dialogue work pretty hard, certainly harder than an ordinary straightforward novel's dialogue. And that kind of challenge always pleases me. I think also, in the novel, you've got to find something you know you're not sure you can do. You have to search your soul for hurdles and obstacles.

Romano: How do you feel the prostitute character will be received by your feminist critics?

Fowles: Well, I was interviewed just before I came here by one in England, a well-known feminist literary lady. She objected to it, and I'm sure strict contemporary feminists will object to it. She complained that I should make a character, first of all, a prostitute, and then turn her into a saint, sort of "overnight," as she put it, and that this was not plausible. But I really chose that somewhat extraordinary change to illustrate that there was this sort of very early existentialism in the 18th century. People were converted from one thing to the other overnight, often by preachers like John Wesley.

Romano: Do you basically accept the traditional existentialist view that people can make free choices?

Fowles: I used to in the '50s, it's dogged me ever since. "Existentialist novelist" is a label I slightly choke over now. Speaking in general, I've become more and more of a determinist, though I'm not as far as Skinner's gone. I tend to think, partly from my own experience of myself, that we are very largely conditioned. But I think, curiously, in novel-writing, you can, if only metaphorically, exercise a certain degree of free will, or what feels like free will—let me put it like that. I sort of like trying to express that feeling that people can occasionally make really moral non-self-interested decisions.

Romano: Do you see yourself as a moralist in fiction? As someone who has moral judgments to communicate?

Fowles: I would say that. In some ways, I wish I had the courage to stand out there and say, "This city is doomed!" (Laughs).

Romano: That job is taken. Every five corners there's somebody with a megaphone.

Fowles: I'm sure there is. But you know, you do feel a kind of moral horror over some things. It was provoked in me the other day on West 55th when we were walking along the sidewalk and I could see a bagel, a whole bagel, lying on the ground, that had just one bite out of it. Obviously, someone had taken one bite and thrown it away. And I did feel like finding a soapbox. This is the society of waste. And the food portions in New York drive me absolutely mad—the way they always give you twice as much as you need to eat or can eat. This is not a new feeling. I've always felt this.

Romano: This is, I understand, your first time over here in eight years. Are there other things about America you're being reminded of, that you like or don't like?

Fowles: I like the forthrightness of the women when I overhear them. This hasn't arrived in England, really, in any sort of widespread sense. I have a feeling it *is* a much more equal society in those sex-chauvinistic terms. And, I suppose, there's something about the freedom and the richness that is nice. I think it's out of hand at the moment.

Romano: Have you mixed much with literary types on this visit?

Fowles: No, I haven't. I don't think writers are ever typical of a country, alas.

Romano: One of the differences between the U.S. and England is the large number of writers who are teaching creative writing here. Is there much of that in England?

Fowles: Some universities have things they call "writers in residence" who are effectively teaching writing. I'm totally opposed to it. I'm probably a ghastly old conservative over this. I don't really believe in it. It certainly produces competent writing. I occasionally read American literary journals. The average level seems to me far higher than in England. But it also produces for me a kind of uniformity, as if everybody is too wise and they know exactly what will find favor. And I don't think that's really how you write original novels, by sort of pleasing all your ex-teachers. We have that in England a bit in many Oxford students. You can sense they're really writing for the sharpest teachers they had at Oxford and Cambridge, and that for me is not a good process.

Romano: Are you in a position now where people make pilgrimages to see you, or deluge you with mail?

Fowles: I get a lot of mail, too much to answer. Yes, some visitors do knock on my door. I'm afraid they don't usually have a very warm reception.

Romano: You're also not thrilled, I understand, by the movie versions of your books.

Fowles: *The Collector?* I do quite like William Wyler. He did make some very fine films. I don't think *The Collector* was one of his best ones. I think it was miscast, unfortunately. *The Magus* was a disaster. It was the worst film of the '60s. Or what was the other one, *Justine?* It was a close race between the two. In *The French Lieutenant's Woman,* I had the director I wanted, and the scriptwriter I wanted, and that was a very pleasant experience for me. I really—well, one can always criticize a film if you're the author of the original book—but I really have no problems. I like that.

Romano: Was *Daniel Martin* too tough to film?

Fowles: *Daniel Martin* has been under option for several years in Hollywood, but that was a little bit written to goad the cinema. I mean, I know there were things about it that would make any normal Hollywood producer feel ill, like having a hero of three ages. It's possible the BBC will do it as a serial, and I think that's more reasonable, because you can't fit a book like that into two hours—it's not possible.

Romano: I know that at the time it came out many people thought it was deeply autobiographical.

Fowles: Oh, no. It had autobiographical fragments, and what I said in it about the cinema was certainly autobiographical. The Hollywood cinema, you know.

Romano: Saul Bellow had, I always thought, a good line about film versions of his work. He said that he'd had the ideal situation for a writer—all of his books had been optioned, and none had been filmed.

Fowles: That's quite a nice way to go on, actually. You get a nice yearly income and no hassle.

Romano: There seems to still cling to your reputation, perhaps because of *The Magus,* and what Nicholas Urfe sees and goes through, some sense of the eerie, or the otherworldly. Is there any chance you'll someday be interpreted as an English Stephen King?

Fowles: That is categorically not autobiographical. I have no belief in ghosts or the supernatural or exorcists or anything like that. I suffered when I was in California. I would get these mysterious phone calls: "Please, will you tell me when you met Ouspensky?", and "Do you write on marijuana or something stronger?"

Romano: Do you see yourself as a rationalist?

Fowles: Yes. But in terms of a novel, I wouldn't stick too close to rationalism or naturalism. I think you have to stay free to write a novel.

Romano: It's certainly a distinctive thing when a writer does take the time and effort to revise an already published work. What has your thinking been when you've made that effort?

Fowles: I did it really out of a sort of feeling of bad faith, that I'd put out a book which I knew was not written as well as I could have made it. I've often used the comparison of, "You've made something like that table there, and you know it's badly jointed, and you know there are all sorts of things wrong with it, so you take it apart and try to make it better." For me, it was much more a personal thing than anything else. I felt I had to do this to live with myself as a writer. And the result has been that many people write and tell me the first version is infinitely better.

Romano: Have you tried to get the first version off the market?

Fowles: I haven't really. I think it's impossible to buy the first version. I certainly wouldn't want to. If Little, Brown wrote and said we're thinking of doing the first version again, I would forbid that.

Romano: I've long believed that for a lot of American writers, there's nothing that they'd really rather be than a great English novelist.

Fowles: Really?

Romano: That they've grown up on Dickens . . .

Fowles: Yes, oh, in that sense. . . .

Romano: That somehow being a great American novelist could never have the cultural resonance of being a great English novelist. I'm wondering if being a great English novelist is all it's cracked up to be.

Fowles: I wouldn't say that it's very much today. I know Hardy's life pretty well, and it strikes you that Hardy really swallowed it at the end of his life, when he was a famous grand old man of literature—you sort of feel he swallowed it all, he believed in it. And that, I think, has become impossible. I think we're all too self-conscious now for that to happen.

Romano: Do you find in England any more reverence toward you, say, than here on the "Today Show"?

Fowles: No. England's a much tougher tiger in that sense.

Romano: What do they say there? *(Feigning British accent)* "Novelist, are you?"

Fowles: Yes! Yes! I'll never forget the first party at my publishers in London, where one of the directors of the firm came up and said, "Are you one of these writer fellows?" It's just that you can't trust writers at business, so we old public school fellows ought to run it. That is dying in London. I have a very good, tough publisher in London, who would beat most Americans for sheer toughness.

Romano: One thing that Bellow, who I think shares certain views of fiction with you, has complained about, is the decline of the writer as public figure, willing to take a public stand.

Fowles: I complained about that in England a number of years ago, but it's difficult. Because everyone in England says, "Well, there's a vain chap. He wants to be on more television," and so on. But I really said it not for me. It seemed to me ridiculous that people like Iris Murdoch, or Angus Wilson, shouldn't really be into public affairs more.

Romano: I wonder if the established novelist is taken seriously in England if he chooses to get on a soapbox, or take a stand. If you called the BBC, or the papers, and said, "I want to have a press conference about Argentina," would reporters beat a path to your door?

Fowles: I would rather doubt it. Some writers—who's the *Watership Down* man—Richard Adams. He's taken up a subject which I feel close to, conservation, fairly well. I think it does his reputation a certain amount of good. But I would rather doubt if that means he's listened to anymore than normally. I think it's part of the general descent of literature in world status, which of course is enormous, with all the new media. I have a feeling it will come back. I don't feel pessimistic.

Romano: Are you ambitious? Are you someone who cares about getting a Nobel Prize?

Fowles: No, I don't care in the least about prizes—that's a thing that doesn't worry me. But no writer can say, "I don't think about what I shall be a hundred years from now." You know, if any writer says I don't care, he's lying. Of course, we all wonder what we'll become, but I don't worry or get neurotic about that. In that sense, I suppose I'm an existentialist in the vulgar meaning. I do really live in the "now."

Romano: Do you feel fortunate in the way your life is now?

Fowles: I feel fortunate that I am a writer, that I can write, and the business about recognition, wealth, *et cetera* . . . I mean, fame doesn't really bring you any happiness at all in my experience. *At* all. It really is gilt, trumpery stuff.

Romano: Do the townspeople in Lyme Regis consider you a regular guy around there?

Fowles: Actually, they probably think me rather a withdrawn person because I don't go into society. I put quite a lot of time into the museum. It's a tiny, tiny museum. It's become a sort of hobby of mine, I enjoy running that, and doing research. But I feel that's just a little gift you owe society back.

Romano: What do you think of the reviews of *A Maggot?*

Fowles: They're predictable, given my past. That is, they're mixed. I've never not had mixed reviews. But I accept that as an inevitable consequence of the way I write. You're going to annoy some people, please others.

Romano: A closing matter. One of the unquestionable marks of your writing is the richness of your language. How much thought do you give to that richness, and the problems it may cause the less adept reader?

Fowles: Language to me is sacrosanct. I won't accept the argument that one must write for the common man. In countless things in life, I'm all for the common man. But I think, with the language itself, there really are no let-outs. You have to make it as rich as you can because you're preserving the richness of language. And that, God knows, at the moment, when everybody's vocabulary seems to be getting smaller and smaller, I think is a problem. I would say that this is a conservationist view.

I get quite a lot of manuscripts from people, and I write back and say, you know, the technique's all haywire—you can't punctuate, you can't spell, *et cetera.*

And you get these terrible letters back, which give their life story. "I had to leave school at the age of 13," and "I wasn't lucky enough to go to university."

And again, I write back and say, "Sorry, I have the utmost sympathy for you, but this is no excuse. You have to learn the language."

Interview with John Fowles

Katherine Tarbox / 1988

From *The Art of John Fowles* (Athens, Georgia: University of Georgia Press, 1988), 170–91. Copyright © 1988 by The University of Georgia Press. Reprinted by permission of Katherine Tarbox and The University of Georgia Press.

You said in *The Aristos* that you would never want to be called a novelist. Are you happy with the name novelist now?

Fowles: I don't think of myself as only a novelist. I suppose I could say the novel is something I happen to enjoy, and I suppose I'm fairly good at it. But I do write novels mainly to discover myself and life. Really, I'm much more just an experiencer of life. I don't honestly mind being called a novelist. In my own private mythology it's rather too limiting.

Q: Are your novels more dear to you than, say, your nonfiction works, or do you care equally for both?

Fowles: Inasmuch as an author can rank his work, I did enjoy *The Tree* very much. It was a great pleasure to write that; that's the one I prefer of the nonfiction. I enjoyed bits of *Islands,* too. Certainly I wouldn't distinguish between writing them and writing novels. But there's always a certain surreptitious excitement when you're writing a novel, because you never know what's going to happen, whereas in nonfiction books you do start with much more of an idea of what you're going to say; and I hate the planned in everything. In fiction there is a certain first-draft mood which comes upon you, which is marvelous and is the nicest of all literary experiences. When you're into a narrative and it seems so full of forks and possibilities, and you're full of ideas, that is marvelous. That's the best of all literary experiences.

Q: What are you working on now?

Fowles: At the moment I have three or four possibilities. I suppose I'm lazy now. I don't feel any pressure to publish, and I also have a strong belief that the longer you keep books to yourself, the better they finally go. So, you know, they're just kicking about, and perhaps one day the mood takes you and you finish them.

149

Q: It's all up to chance?

Fowles: No, well . . . no. I think probably deep down it's not up to chance, because the unconscious is such a large part of every artist. There are probably unconscious things that make you slow about finishing a text or make you feel you must absolutely finish it, as I did with *The Collector,* for instance. I wrote *The Collector* in one month—the first draft. But I don't think I could ever do that now, because the whole business gets more difficult as you grow older. It was just that the idea hit me, and once it started it demanded to be sort of raced through. When I say I wrote the first draft in a month, it went through lots of revisions afterwards, but the basic story did come quite exceptionally fast for me.

Q: Do you feel that writing is a calling? Are you driven to write, as the cliché suggests?

Fowles: Yes, absolutely. In old-fashioned terms it is a vocation. With a lot of writers, of course, I don't think it is a vocation, but I would say for every writer I admire it is truly a vocation. Of course lots of writers write to make lots of money, and it clearly isn't a vocation for them. It's just a trick they've picked up and a straight profession like any other.

Q: What's the most difficult part of writing for you?

Fowles: I should think the revising part. I write lots of drafts, but so does almost every writer I've ever heard of. I don't know anyone who can sit down and write a perfect text. I've quoted quite often the hypnotism chapter in *The Magus,* which I left out because I couldn't cope with it. All it was in the typescript was just a page with a note "Conchis hypnotizes Nicholas," or something like that. I couldn't actually see how to do it. I did it right at the very end; I wrote it in one morning, in fact. The accursed Erato was on my side on that occasion. This does happen in narrative: you'll get a chapter down very fast and then the most ridiculous little thing in some other one causes you hours and hours of problems. On the whole, dialogue is the most difficult thing, without any doubt. It's very difficult, unfortunately. You have to detach yourself from the notion of a lifelike quality. You see, actually lifelike, tape-recorded dialogue like this has very little to do with good novel dialogue. It's a matter of getting that awful tyranny of mimesis out of your mind, which is difficult. Evelyn Waugh is the man I admire. I don't like him on social or philosophical grounds, but I think he was an admirable handler of dialogue.

Q: All through your books there is a great deal of emphasis on music and painting. Do you paint or play?

Fowles: No. Well, when I say I don't play, I can just about get my fingers around a recorder; and, oh, I've tried to draw, but I have no skill.

Q: How do you feel about the fame you have achieved? Have there been adverse effects?

Fowles: Yes, many. I don't like it. I don't suffer it here because I have a sort of understanding with the town. They know I don't like being treated as famous. Yes, it has all sorts of problems, especially with old friends. I used to resent it because I used to think relationships had changed with old friends; but I realize that it is a traumatic experience for them, in a strange sort of way. And I think it's disagreeable because you can be taken too seriously, and you can get the feeling that you're being treated as if you were already dead—which I hate. I also get a very large correspondence, you see, especially from America. It takes—if I answer it all—too much time. Lots of well-meaning people write really rather lovely letters to me, and I can't answer them as humanly as one should. And the nicest letters are often the most difficult to deal with. You get a lot of other minor things like autograph hunters. Or "Will you please trace your hand?" and "Can I have a signed photograph?" That last is the one I particularly loathe—as if you're a pop star. I have a basic sympathy with writers like Salinger or Pynchon, who have a kind of shyness, or a neurotic complex, about all this. I fully understand it; I feel it myself once in a while. It's because you've had so many bad experiences, unfortunately.

Q: Do you still have a great interest in films?

Fowles: I see a few when I go to London, usually Continental films, because we never see them here. Yes, I enjoy films very much.

Q: Are you aware of all the cinematic qualities in your work?

Fowles: Yes. Films must have altered literary imagination greatly, I think. I did have periods in my life when I was seeing an enormous quantity of films, several a week. You can't pick up a modern novel without seeing techniques of editing—cutting, and all the rest of it. Flashbacks. The funny thing is, of course, that the cinema in fact got them from literature in the first place, so I don't feel bad about this at all. I just think it's a curious feedback, in effect, from how the cinema directors first used literature to develop their own art, and now we've got this sort of repayment from them.

Q: You've put yourself in exile down here in Lyme?
Fowles: In exile from literary England.

Q: Well, you've spoken several times about a feeling of alienation, a feeling that you've come from another planet, and that sometimes you don't understand the beings around you.
Fowles: Yes, I do feel that way. That's really not so much why I live in Lyme, but has to do with my whole feeling about nature. In many ways I have closer feelings to nature than I do to other human beings. I suppose living in a comparatively remote place like this is a kind of exile. But I think most novelists are implicitly in exile from most of society around them because of the elements in the novel which require you to look at your society objectively and criticize it. That immediately makes you different from most other members of that society. Therefore, that is a kind of inner exile which I should have thought every ordinary novelist would have felt. I mean, we do see life differently from most other people—and not only in a political way or a social way. We're so . . . what's very important for us is this whole business of writing. You've read up deconstruction, no doubt? The distinctions between *lecture* and *scripture* also put you in exile. We're all suspicious, you see, and we're always thinking in printed text terms, whereas most people, I suspect, think much more in terms of spoken, oral speech. I suppose I've always enjoyed being something of a solitary, anyway. There is certainly something in my private character, but it seems to me inherent in the fact that one is a writer.

Q: How different do you feel to be Fowles-the-man from Fowles-the-writer? Is the implied author of your novels significantly different from yourself?
Fowles: I hope not too different. I mean, it's part of the con man side of writing that of course you try to present yourself to the reader as enormously sensitive, intelligent, and perspicacious. But I suppose I would have to say that I really feel I *can* see through things sometimes better than most people around me. So in a sense I share the notion of—Thackeray was the one, wasn't he—of being the urbane compeer of human life. I suppose part of that is part of my private self inasmuch as that's an image I like to present to the world. I would say that on the whole a strong "voice" is usually very closely linked to a highly personal style, which I don't have and don't want. I hope my public "voice" is fairly close to my own; but of course you know you're being read, and I think you are probably slightly tainted by the fact of the

whole business of the reading of a text, and that it goes on out of your sight. It's very difficult to impress what you really mean on somebody you can't even see and you won't know. Anyway, we don't know what goes on when people read. That's the great mystery. You can't do it yourself, you see. You can't say, well, I'll read a passage and analyze what I think. It's like the same situation in physics—as soon as you start observing and thinking consciously, how do I read myself as I read, it's all distorted. It's a very strange blank. It's a dead end; you can't get past it.

Q: There's no right reading of a text?

Fowles: There's no right reading of a text, certainly not. And there's no way, I think, of knowing what actually happens mentally as the process is going on. We don't know to what degree people visualize, for instance.

Q: The act of reading, you think, is as creative as the act of writing?

Fowles: I'm all with deconstruction on that side. What I don't like is the corollary they've made. You know, the author is a mere irrelevant detail, who sells half a pound of text like half a pound of sugar. I rather object to that. I still haven't got over J. Hillis Miller's book on Hardy—when he said that all the biographical data are irrelevant to the true understanding of Hardy.

Q: Do you think you can be more honest in your writing than in ordinary social life? Are you ever inhibited in your writing by outside circumstances: social relationships, personal circumstances, and so forth?

Fowles: In writing? In what I say? No, no, I don't feel that. This is a problem for many young writers. I mean I did feel that at the time of *The Collector.* You have your close friends and your parents, your teachers—your dreaded ex-teachers—and I think that is a difficult period for many writers, younger writers. All art *must* be a kind of striptease. I don't, thank God, get sent many novels to read, but I would say it's the commonest fault: inhibition caused by private circumstances. It's very difficult to get over. The wife is a very special category, I think. One is still frightened and apprehensive about how the person who knows you best is going to react, and that is a problem. It's far worse for young writers who haven't really got out of what is the natural human position, which is to fear your neighbors and elders. It's another reason we're in exile. We've said forbidden things. I think a bad category here, especially, are one's ex-teachers, because they have generally taught you some traditional standards, certain rules which must be obeyed in art. And it's very difficult to shake off that whole credo they've fed you. To break rules, especially aesthetic rules. They're very difficult to crack. That's another sort of incubus you've got to shake off before you can write.

Q: You are conscious, I assume, of an audience when you are writing. Who is your audience?

Fowles: Well, I try not to be too conscious because the audience I usually try to keep in mind is one other person. This is because the reading experience is always, however many million times it takes place, one to one. There are just two people present: me and the person who is reading my book.

Q: Who is that person?

Fowles: It's a . . . you see, I can't describe it because it's the sum of all the many letters, the many thousands by now, I have received from readers. I would say in general they are people who like narrative, they're at the university level in education (although I've had very touching letters from people far below that), and I'd say they usually share my concerns about the bad social values in the U.S., or whatever. And I think most of them have a sense of humor. They enjoy the kind of games I like to play with readers. I think this is a mistake that some novelists make: they sound as if they're addressing huge crowds. You know, Ronald Reagan talking about the state of the union, when in fact the experience is always one person—one person.

Q: How do you deal with the feeling that your reader has expectations of you—that you tell a story, that you end a book, and so on?

Fowles: I hope they'll follow me in that department. No writer is in control of how people read his books, and this, in some moods, is the delicious thing about the book; because, no matter how precisely and fully you describe something, you never, never know how the reader's going to read it. Your first reader, and your most important reader, is always yourself, in fact. So I basically write what I know is going to please *me,* what *I* am going to enjoy. Sometimes I'm right, and sometimes, as I generally was with *Mantissa,* I'm wrong. This is the risk. You can't go through life—even gamblers don't go through life—betting always on the favorite, the obvious choice. There has to be an outsider principle. You must say, well, probably most people won't like this book, but to hell with it.

Q: Do you feel the same way about making concessions to the reader's understanding? That is to say, your novels are very complex; are you ever afraid that you're being too obscure?

Fowles: No, because another thing that is very important for me in a novel and in the cinema, for that matter, is the gaps in understanding and narrative. Reading a novel is an equally creative experience, and the one thing the fiction reader does not want to be given is something where every question is answered; surely one of the most important functions of the novel is to create, not exactly a sense of mystery, but to leave spaces which the reader has got to fill in. It's . . . it's a kind of discipline—not a discipline so much as—it's a kind of joyous experience, a kind of *jouissance,* in Barthes's terms, that I think the reader deserves, you know. Only a very elementary kind of reading mind complains when it doesn't fully understand a novel. That doesn't mean I like willful obscurity, but I think ambiguity is a very important part of the experience. That's why I like nature. There's so much of it we just cannot understand; we can only guess at the possibilities. Nature is full of gaps and is very bizarrely and asymmetrically designed. This is rather like all those Americans who write to me and say, how dare you use foreign words. They often will send very odd, pathetic pleas: "I had to leave school at the age of thirteen"; "I never had a good education, so how dare you use French words or Latin words." I'm a socialist, but I have no truck with that at all. Language is primary. Nothing must . . . nothing must attack or diminish language. Oh, occasionally, perhaps, if a passage is too obscure, or perhaps a highly unusual word is a bit much, or perhaps I am suffering from, as I tend to (as I'm half brought up in the French culture), the French flu, then I will alter things. But I'm all for richness in language, and if people can't understand then they can bloody well go elsewhere. Buy a dictionary or something.

Q: When you write, are you more conscious of form or idea?
Fowles: Oh, idea. Idea and feeling, I should think.

Q: Will the idea and feeling control the details of the book?
Fowles: Yes. Much more so than the other way around. I try to be very careful about fitting details in with the general mood, or certainly in giving things like dress color or speech patterns a symbolic value. Another great problem in novel writing is names. I think most novelists find that. It's very mysterious the trouble you have with names—when perfectly plausible names for some mysterious reason sound slightly wrong. That's always been a mystery to me. Some complicated little computer in one's unconscious will reject what seem perfectly good names on all other grounds, and then it will suddenly click and you find you've got the right one.

Q: So the idea will control the details almost autonomically?
Fowles: I don't know if I would call it the idea, it's much more than that.

It's a very general gestalt kind of feeling about what the mood ought to be. This usually comes up naturally and unconsciously in the writing, I find. All passages of narrative are set in a kind of musical key, and usually you won't put in accidentals unless they have some special reason, they seem to work. It's mood.

Q: You've said that Raymond Chandler occasionally writes perfect prose. What is perfect prose? What does a writer look for in another writer's work?

Fowles: Well, perfect in the context of what he is trying to do. It's certainly *le mot juste* in part, but it is sensitivity to what we've just been talking about. And absolutely accurate choice of words is important. I'm against Hemingway for many reasons but I do admire many of those short stories he wrote—I think they're an example of that. And Flaubert is a great master of this. With most novelists I can read a page and see hundreds of things I would change. In some of Hemingway's stories you can't change a word. Evelyn Waugh was able to do that; Greene also, I suppose. I don't know if it's really terribly important. I think many very good writers didn't have that accuracy. Dickens, for example. There's something to be said for sometimes being dull and boring—it's actually rather an important part of the reading process. In my opinion Jane Austen is an awful bore—very often. A very second-rate writer. Then suddenly she'll get one page, out of dozens of pages, where every word is perfect, and you couldn't in a million years improve it. It's that sudden rise from a very flat, normal level to these superb passages, I think, that's part of her achievement. I like that.

Q: How do you feel about writing in the modern literary climate—if you believe there is such a thing? Do you imagine that it's any different now than it's ever been, given the impact on literature of such things as television or burgeoning academic criticism?

Fowles: I don't think so, really. I used to think so at one time, but I don't now. Literary people, whether academics or writers, are extremely jealous, envious, and back-biting. They've always gone overboard for new theories. I see literature much more in natural history terms, with a whole natural order of genera and species, if you like; and I don't like the idea that you must despise this genus or admire that. You know, there's a parity among them all.

Q: There's nothing inherent in the times that affects the way you write?

Fowles: I think obviously one's influenced by the ideas from outside, often in a very positive way. I think you can very often pick up ideas which intrigue you. In a way, all novelists are information-gathering machines, and all this makes your stock in trade richer. I wouldn't call myself an existentialist now, but certainly that was very fruitful for me at the time. And I find structuralism and all its children quite interesting, inasmuch as I understand it.

Q: How do you feel about experimental writing?

Fowles: First of all, I think what used to be called the avant garde, when I was a student, is dead now. The theory then was if it was avant garde, it must be good. That's an absurd viewpoint. I don't mean I reject experimental writing, but I think the same law applies as to every other kind of writing. A tiny fraction of it will be good, and the great part will be bad. I've watched too many highly praised experimental writers sink beneath the waves. That all good resides in being experimental—that belief now seems thoroughly provincial to me. Some academics still set such great store in experimental writing. I should have thought the interest now is how you can restructure traditional modes.

Q: How do you feel about critics?

Fowles: You can get briefly hurt by critics, if you're talking about adverse reviews.

Q: Not so much reviews, but serious academic criticism. For example, do you think that writers will sometimes write for critics?

Fowles: I think this is a perceptible fault. I find it in reading the occasional American university literary review. I do detect it in some of the short stories and in the poetry. You get the impression that they're not really writing out of their true selves, but writing out of a campus ambiance; or writing to their creative writing teachers. I think that is a danger, and this is why I am highly suspicious of creative writing classes.

Q: I've heard you mention that several times. Have you ever sat in a creative writing class?

Fowles: No, no, I'm like most critics. I'm speaking absolutely from an armchair view. Actually, a very good friend of mine, Malcolm Bradbury, has really had quite considerable success at the University of East Anglia here. He's produced rather an impressive list of good young writers. I enjoy most academic papers. I've got stacks upstairs, but I haven't read all of them by any means. But those I have read I've practically always enjoyed. There's a certain narcissistic and masochistic enjoyment: how nice of this person to take me to bits. But what I dislike, more in the English than in the American critics, is the old sort of paradigm which is the curse of this country; that is, that every critic feels he must be a schoolmaster. And his subject must in some sense be a rough, backward, and far-from-perfect pupil. This awful—I may be wrong—but this awful image of the schoolroom haunts literature on this side of the ocean. It haunts reviewing also. So the poor writer always feels he is somewhere at the back of the class. And there's this weird feeling that I have disobeyed authority, and that the true basis of authority must lie in the analyzing academic. Now that I hate; that I hate. And I get a sense, certainly from reviews in America, that even when an American reviewer doesn't like your work, at least he treats you like another adult. You never get this in England. No, you always get put down as somebody who belongs to an inferior order in reason. It's a weird part, I think, of the English class system.

Q: You're on the record as having a very disdainful attitude toward critics. I know you've said the whole lot of British critics should be thrown into the sea, but . . .

Fowles: No, no. I find certain kinds of academic activity incredibly wasteful and jargon-ridden. I mean, I've had many things written on me which really make me vomit in a literary sense, because they're so badly written and all the rest of it. And in the sense that it's become a kind of campus industry, I'm hostile. If we're talking about really serious critics of literature, from I. A. Richards or F. R. Leavis right up through Roland Barthes, I certainly don't have a scorn for them. I do have a certain scorn for some of the French because they are so appallingly obscure. I don't mind obscurity in the novel, but I find obscurity in writing about the novel intolerable, and I think there's no excuse for it.

Q: What should good criticism be?

Fowles: Well, I get lots of letters also from students who write to me for help because they are doing a thesis or an end-of-term paper. And I always write back and say, far more important than what *I* think it means is what *you* think it means, because if criticism of literature or any art is not self-learning, then it is nothing. It's wrongly conceived. So, I would really rather read the silliest paper about me, which at least shows self-thought and gives personal reactions, than the cleverest paper full of all the current theories and the right jargon. For me, good criticism must induce a feeling of greater knowledge of himself or herself in the reader. I must say that is far and away the most important thing.

Q: Have there been good things written on your work?

Fowles: Oh, there's so much of it that I haven't read, really. I think I'm overstudied. It sounds rude to say that to you, but a lot of it is repetitive, that I have read. You get the same ideas coming up again and again. On the other hand, its breadth, in treatment terms, is quite interesting. People do see so many different things, some of which I never imagined. I've just had a paper yesterday on the influence of Chaucer's "Miller's Tale" on *The Magus.* A very good case, truly. Nicholas and Alison—very good case, an excellent case. But I didn't read Chaucer at all till about six years ago. Who was the first man to write a book on me? William Palmer. He sent me the proof to criticize before it was published, and there was a whole lot about the influence of J. S. Mill in it. I wrote back and said, sorry, but I hadn't to my knowledge ever read a word of J. S. Mill. Then I sent this back thinking, well, he'll have to drop all this. Damn me! Then the finished copy comes and it's all still in there! I wrote to him and say, "What the hell are you doing?" His answer was, "I thought you *ought* to have been influenced by J. S. Mill"! I've had a great deal of "ought to have been influenced." I have very peculiar reading knowledge, I'm afraid. The classics I haven't read—the list is disgraceful.

Q: Does it bother you when your books are misunderstood, given the prodigious amount of thought and care you put into them?

Fowles: No, no. I don't think so. I was hurt because this was a common thing when *The Collector* first came out. A lot of English critics said Miranda deserved everything she got, she was such a young prig. I had intended to show she had the faults of that age: idealism and a certain amount of priggishness. That's still the worst wrong reaction I can remember. But I realized later that it was something to do with the England of that time, which had an absolute horror both of the priggish and of idealism. It didn't happen in America; none of the American reviewers felt that. *The Collector* was reviewed universally in England in the thriller column. That sort of mistake is one of the hazards of the literary life.

Q: Is freedom still your largest concern?

Fowles: No one is free, really, except in some very minimal way.

Q: What in your background has made you so concerned about freedom?

Fowles: I think it probably was a personal thing—being brought up in very cramped suburban surroundings as a child and adolescent. I hate suburbia all through the world with a passion I can't describe to you. You know, I hate same streets, same houses. They bore me to death. And the kinds of minds they produce, too. And certainly the notion of escape from what you seem destined to be has always fascinated me. In a sense, I suppose, becoming a novelist (because, heaven knows, nobody ever thought that was likely), that is the freedom I've got. But, of course, all you do really when you come to be what you've always wanted us to be is to find yourself in a new series of chains. The actual experience of writing a novel is a very imprisoning thing. It's also busy writing you as you write it, biting back at you.

Q: Your books are full of the existential individual. They show an individual finding himself through deconstructive and reconstructive processes. You know, being taken apart, then putting himself back together again through remembering, usually as a result of some fantastic godgame. Since we all don't have access to magi, how do ordinary people go about the same process?

Fowles: The basic idea that lay behind *The Magus* was that we are all in fact in a godgame and we're always in close contact with a kind of super-Conchis. This is the very basis of human existence, for me. There are mysteries, there are weird lessons being taught to us by ordinary life itself. I don't think that I ever got that idea across. I know most people read it as a sort of unique, peculiar experience that could only happen to one person in one particular place. But the idea behind it was that whatever first principle one puts behind human existence, it really does have some of the features of a Conchis, which always teaches slightly ambiguous lessons, and at best we don't know what it's trying to do or "say." And that was an existential proposition. Certainly that was, as I was writing it, the major idea behind it. And I still feel this is true but, of course, it's difficult to see, for most people.

Q: How do you go about discovering the lessons?

Fowles: I suppose by examining events, learning to read other people's motives, above all learning to read yourself, realizing there's a huge component of hazard and very real mystery in *everyone's* life. Life does condition us so frightfully that it's terribly difficult to sense this—to sense the underlying nature of existence. You know, we are caged more and more by present society in roles, and I think being able to see through the roles is most important. I once suggested it was as if we were all acting players. What we've lost the trick of is seeing through these public roles and discovering the actor's true self underneath—the experience every real actor has to deal with.

Q: Have you done that yourself?

Fowles: I hope so, yes. You know, one can never do it completely. I think, yes, I play roles, but I don't really believe them, except in the sense the actor has to believe.

Q: Are you interested in political freedom? Your novels suggest that if more people were free, in the existential sense, there would be far fewer problems. Is that true?

Fowles: Well, you have to define freedom very carefully. The first thing, if you do have a sense of freedom, is that in a way it is a very limiting thing. That is, if you gain a sense of freedom and you believe in it and wish to act on it, then you realize it puts appalling limitations on you. In a strange way, freedom is one of the least free things in the world; and so that is the political sense in which I use it. By freedom I don't mean that I think everyone should have the freedom to be as rich as they like or to behave as they like. That is an awful capitalist misunderstanding of freedom.

Q: You seem to assume that there is some sort of innate goodness or right sense about people that will guide their freedom. For example, you suggest in *The Magus* that if more German people had been true to their selves, World War II would not have happened. That implies a tremendous social side to existentialism.

Fowles: Freedom for me is inalienably bound up with self-knowledge. I would say the two words are almost synonymous in this context. And so it's really *that,* you know, the ability to withstand the appalling brainwashing that we all get now through the media, to think of yourself and know yourself. I must see that as a vital kind of freedom. And, honestly, it's an unhappy freedom at the moment because it doesn't exist very much. That's certainly how I see political freedom. It's more self-knowledge, and thus knowledge of others, too, and that's why I'm definitely on the socialist side.

Q: Existentialism, then, could be a strategy for effecting social evolution?

Fowles: Yes. Well, Sartre more or less argued that. I wasn't in agreement with his complete conversion to Marxism, but I certainly think existentialism is an argument for socialism.

Q: Since we're not a society of existential selves and free people, how does the existential individual get along with the rest of his fellows?

Fowles: Badly. In exile from them. Most people like to be conditioned. Unfortunately, it's a fallacy that everybody wants to be freer in the sense we're talking about. They're much happier, I think, having fixed routines and a limited way of life. I haven't really changed from what I said in *The Aristos.* I see no hope for change unless our educational system is changed very extensively.

Q: How do you do that?

Fowles: Well, all state systems pursue—it may not be complete chauvinism—they pursue notions which will bias the individual toward society; so that they will create a "good" or obedient social being out of a child. But that so often becomes merely chauvinistic and merely advantageous to society, to help society run more smoothly. I mean, we don't actually educate to create awkward cusses and bloody-minded people. I'd rather see more of that. I think one can do it by (again I'm slightly tainted by the general English situation) allowing far more free discussion among students and showing them, if one can simplify it enough, the sort of thing that deconstruction is trying to do—you know, the implicit contradictions in texts or social institutions. And certainly by putting far more stress on self-knowledge and less stress, I think, on just feeding absolutely useless external knowledge. There still is a bad split between science and the arts. I suppose I'm lucky because I've always been interested in the scientific side of my interests. It's teaching people to resist fixed ideas which is becoming the urgent problem, and this is because of the enormous power the media now have. The last election in England was very interesting because it was our first media election. It was the first time the country had been swung by clever media manipulation. It's also been called the first American election. It's all very mild, actually, compared to your system. But one must really start teaching societies the danger of all this. So in that sense I'm antisocial, antisociety, as in one or two other things. I'm not sure this should be a right function for a politician but I think it is an eminently right function for a novelist to do this, to be like this. So I don't care if I am quoted as liking birds more than human beings or having peculiar political views. I think this is our function. We must, in a way, try to be different from other people.

Q: I know mystery is very important to you, but what is it exactly that is mysterious? What is the great mystery?

Fowles: There's a lot of the occult in *The Magus,* but I regard all that as parody. I have no, absolutely no interest in the supernatural or mysticism or gurus or all these new Californian occult therapies, all that stuff. It bores me into the ground. A mystery lies at the base of all that is in nature. I see countless mysteries: Why do things behave as they do? Why do things happen as they do? All sorts of things like that. Why is death so important? And in literary terms I think the inexplicable, the gaps, are also very rich. This is partly because of the nature of the writing-reading process. I don't think of mystery in the now-bracketed sense of the mystery book or "the mystery." Mystery really lies in things the author doesn't say and in gaps in the story; that has much more to do with it. I regard all that in books as symbolic of the general mystery in cosmic, existential terms. I rather like stories that begin with an impossible situation or fact that you can make plausible. I'm also interested in brain surgery and in what they are discovering about the nervous system or the brain. There is some extraordinary work going on, especially in America, about brain lobe function. And it begins to seem very likely that one might be able to classify or even predict writers, because they have a reverse lobe domination from the normal. Brain surgery made a gigantic leap in the last world war when they suddenly realized that the two lobes are not one superior, one inferior—specialized, but capable of supplanting each other—they are, in effect, equivalent. They had various cases where a whole lobe had gone and then somehow, mysteriously, the supposed different lobe began to assume all the functions of the other. The Russians have also done some work. It's things like that I begin to find rather fascinating to write about. In a way, such ideas seem absurd, almost gothic, but I feel a fertility in them. Rather like Ray Bradbury, whom I rather admire. I was delighted when I heard he couldn't drive.

Q: You don't drive?
Fowles: I don't drive.

Q: Never?
Fowles: No, I'm too absentminded to be safe on the road. I'm also like every naturalist—I adore watching hedges and looking for plants and birds. That's not helpful.

Q: In your love of mystery you seem to be going against the grain of the major intellectual trend of this century—a structuralist kind of trend that seeks to demystify. Do you feel a tension between your love of having things unanswered and an intellectual current that demands answers?
Fowles: Yes. Yes, I do. That doesn't mean it isn't enjoyable when you're writing to try to explain or make some shrewd comment on something in society. But I would hate a world where everything was explained. You see,

this is missing out, as I explained in *The Tree*. It seems to me that there's an art of living and of knowing, and this is what the scientists really won't accept. They won't accept that there's an art of knowing. It's all rational or logical, or not. And I feel this completely betrays the actuality of what goes on in one's head during any few moments of existence. One's mind is full of an indescribable complex of feelings and reactions and past influences and all the rest of it. I think it's bound up with the reader's notion of such present-ness, you know. That's how he or she reads.

Q: It's obvious that you do object to a scientific attitude toward life, and yet you are a scientist yourself. How do you explain that?

Fowles: I greatly admire good science, and I recognize that what I know about things as an amateur scientist does help in the actual enjoyment of them outside. But the enjoyment of them always seems to me a whole world which hasn't really been explored. Sometimes the scientific side of it will be dominant. You see some completely new species, and the thing uppermost in your mind when you've looked it up is probably a Latin name and what the scientific handbooks will say about it. But that tends to exclude all familiar species, you know. Scientifically you know them, so nothing is learned. But I have taught myself over the years that this is completely wrong. I can go and look at the flowers in my garden. I've seen them a hundred thousand times, but I can still . . . something is there beyond all the science. It's made up of, most obviously, all my past seeings of it. And there's a kind of "thing in itself." I was rather hooked on Zen for a time and this is a very useful trick. I don't regard it as anything mystical, but simply being able to float without an identity yourself and to have all sense of identity in the thing you are looking at. It just needs practice. I don't regard it as anything transcen-dental, something you have to pay a thousand dollars for on some California ranch. Anyone can do it.

Q: There's nothing contemptible about science itself, then. Only science that excludes these other feelings?

Fowles: There's nothing contemptible about science which acknowledges it is working within the context of science. No, that is admirable. But what worries me is when the scientific view of life is applied to everything else; then I get upset and very often angry. It's because I think existence itself is not scientific. Even the purest scientist can't actually live his own existence that way. It's not possible.

Q: Are you still very interested in psychology?

Fowles: If you mean, do I keep up with the movements, the journals, and so on, no, unless somebody sends me something. But I owe a great deal to Freud and Jung. I've often said that if I felt I needed psychiatry I would certainly go to a Freudian. Freudian theory does interest me. I still find it a very satisfying kind of symbolism. Whether it's actually true or not, I don't know, but I like its mechanical structure. I think for a writer, Jung is actually the best person to read. He's very fertile and fruitful.

Q: Why is there so much stress on anima in your works?

Fowles: Anima . . . it's very difficult for me to say where it came from originally. I'd have to be analyzed to do that. But it's the idea of the female ghost inside one that's always been very attractive to me. Perhaps it's bound up with my general liking for mystery—the idea that there is a ghost like that inside one. In historical or social terms I've always had great sympathy for, I won't quite say feminism in the modern sense, but for a female principle in life. It doesn't always tie in with modern feminism. My wife would deny point blank that I'm a proper feminist. But I do, more for obscure personal reasons, hate the macho viewpoint. This is the one thing I can't swallow in America, both North and South. I find it detestable.

Q: What do you think is the function of fiction today? Is it any different than it's ever been? The real question is, why do you publish books? Not why do you write them, but why do you publish them?

Fowles: Well, I suppose in a way I am a good test case because I really don't have to publish for economic reasons any more. I think you must presume that there is a kind of devil in you that always enjoys going on show, even though an outward part of me dislikes much of the publishing side very much. But one does think of the future and, you know, it's nice to think this book will be on the cheap shelf in a hundred years' time, in some obscure bookshop. And I also hope there is something good in it. You hope to bring a certain amount of instruction and a certain amount of pleasure, too, because one cannot remove the pleasure principle, I think, from the novel. It must be an entertainment. I was delighted, I remember, in Cairo, to see the old professional oral storytellers still at work.

Q: Are you after any kind of proselytization?

Fowles: I think all I would attempt to do is to try to help people to see primarily themselves and then the world slightly differently. I had a letter

from a young man the other day who said *The Magus* had made him—he had
been in a seminary—it had made him drop the priesthood. He had read somewhere that I'd said novels can't change lives. He said that in this particular
case it had very deeply changed his life. But I had to write back and disclaim
most of this because, I think, as I pointed out, all the time he was already on
a certain road. He did admit that he'd had grave theological doubts. All *The
Magus* was was a signpost which happened to hit him at a certain point and
which probably in retrospect he sees as more important than it really was.
But I've actually had quite a lot of letters from various people like that, and
it's tempting to be very vain and say, "Great, I'm superman." But I'm very
suspicious of such claims. I think all a novel can do is, if people are inclining
in a certain direction, then push them slightly more quickly towards it. But
in general I want to propagate, I suppose, humanism.

Q: Are you happy with *The Magus* now?
Fowles: I'm happy with it now. I've always been fond of it.

Q: Is it your favorite novel?
Fowles: In the sense that one might love a crippled child more than normal
children.

Q: Do you really believe it's the product of a retarded adolescent, written
for adolescents?
Fowles: Well, as I put the phrase, it is pejorative. I have a very firm belief
that writers have to have another kind of animus inside them that is still
charmed by existence—under its charm, still adolescent, still a young man,
and so on. This is another thing that puts us in exile. All my contemporaries
seem much older than I. They don't see it, but I feel it. All the time. They're
now getting a dignity and a sort of maturity which I shall never have.

Q: Were you happy with the film of *The French Lieutenant's Woman?*
Fowles: Yes. Well, I could fault it on one or two minor things, but I thought
it was a very interesting experiment. And it's been much, much better dis-
cussed in France than anywhere else. They, on the whole, really loved the
film and some very good stuff has been written on it. I was happy with that.

Q: I am curious about the background of *The Book of Ebenezer Lepage.*
Fowles: Yes, I know. I'm the world's greatest living authority on that!

Q: What were the circumstances behind your bringing that out?
Fowles: I didn't bring it out. I only came in when the publishers got the

manuscript and decided to publish it. If I'm honest with you, I didn't altogether admire it, but I felt it was categorically a book that ought to be published. I thought it was rather extraordinary in terms of the circumstances in which it was written. I never thought and I don't think it's an undiscovered masterpiece. I don't think it's anywhere near that. I would have cut it by at least a quarter. But I did feel it was definitely a literary curiosity. We've since learned a good deal more about him, G. B. Edwards.

Q: Where did *Mantissa* come from? Are the Muses really so cruel to you?

Fowles: Another side of me has to regard most of writing as a game. I've always had this, I suppose, half-unconscious feeling that when you're writing there's a tease element: that something is always teasing you and making you have pratfalls. There's some mysterious enemy who one knows also helps, but who can cause all kinds of problems and give you all kinds of misinformation. *Mantissa* came partly from that sense; partly, I suppose, from the sense that I think modern literary criticism has altogether got too serious and pious. I get this from so many of the papers I read—that there's really no fun in writing, it's all got to be taken with seriousness. I suppose I'm a paradoxical person. I do love realism on the surface, but I also love the enormous artifice writing involves. In many ways it is a kind of natural thing, engaging in it is a natural process. But once you're engaged it becomes highly artificial. I get a kind of pleasure out of that. If there were such a thing as a Muse, I can't imagine she would be that dreadful, wishy-washy figure of legend. I think it would be . . . it's your anima, obviously. And extremely naughty and unhelpful a lot of the time. That really is the literal feeling you get, on the page—that whatever inspires you can also be a terrible obstacle, a confounded nuisance. And also, I suppose, I wrote the book because I knew it was a book most people would disapprove of. Really, I wanted to give people an opportunity to kick me—which they duly did.

Fowles on Fowles

Susana Onega / 1988

From *Form and Meaning in the Novels of John Fowles* (Ann Arbor, MI: UMI Research Press, 1989), 175-90. Reprinted by permission of Susana Onega. This interview originally appeared in *Actas del X Congreso Nacional de A.E.D.E.A.N.*, 1988, 57-76.

In an interview published in *Counterpoint* in 1964 you placed Frederick Clegg, the protagonist of *The Collector,* at the end of the line of "angry young men" which starts with *Lucky Jim.* Have you ever thought of yourself as a member of "The Movement"?

John Fowles: Could I please start by saying that if we had been in China I should get up now and clap you back. It is lovely for any novelist, even something of a hermit or a recluse like myself, to see such an audience as this. I have been in Spain before but it is very pleasant to be back again, after a long interval in my case.

Angry young men. I was never really an Angry Young Man myself and I do not think I could be put into that movement. If we are talking about it in general, I am grateful that it did happen. The typical novelist, I suppose, of that movement was Alan Sillitoe, of whom I spoke rather badly in one of my novels, but that was because of the needs of the novel. It was not really my personal opinion. The Movement had an important effect in the English theater and the English cinema; it was really a kind of "cleaning" of English art in general, and a valuable one, working-class in its inspiration and with a tiredness for all the old classical ways of English thinking about the arts. It was like a kind of minor fire in a house and it burnt some rooms which needed burning. I come from a small town in Dorset which had a bad fire a hundred years ago. The fire is now regarded as a blessing; it completely destroyed the abominable poor quarter of the town. Things that are tragedies in one way can be very beneficial in another.

The trouble with the Angry Young Men is that unfortunately, because I am really a socialist of a kind by conviction, there is a richness in the middle classes and the middle-class field of life, for the novelist especially, that confining yourself to the working-class view of life, the proletarian one, rather restricts. This was the case with Alan Sillitoe, for example; another

English novelist, David Storey, is another case. They tended to get themselves into a corner and found they lacked a richness of subject. This I regard as less political than biological; it is just for me that, perhaps unfairly, the middle classes lead richer, wider lives. This will not satisfy any Marxists or Communists who are here today but the Angry Young Men are for me a historical movement. It performed a useful function but now it is over. It is not a phrase you hear any more in contemporary discussions of English literature.

Susana Onega: *In an interview with Lorna Sage you talked about a tension in your work, an opposed pull between the English, realistic tradition, and your French, experimental background. What are the basic ideas you have accepted from each and to what extent have they conditioned your literary evolution?*

John Fowles: When I was much younger I taught in a French university for a year and I was supposed to teach English there. Now I was a disaster as a lecturer at that university because I really knew nothing about English literature. I did know a little, I had been to Oxford and had studied French literature and I knew French novels and that country historically quite well, but when I suddenly had to get up and start talking about Shelley, Keats, Byron, and Rupert Brooke, whatever was on the French syllabus in the English Faculty, I was absolutely at sea. I ought never to have been appointed. In fact, at the end of that year the university said goodbye to me with no regrets at all.

I then went to Greece, and the school in Greece where I taught also said goodbye to me at the end of my stay there—in other words, I was sacked, or fired. That was for rather different reasons but I think, in general, it is quite good for novelists to have failures like that early in life. What you have to do if you are to be a novelist is *not* to be a teacher.

There is a theory in England that if you want to be a novelist—and it is even stronger in the United States—that all would-be writers go "on campus." They go to university and they do not earn their living from books, they earn it from some job they have in a university. I think teaching is a very bad thing for a creative writer to do, if we are talking about it as a career, and whenever young novelists in England say, "What advice have you got?," I always say, "Anything, but don't be a teacher." It is curious because obviously teaching a language with its literature and writing might seem to be parallel and close activities, but in some ways teaching literature is a very bad basis for actually writing or creating literature. This is why you do not get many professors of literature who are really good writers in a creative sense. There have been one or two. We have two famous professors of English in England at the moment who are also good writers. One is Malcolm Bradbury and the other is David Lodge, but they are exceptions to the rule. There have been one or two in America, too. Lionel Trilling in America was a famous critic and teacher of English as well as a novelist, but on the whole you do not learn to write books by being good at analyzing them and explaining them. That may seem strange to you, but, believe me, it is true.

Susana Onega: *Do you think every novelist, even the most experimental one, should write only about things and places he has firsthand knowledge of? Or to put it another way, do you think that real life experience is as necessary as genius?*

John Fowles: I think for the young writer it is important. I am greatly in favor because I am an internationalist by spirit. I think it is very important for young writers, I would say for all young people really, to travel. I traveled a lot when I was young, but I am now at an age when I have a little bit of that complacent syndrome, I have seen everything and I have read everything. This is a danger when you get to my age. I am sixty years old at the moment. You think you have travelled everywhere and you will get no new experiences, but this is not true, as I have just learnt in Spain *[S. O.: Yes, Las Ramblas, unfortunately]*. It is really more than that. I am at the moment thinking, no more than tossing around in my mind, an idea for a new novel and I find coming to Spain lovely and fertile for the writer. All feeds in, objects you see suddenly attract you and you think, "My goodness, I could use that!" or "That's something I must remember." So, this is why I am always persecuting my very kind hosts here about strange words I see, or habits. Novelists are magpies and steal objects if they can. We really have to be magpies, and amass masses of information we will never put in our books and perhaps will never use. If you have a novelist's mind it is rather like owning a junk room in a house or an old *brocante,* an old second-hand dealer's. In some way you have got to have this room full of old furniture, in our case events and characters, characters you have never developed. Then suddenly one day you feel there will be a place for such and such a character or event. This, I think, is one important way we really are very very different from professors, teachers of English. I feel I am a sheep among goats here in Zaragoza, or a goat among sheep. A novelist is truly very different from an expert on literature. We do not have to have ordered minds, we do not have to know Derrida or Barthes or the great theorists backwards, we have very loose ideas, a mass of mixed information that is really of no use to us or anybody else, but we have to carry round our minds stuffed with these facts. You have to have a private treasury, a house which is full of objects or memories that one day may be useful, may be useful, you may use them, or they may disappear and sink out of sight. It is by writing like this that we get an important response with that other person the reader. The novelist does not have a relationship with readers, in the plural. We have to remember it is always with one reader and that reader you have to tickle as you "tickle" a trout, you have to evoke a world, to tease their emotions. You are appealing in most novels, I think, to the corresponding junk-room nature of the reader's mind from your own. It is not by theory, by logic, by order, as a rule, that you establish this communion with this one reader who is your brother or sister in the experience of reading a book.

Susana Onega: *You have often explained that some of your novels developed from a single image:* The French Lieutenant's Woman, *for example, developed from the image of a woman standing on the quay at Lyme Regis, and looking out over a rough sea; or* The Collector, *from a piece of news in the papers about the kidnapping of a young woman who was held prisoner in an air-raid shelter in London. Did any of the other novels also originate in a similar way?*

John Fowles: It used to happen to me by something like a cinema "still." I used to get one vision. In another novel, one of my favorite novels in fact, *Daniel Martin,* I did have an image that in the novel is at the very end of the book. It was of a woman standing in a desert somewhere. I did not at that time even know where it was. She seemed to be weeping, to be lost, a moment of total desolation. It is from tiny images like that, very like cinema stills, say good Buñuel stills or Eisenstein stills, the way they can evoke the whole film even though there is only one frame, one picture . . . and that seems to have some effect on me. I do not think this is true of many novelists . . . it is just a peculiarity of my own. I am a visual person in other ways, I would normally much rather go to an art gallery than sit on a literary discussion. Pictures have always spoken to me, in emotional terms anyway, and I think that is all I can answer.

Susana Onega: *In* The French Lieutenant's Woman *the narrator protests that he cannot control his characters, and that once created, they are free to*

choose what they do; if you agree with your narrator, the obvious conclusion
is that you do not have a preconceived plan when you start writing a novel,
that you haven't decided the ending beforehand. Is that right?

John Fowles: Yes. Again please remember this is one person speaking to
you and that you must not take this as applying to all novelists. I know others
do write to carefully preconceived, prepared plans, and if you read books on
how to write a novel, usually they will say, "Make a careful plan and keep
to it." I am completely different. I am, I suppose, a wanderer or a rambler.
The Rambler was a famous eighteenth-century periodical in England and the
title has always attracted me. The wanderer, the person who strolls and devi-
ates through life. I always think the notion of the fork in the road is very
important when you are creating narrative, because you are continually coming to forks. Now, if you write to an elaborate, prepared plan, the choice is
taken out of your hands, your plan says you must take this fork to the right,
you must take this fork to the left, but I do not like that. I like, in the actual
business of writing, this feeling that you do not know where you are going.
You have in this to know deep principles or feelings that guide you very
loosely, but on the actual page you often do not know when a scene is going
to end, how it is going to end, or, if you end it in one way, is it going to
change the future of the book. This, you see, is a state of uncertainty, or in
terms of the modern physics, indeterminacy. . . . You are never quite sure
where the concrete facts and characters that the narrative develops in a book
are going to lead. You sometimes have extraordinary mornings and these are
the only times in my life when I would, very modestly, claim a genius. That
is when ideas flow in on you with such force that very often you cannot write
them down, they come so fast, in my case often fragments of dialogue, so
fast that you literally cannot write them down. They are very rare, these
moments; you pray for them, you can't create them in any way, they just
come; and I have noticed, rather oddly, usually when you are feeling ill and
depressed. I do not know whether you know the French religious philosopher
Pascal, but Pascal once had a religious experience like this which he could
never describe. He just had to say "Fire! Fire! Fire!" He means "I was
flooded with fire and it was beyond description." Very occasionally you have
these feelings, almost visions, when you see the whole book. You see all sorts
of developments and these moments give you an extraordinary feeling of
euphoria, of happiness. Very often later on, when you look at things you have
scribbled down frantically, you realize they were nonsense, but usually you
get one or two grains, sometimes much more, that are important in your

book. This is another distinction between creative writers, poets, and teachers of literature. These are not rational moments, they are much more shamanistic. A shaman, if you remember, in Stone Age and earlier times, was a kind of tribal magician, a tribal priest. Somebody in England at the moment, a writer called Nicholas Humphreys, who is really a zoologist, he studies animal behavior, has recently written a book suggesting that playwrights, poets, novelists can all be associated with the notion of the shaman speaking both to and for the tribe.

Susana Onega: *But if this is so, how do you explain the structural perfection of your novels?*
John Fowles: I do not think they are perfect.

Susana Onega: *Yes, for instance, the symmetrical embedding of Miranda's and Clegg's complementary narrations in* The Collector. *This cannot happen by chance. Or can it?*
John Fowles: Well, perhaps I could answer rather obliquely. There are two stages in writing a novel; there are many stages but there are two broad ones. One is the slightly shamanistic first draft. To say that one is inspired by the muses, as they used to in the eighteenth century, is ridiculous, but this is an area where you have to suppress the teacher, the censor, the critical part of you. Many very clever people linguistically cannot write novels because you have to learn to be two people. One has to be innocent, self-hypnotized, and the other has to be very stern and objective, a kind of professor of himself. I once had a letter from America from an American student who said, "Dear Mr. Fowles, I understand you are something of an expert on the fiction of John Fowles." Now that amused and interested me, because he obviously thought there must be two different people. One was a kind of unofficial professor of John Fowles and there was this other chap, Mr. Fowles, who he had to write to. But that schizophrenia he had, you need yourself. In that second period or self you have to be very stern, you have to have your blue pencil in hand. The old rule in English is, if you are going through a page of your own prose, the first thing you strike out is what you think is the best sentence in it. There is some sense in that. You very often get so attracted by one single phrase or sentence that you cannot see it is distorting the whole page, or even a chapter. The best solution is often to drop it.

Susana Onega: *Thank you. And the open endings of* The Magus *and of* The French Lieutenant's Woman *aren't meant to echo the thesis of the novels that the existentialist hero's quest is the quest itself?*

John Fowles: Yes, I was when I was younger, when I was well below half of my present age, we all were in England at that time . . . we were on our knees before Camus and Sartre and French existentialism. It was not because we truly understood it but we had a kind of notion, a dream of what it was about. Most of us were victims of it. I quite like that philosophy as a structure in a novel and in a sense I still use it. I would not say now that I am any longer an existentialist in the social sense, the cultural sense. I am really much more interested, in terms of the modern novel, in what fiction is about. I read quite recently most of Italo Calvino, the Italian novelist. That had a considerable effect on me because I felt he was doing what I am trying to do, or what I have tried to do. We writers are of course always slightly jealous and envious of each other and we can stab each other in the back very often, but there are some writers with whom you feel a brotherhood, a fraternal or even sisterly feeling, and Calvino is one of those. I feel great sympathy for Márquez, too, for Borges, the whole South American influence on the current European novel. I think this is for me the major influence on fiction today. It is much more important than that of Beckett or the black novel, the absurdist novel, and also the existentialist novels, Sartre's theater and so on. I really feel that has passed, that is gone.

Susana Onega: *In* The Collector, The Magus, *and* The French Lieuten-ant's Woman *the heroes are invariably left in a "frozen present," but this is not so in* Daniel Martin. *Would you say that the happy ending at the end of this novel expresses your jump beyond existentialism?*

John Fowles: Well, this is slightly difficult. When I was writing that book I had got very fed up, very displeased with the whole black, absurdist strain in European literature. I do sincerely admire Beckett as a writer, but I suppose Beckett would be the obvious representative of that, Ionesco and so on. I suddenly felt, "This novel I am going to end happily," and believe me, in our age it is a difficult thing to force yourself to do because the whole drift of modern intellectual European life is that life is hell, it is absurd, it is tragic, there are no happy endings. God knows it has been tragic in a very literal sense, but I somehow thought I would like to end the book happily, just as the Victorian novelists did. The Victorian novelists often tied themselves in knots so that they could have a happy ending, but I felt I would like to try that in a modern British novel. *Daniel Martin* was very much against Britain because, like all good English writers, I hate many aspects of my country. It seemed right somehow that at least it should end happily when I had said so many things against Britain, and America also, incidentally. It was a very anti-Anglo-Saxon book.

Susana Onega: *The hero, Daniel Martin, finally decides to give up script-writing in order to write a novel, after he has succeeded in recovering the love of Jane: are love and creativity the two antidotes against the void?*

John Fowles: Well, love, obviously, I should have thought. But creativity, you see, is so unkind. I mean, we can talk about how good democracy enhances many things, but, as I know from the manuscripts I get from other would-be writers, very often they are very handicapped. They have defects of body, or of mind, or of career, they have had to leave school early or whatever it is. Clearly life is cruel, you can only say, "I have sympathy for your problem." But when it comes to actually judging the novel, I am afraid aesthetic justice is without feeling. You have to say, "You can't write" or "This is badly written" or "This is a cliché." Only the Marxists allow clichés, political in their case, to count. Really, I do not know how you deal with this, but there are points when you have to say to people, "You can't write, " "You can't think," or even more important, "You can't imagine," because this is a part of the human mind we know very little about: why some people can imagine vividly and why some people can organize that imagination, because creation does need a certain amount of organization. Why some people can do these things and also learn to suppress themselves, because novelists cannot do everything they like. You soon learn when you write novels that you are in a prison. I do not deny for a moment I am in a prison when I am writing a book, but it is really like being in a prison that is perhaps six-by-four and you think, "How could I make it a little bit larger?," perhaps seven-by-five. In other words, you try to create a little bit of freedom, as a prisoner might do in prison circumstances. It can be intolerable when you are writing a novel, when you know you are in this cell, you do not know how to get out of it. Occasionally the escape attempts are what makes the novel, you have got yourself into a kind of fixed code, a fixed theorem, like a geometrical theorem, and it is escaping from that which, I think, often produces remarkable books. Beckett is a good example of trying to get out of the prison we are all in.

Susana Onega: *At a given point in the novel, Daniel Martin says: "I create, I am. All the rest is dream, though concrete and executed." Would you say that* Mantissa *fictionalizes this statement?*

John Fowles: *Mantissa* was meant to be a joke. It was first going to be published by a Californian private printer—he prints very nice books—but unfortunately I was under contract with large British and American publishers. They turned cruel on me, they said, "No, we want this," and this nice little Californian publisher was just pushed out by these large publishing houses. In America and Britain it was really taken much too seriously. I like the French idea of the *jeu d' esprit*, the lighter book. Something you suffer from in America is this belief that your novels must get larger and larger, longer and longer, more and more important, bigger and bigger in every way. This is blowing up a balloon of hot air. I liked the much more European idea of producing very minor works, something you enjoy doing perhaps, do not spend a great deal of time on and that you will not go to the stake for. You will not be martyred for this book. *Mantissa* was really meant to be a comment, no more, on the problems of being a writer. I have always had a kind of belief in the muses. Of course there is not a muse of the novel, but I chose Erato, the muse of lyric love poetry in ancient Greece. The notion that she was locked up with a would-be novelist and of course they really hate each other.

You get this kind of problem when you are writing, or at least I get it, because I am a man often very attached to women characters. You just do not know when you are writing dialogue—dialogue is the most difficult part, technically, of any novel—you do not know what they are going to say. I had a famous case in *The French Lieutenant's Woman.* I remember spending a whole day, I needed one sentence that Sarah, the heroine of *The French Lieutenant's Woman,* was saying. I tried sentence after sentence, all in the wastepaper basket—and then I realized she was actually saying, inasmuch as a literary character can be real, "I don't say anything at this point." She was saying, "Your mistake is thinking that dialogue here is necessary. It isn't necessary," and so, that is how it is in the book. She is silent. This relationship you have with main characters is slightly like the dialogue I put in *Mantissa:* they often seem to be fighting you. They say, "I'm not going to walk down this road," "I'm not going to be burgled," whatever it is. In a strange way you have to listen to this. It is a little bit as it is with schoolchildren. Occasionally you have to smack them and say, "No! You're going to do what I tell you to do!" but, like schoolchildren, occasionally they are telling you something which you had better listen to if you are going to be a good teacher.

Susana Onega: *What was your real aim in writing* Mantissa? *How consciously did you have Roland Barthes's* Le plaisir du texte *in mind when you were writing it?*

John Fowles: I do not think particularly. Dr. Federman yesterday was giving his views on Derrida, Lacan, Barthes. . . . I am exactly like him. I have read quite a lot of them on deconstruction and post-structuralism and all the rest of it. I really do not understand what it is all about. I speak French and I read French quite well but I am afraid most of it is absolutely over my head. A much more scholarly English novelist than myself is Iris Murdoch. I heard her saying only the other day that she regarded it as philosophical nonsense, very largely. Of course it can be very elegantly expressed; especially Roland Barthes I think is a good writer, but I am really very doubtful whether all of that has had much influence on me. In *Mantissa* I was making fun of it, rather crude fun in places. But I was really expressing the old English view that most of French intellectual theory since the war has been elegant nonsense . . . attractive nonsense. This is the old business of the practical English never understanding the very rhetorical and clever French. France and England are undoubtedly the two countries in Europe that are furthest apart, although they are so near geographically. The English are much nearer to Spain, Italy, Greece, than England and France will ever be.

Susana Onega: Mantissa *also brings to mind the deconstructivist theory that there is a unique, all-enveloping written text, a text that is prior to the writer himself. This reduces the role of the writer to a mere "scriptor," somebody whose only task is to endlessly rewrite this unique and polymorphous text. Would it be right to say that, for all their thematic and stylistic differences, all your novels are simply "variations" of the same novel?*

John Fowles: Yes, in one sense. I have often said I have only written about one woman in my life. I mean, I feel that. I do not put it in the novels but I feel when writing that the heroine of one novel is the same woman as the heroine of another novel. They may be different enough in outward characteristics but they are for me a family—just one woman, basically. Novels, where they come from in your mind, whether they come from some prior unconscious text, I think I would really not like to say. I am not sure. I think also we are touching on an area where it is dangerous for the novelist to be too clever. It is like the old story of your watch being slow and you take it to bits to improve the time—and of course you have finally no watch any more. By trying to repair it you have lost it. Usually, when I am asked this kind of question, I say I would rather let others judge, as they certainly have in the past. I think this is a job for the critics. They can say that I have certain characteristics of fictional literary behavior and structure and so on. It is not for me to discover that I am a poor conditioned guinea pig or rabbit. It is safer that I keep that at a distance.

Susana Onega: *Most of your novels seem to have been written with a view to parodying well-worn literary traditions: the "confession" and epistolary technique, in* The Collector, *for example; the historical romance, in* The French Lieutenant's Woman; *or the "Examinations and Depositions" of convicts in* A Maggot, *which strongly echo the reports made by Daniel Defoe at Newgate. Also, in all your novels there is an explicit reference to certain writers of the past, like Shakespeare, Dickens, Thomas Hardy, or T. S. Eliot, and they even include literal quotations from their works. Why do you do this?*

John Fowles: Do you mean in *A Maggot?*

Susana Onega: *In general; specifically in* A Maggot.

John Fowles: *A Maggot* is set in the year 1735 and what I did, although the novel itself is fiction, I suddenly thought one day, I have never liked historical novels—why I have written two I am not quite sure but in general I am much more interested in real history. I would much rather read the historical texts of the period. It occurred to me that in *A Maggot* it would be nice, because I am imitating eighteenth-century dialogue, to give the reader passages from a wellknown magazine of the time called *The Gentleman's Magazine,* which all educated people once read. It is also useful because it does give you many authentic facts of the time, and shows how they were printed. English printing was then different. And an impression of the cruelty of the time, because the English then had a barbarous judicial system. If you stole a handkerchief or a spoon then you would probably be hanged in eighteenth-century London—an awful system. I have also always liked the old trial report, where trials are reported in dialogue alone: purely question, answer, question, answer. That is quite common. It did not start with Defoe by any means but I like it, as a novelist, because it sets you an enormous problem. This is another strange thing that novelists have to do to themselves. They have to set themselves difficult situations. If you use this trial technique—question, answer, question, answer—you lose half your arms, half your weapons as a novelist. There is no description of what people are doing ... "She smiled," "She lit a cigarette" (not in the eighteenth century!); but anything you can say in an ordinary novel is forbidden by using this technique of the trial report. I like that because it also makes your dialogue much better. You have to express far more through your dialogue than you will in

an ordinary conversation. A friend of mine in England is the playwright
Harold Pinter, and I think he is the chief exponent of this in English. That is,
really cutting down to an incredible degree—that is why he is such a good
scriptwriter in films—unnecessary dialogue by making every line of his dialogue really work. Every word of it works, even the silences, in his best plays,
work. I really wanted in *A Maggot* to use that difficult power of pure dialogue
a little, although he is a playwright and of course I am a novelist. I think that
the novel has not caught up with the modern world in the sense of what the
novelist can leave out. This is one of the great qualities a novelist must have,
knowing what to omit, what to leave out. Many novelists, I am afraid I would
accuse the Americans a little bit here, write far too many words. They do not
let the reader do any work. You must, you see, get the reader on your side
and the way to get people on your side is to give them pleasant work or
intriguing, interesting work. Therefore, all that you leave out, all the gaps in
your text, are so much fuel for this one-to-one relationship you have with the
reader. I am guilty of this fault myself. I look through old texts I have written
and think I ought to have left many things out. You realize you are much too
fat, you are much too rich always; you can be sparer. I was reading a little bit
of Cervantes, *Don Quixote,* the other day. Of course that is historical, but I
was tempted even then to pick up my blue pencil. There are whole passages
where you think, "Well, he doesn't really need that." He is a great writer and
of course it is historical and enjoyable, but from a strictly modern point of
view—the same is true of Defoe in England—it is their prolixity, their unnecessary prolixity, that strikes me personally when you reread them.

Susana Onega: *Another recurrent feature in your novels is the existence
of two complementary and opposed worlds. One seems to be described in
realistic terms, while the other is symbolic and mythical. Invariably the mythical realm is an untrimmed garden, a valley, or a combe. This dichotomy
between the city and the green world is a traditional one in literature, but in
that delightful little autobiography of yours,* The Tree, *you describe the green
world as something real and at hand, you even use proper names, such as
Ware Common or Wistman's Wood. Should we take it that there are no
boundaries, then, between the real and the unreal?*

John Fowles: Well, the real in the general sense, the real for me does not
lie where we are now, in other words, in cities. It lies for me very much in
the countryside and in the wild. They had a phrase in medieval art, the "hortus conclusus," that is, the garden surrounded by a wall. Very often the Virgin

Mary and the Unicorn would be inside this wall and, you see it in medieval painting, everything outside the pretty little walled garden is chaos. I must not get on to ecology and conservation terms. We have ruined the nature of Europe very largely and of course we are busy ruining it in South America and elsewhere now. Man really hates everything outside the "hortus conclusus," this walled garden. We do not like the wilderness, the chaos. The Church was against it for centuries because it was where sin took place. In England, for instance, it was hated because of the Puritan ethos; because man could not get profit, he could not make money out of the chaos, the wilderness. This has always hurt me very profoundly, that we have this profound schism, the schism between us and wild nature. I loved the countryside on the way here to Zaragoza from Barcelona. That, for me, is a kind of paradise still, bare fields (not enough trees, though), a few shepherds, sheep. I really prefer that, I am afraid, to great congregations of human beings. I do not really like speaking to you like this. I do not like crowds of people. If it were possible, I would rather have had half an hour alone with each of you here because that, for me, is where all the reality is. It is in small groups of human beings, ideally in the "I-thou" two-persons confrontation. I really fear for Europe, its increasing cultural and economic madness, the greater crowds, the greater masses, the appalling tendency all over Europe to go to the big city. I know there are wage reasons and all the rest of it, but I am all for getting back to the country. I am all for depopulation. I should not say this in a Catholic country but I find the world population growth abominable. It is one of the worst problems the world has at the moment.

Susana Onega: *Women also seem to have a double nature in your novels: Alison's "oxymoron quality," for example, expressed in the splitting into twins, in* The Magus; *Sarah's baffling double nature, alternately innocent and corrupt, like Rebecca Hocknell in* A Maggot, *etc. Are women as complex and polymorphous as reality, or literature?*

John Fowles: I have always found them quite exceptionally difficult to . . . well, "handle" is rather an ambiguous word in English. Let me say, to have relations with. I am not a "feminist" in the fiercely active political sense it is usually used in England and America nowadays, but I have sympathy for the general "anima," the feminine spirit, the feminine intelligence, and I think that all male judgments of the way women go about life are so biased that they are virtually worthless. Man is really being a very prejudiced judge of his own case and of course when judging against women. It is counted very bad taste in England now to talk favorably of women's intuition. The real feminists in England do not like this sentimental talk of female intuition. I am afraid I still have some faith in that. Women cannot, I think, sometimes think as logically or rationally as men can, but thinking logically or rationally often leads you into error. It is by no means certain that the result is any worse in a woman, if you like, muddling her way through to a decision, or feeling her emotional way to a decision, than that of a highly rational man. My impression in Spain is that feminism has not really quite got there to the same extent it has with us. Perhaps that is to come.

Susana Onega: *There are so many more things I would love to ask you, but I'm afraid the old tyrant, time, won't allow me more than one question before I hand over the microphone to the audience. Let's make it a naughty question: At the end of* Mantissa, *the mental walls of Martin Green's hospital room become solid again, trapping the Staff Sister within them. Assuming that she stands for the prototypical literary critic, do we have any reason to hope that there is, after all, a little corner reserved for her within the creative mind, that she is creative in a way?*

John Fowles: Well, the whole of this book, *Mantissa*, takes place in a cell, but of course the cell is the human brain. It all takes place in the brain. It is supposed to be a lunatic asylum and this is where the hero, or anti-hero, of the book is incarcerated. If I could just say, there is an Irishman—we talked a lot about Joyce and Beckett yesterday, but there is a third Irish novelist who I could put very near their level—I do not know if he is known here, his name is Flann O'Brien. He was a journalist, a very funny, humorous journalist also. He had several pseudonyms. Flann O'Brien, I think, was a genius at really absurd humor and that book was behind *Mantissa*. If I went in for dedicating books to other writers, I would have dedicated it to Flann O'Brien. I suspect his humor is very difficult indeed if you are not Irish. Even the English have a little trouble with it. The Irish are a marvelous literary race. Everyone who is not Irish issues a secret little prayer, "I wish I were Irish." They really have superb writers. We owe them a great deal in England, Wales, and Scotland. Sorry, now I have forgotten the question.

Susana Onega: *No, that was a very diplomatic answer. I was asking whether the literary critic has a right to have a corner within the creative mind.*

John Fowles: Yes, yes, I think so. If you remember, a part of the muse herself is a critic. Whatever inspires you also usefully criticizes what you are.

John Fowles: The Art of Fiction CIX

James R. Baker / 1989

From *The Paris Review*, 111 (Summer 1989), 43-63. Reprinted by permission of James R. Baker and Russell & Volkening as agents for *The Paris Review*. Copyright © 1989 by *The Paris Review*. Interview originally appeared in *The Paris Review*.

Interviewer: Is it accurate to say that you did not begin to establish an identity as a writer until you went to Oxford in 1947 and entered into a rather fashionable revolt against the limitations of a suburban middle-class background?

John Fowles: Yes, completely accurate, though I think the notion of joining "a rather fashionable revolt" is a little bit wrong. You must remember my generation—I was born in 1926—had spent our late adolescence and early twenties in wartime, followed by a period of national austerity that remained psychologically like war. Oxford in the late 1940s was I think, to all of us lucky enough to be there, a kind of wonderful escape from all that—a happy dream, an alternative world . . . in a sense a novel we had heard of, but never actually read until then. Where the individual was paramount, not the nation. I came out of the strict "order" and discipline of the British Marine Corps into the ancient indulgence of Oxford; it was a heady experience for all of us, an intoxication, hardly a matter of revolt.

I should add that in my teens I had a somewhat unusual experience for a youth, having become head boy of my large public school (in Britain really a private school, of course). Head boys were in those days responsible for all minor discipline in the school outside of class, able to give punishments and cane delinquents; we were, so to speak, appointed heads of Gestapo, with a body of lesser prefects to help us spy on and patrol, cow and bully, the several hundred other boys. It was really a very bad system, and I wish I could say that a more sensitive side of myself had revolted against it at once. It did not. The power went to my head, and it was only afterwards—when I had left the school—that I rejected it completely. I have indeed hated all forms of public authority ever since—oh, not every individual representative of it, but the general idea behind it.

Apart from anything else, head boys were largely excused from any other kind of work, and that had fatal results on my own proper "academic" career. We were also supposed to stand as models for the whole system (in my particular school, producing eventual administrators of the already dying British Empire, stiff with every supposed middle-class virtue), and that was a role I came to realize I despised and did not want. This happened in the two years or so of service in the Royal Marines between leaving school and going to Oxford. I arrived in that latter place, in other words, in a state of full rejection of everything I had been earlier taught to believe in. Oxford handsomely confirmed the revolt, rather than initiated it.

Interviewer: What induced you to read in French during your four years at Oxford? What writers particularly impressed you? Was Montaigne, for example, an influence and a model in the formation of your humanistic philosophy?

Fowles: This was largely pure chance. I had been fairly good at modern languages in school, and had a very sympathetic master there. It was sort of taken for granted that I would later do them at university. Those were, of course, the days of compulsory conscription. So I was in the Marines from 1944 to 1946, ending as a lieutenant training recruits who hoped to become commandos. I was at the time a little bit torn between joining the Marines permanently or taking the place I had been promised at Oxford. One day we had an official visit from a famous lord mayor of Plymouth, Isaac Foot. I was appointed his temporary ADC for the visit, and took the opportunity to ask his advice about my dilemma. To my surprise—we had all been brainwashed in those days into thinking the only thing that mattered was one's middle-class national duty—he said very crisply that only a fool would find it a dilemma. If I had a place at Oxford, *of course* I should go for that, not the Marines. Spurred by what Isaac Foot said, I applied at once.

My first year at Oxford I "read" both French and German. I liked my French tutors, did not like the German ones, and so dropped German . . . something I have regretted somewhat ever since. Despite grim experiences in the trenches and afterwards in the occupation army in Germany itself during the First World War, my own father was much more fond of German literature than French. That decision of mine did not please him. In a sense I was going against family (or Victorian) tradition in turning my back on Germany and German. But I am sure now, forty years later, that it was basically the right decision. I think it is much more useful for the future novelist—for any seeker after culture—to get to know the Latin side of Europe well, rather than the Teutonic and Nordic one. The Germans are too like the British, and the French so richly different. We need what we haven't got by nature.

I had student "love affairs" with various French writers, although some took years to take effect. I very much liked Montaigne, although I haven't read him for years now. He seems to me one of the sanest and intellectually most attractive Europeans who has ever lived and he set me on the course of humanism that I have followed ever since. We had at that time to spend a great deal of time on Old French, and used to rather groan about it linguistically; but there seeped into me eventually an affection for the early storytelling—for Marie de France, Chrétien de Troyes and the rest, the fathers and mothers of the European novel. I also liked the French comedy, especially Molière and Marivaux—not Racine and Corneille, I'm afraid, and I liked the late nineteenth century poets, Baudelaire, Mallarmé, Laforgue. I also particularly fell for that elegant, precise tradition of the *pensée,* the carefully framed apothegm and wisdom, something we've never really mastered in English— Pascal, La Rochefoucauld, Chamfort, all the rest. That admiration ruined a book I wrote later, *The Aristos.* I learnt my lesson there. It is not only wines that won't travel between our two countries.

By and large, I have never had much enthusiasm for the classical side of the French tradition, whose apotheosis is, I suppose, Racine. Even at Oxford I seemed to get endlessly lost in the byways, things I should not—at least for exam purposes—have been reading. I have never been particularly interested in French contemporary literature. Though I love the language, I have never learned to speak it well, though I would claim I am quite a good reader of it. But that was, I think, the aim of the old Oxford at that time: to teach one to understand France and the French, not to speak the language currently and fluently. That for me remains a vital difference between proper university "French"—or any other foreign culture and language—and its language-school variation. They are, or should be, two different things. One is for human beings, the other for business people. I don't think modern educationists have ever understood that, at least in this country.

Interviewer: But weren't the existentialist writers—Sartre, Camus, de Beauvoir—important in fostering your bid for freedom from the rigid structures of your conservative background?

Fowles: Those writers certainly came to us after the war as strange and exciting. I always liked Camus best. Sartre I often found hard to understand. I can remember giving up *L'Etre et le Néant* in a mixture of despair and disgust. It wasn't just a language problem, more a philosophical one, not knowing what he actually meant in real life. That applies to most of the gurus

since. I don't recall having read Simone de Beauvoir then. I think the "influence" was partly from the endless amount of talk in Oxford about "the existentialists," "authenticity," being *engagé* and the rest, all the implicit
condemnations of the bourgeois view of life, that affected me. It corres-
ponded to feelings inside myself that I think would have emerged anyway,
indeed had already emerged, if confusedly, but were certainly quickened by
the existentialist writers.

Students of my work often make rather a lot of existentialism, a good deal
more than I ever felt is true of myself. But that is a familiar feeling, for me,
anyway. You are presented as something you never really were. Of course
it's flattering to be extensively studied; but I'm not altogether happy about
the intensive pursuit of living writers that seems so popular now with literary
students and teachers. I write for other reasons than providing fodder for the
literary faculties.

Interviewer: Did you read Jung? Could his influence be linked with the
theme of psychological growth so apparent in the early novels?

Fowles: I did dabble in him, from Oxford days and after. But not as a
serious student might, much more as a dilettante, picking up the ideas I
needed and that appealed to me rather as a spoilt child might pick out of a
lucky dip if he or she were given free range and choice. For me Jung has
always been the most fruitful psychologist, that is, most fertile in his effects
on any subsequent fiction. I suspect a straight analyst, more or less in Freud's
footsteps, would suit me better medically, if I ever needed such attention—
which perhaps I do . . . like every other novelist!

Interviewer: You have said that you started writing *The Aristos* as a sort
of student's notebook or "self-portrait in ideas" at this time. It seems an
indispensable book for the serious student of your early fiction, *The Magus*
and *The Collector.* Did it precede any extended effort to write fiction?

Fowles: Like so many Oxford students, I developed very timid literary
ambitions there. Such as they were, mine had far more to do with poetry than
the novel. Poetry lasted as a long dream, long after I'd left university, of
which the *Poems* that were published in 1973 were a funeral relic. I still
occasionally get the urge to write poems, but usually sternly resist it. I didn't
attempt fiction till the mid-1950s, and then not very seriously; it long remained a kind of second best, or *faute de mieux* to me. *The Aristos* I did
begin in my last year at Oxford, 1949. I also began keeping a personal diary
about that time. I am a great believer in diaries, if only in the sense that bar

exercises are good for ballet dancers: it's often through personal diaries—however embarrassing they are to read now—that the novelist discovers his true bent—that he can narrate real events and distort them to please himself, describe character, observe other human beings, hypothesize, invent, all the rest. I think that is how I became a novelist, eventually. It's certainly how I tend to see my older books when I reread them, which is not at all often: that is, as a sort of past diary about myself. So that's how I felt and thought then. Not always a pleasant experience! *The Aristos* certainly preceded my novels, and yes, often bears heavily on them.

Interviewer: You have said that you wanted to be known as a writer and not simply a novelist. You continue to make it difficult for us to separate the fiction and the nonfiction in your work. Is this a result of the early humanistic idealism—being a "renaissance man," a generalist, rather than a devotee in any single genre?

Fowles: I've always felt that expressing myself in other literary forms is natural *and* desirable. Or putting it most generally, that all novelists should live in two different worlds: a real one and an unreal one. That is perhaps why my taste in fiction is towards a fair degree of realism in style and my taste in non-fiction (say in what scientists and academics write) is towards those who can exhibit qualities like tolerance of hypothesis, dislike of the rigid interpretation, a general fluidity of attitude and a basic sympathy towards a subject . . . a touch of ordinary humanity, in a phrase.

Very important for me also is the collection of "old" books I have gathered over the years. I am a lousy bibliophile in the proper and normal sense. What I like about picking up old books is their enormous variety and the glimpses they can give into past and lost worlds and cultures. I do this quite indiscriminately, with whatever takes my fancy; the returns, in a literary sense, are infinite, but difficult to categorize. An American student to whom I mentioned this asked if she might have a list of what I had read or collected over the years. I told her it was impossible. I keep no such list. But this very miscellaneous reading I have done over the years has become a major influence for all its maddening vagueness for the students. Students nowadays seem to want to "place" precisely, to locate precisely, everything about a writer's work: what he is, what has made him or her what they are, and so on. It seems to me that to imprison it is to deny something very essential about writing. Rather the same thing has taken place in nature, or natural history—the mania to place everything in a precise species or sub-species, to discover exactly how it works, all the rest. I am opposed to the scientization of nature, the reducing of it all to species, ecological distributions, biochemical mechanisms, and so on. I feel this very strongly about writing and writers too. The world wants us caged, in one place, behind bars; it is very important we stay free.

Interviewer: Like Forster, you have always distrusted Jamesian perfection of form, or at least you seemed to reject it as a worthy goal after the two early novels. Why?

Fowles: I'm not quite sure what "perfection of form" means, unless it means obeying whatever "ideal form," that fickle thing, that the general educated taste, and in particular its leading determiners, the literary professors and serious critics and students, have decided their age must judge as "ideal." I dislike intensely the notion that a perfect form, like a sort of god, hovers over all of us, which we either cling or pay lip-service to. I think whatever form is chosen by each writer is "perfect" for him or her, however imperfect it may seem to those under the delusion of some general "perfect form" and its attainability. That sort of myth of a perfect form, applicable to all, seems to me one of those things modern art has sunk beyond resurrection. I certainly try to make the form I put things in suit their matter, but I agree totally with Forster that forcing that matter into some supposed general ideal of the form best suited to it is wrong. Novels in a sense are like new scientific theories. Of course there are ways in which they have to pay homage to the past, to high past standards; but they have also to disobey and question them, to break new ground. Nothing in their cultural pasts could have allowed for or predicted, say, *Tristram Shandy* or *Ulysses*.

Interviewer: I meant to suggest that the two early novels are quite highly structured compared with the later ones. They're both allegories on power, aren't they? Both novels reach for the "living myth"—the archetypal and perennial confrontation of the "aristoi" with the "hoi polloi." They're set pieces, world-weary. Doesn't *The French Lieutenant's Woman* show a new openness in form and mark a real change in your conception of the novel and novelist?

Fowles: They may be allegories on power, but I really don't think I saw them particularly so at the time. The younger novelist is really so excited by the powers he discovers he has—in part—that novels grow closer to love affairs—between novelist and subject—than to the sort of serious theme you're suggesting. This is perhaps why they come to you as world-weary set pieces; they were both written in a state of excitement! In a sense the young novelist finds himself in a gymnasium, with apparatus for set exercises, and wants to try his hand at some or all of them. I think it is only when he at last has mastered that side of it, that the real work, and the freedom we all fundamentally covet, become possible. Certainly I hope that in that way *The French Lieutenant's Woman* marks a real change and a new openness—what the Russians now call *glasnost,* transparency.

Interviewer: You insist in these early works on the natural inequality of human beings, but at the same time you lean toward socialism. How do you reconcile your social egalitarianism with the rather snobbish idea of an "aristoi" or elite few set apart from the many?

Fowles: This is something of an eternal torment, or split, in my life. The idea of an elite few is, of course, nowadays something no one likes to declare a belief in. On the other hand I am absolutely sure that it is a biological, if you like Darwinian, truth. So I am torn between this "cruel" but necessary truth: that some—perhaps most strikingly in the arts and sciences—are clearly better endowed or adapted than the others, and then by that other, kinder truth which asks equality and equal justice for society as a whole. In general I confess I much prefer the company of reasonably intelligent and educated people, but I still basically hold with the contention I made in *The Aristos:* that being "superior" in intelligence or education does not excuse an indifference to *hoi polloi,* the Cleggs and "fools" they have to live among. On the other hand, some of the recent calls for greater egalitarianism seem to me absurdly unreal. You can't legislate stupidity and ignorance out of existence, or deny they aren't evolutionary disadvantages. But perhaps we'd better not go into that!

Interviewer: Have your work habits and methods changed or evolved since you wrote those early, idea-driven novels? In your "Notes on Writing a Novel," you say *The French Lieutenant's Woman* had its genesis in an image that simply welled up from the unconscious. Just how do you now proceed in the task of writing fiction?

Fowles: I don't think my methods and habits have changed. When I do write fiction it is still much more by instinct and feeling than by some kind of theory. I am at the moment toying with the idea of a novel about French counterrevolution in La Vendée in the 1790s. That also has come to me by something very like an image. I may not do it, but what attracts me are these image-constituted kernels of a story. How shall I put it—they seem inherently rich, they promise all sorts of potentialities in how they might grow. What is rather terrifying at my age is the prospect of all the work you are setting for yourself by allowing such images to haunt the mind. That *has* changed. Some stories in the past one couldn't wait to get into; the energy needed, all the hard work, seemed nothing. Now it is frankly much more difficult. My last novel, *A Maggot-La Créature* in French—is currently having some success in France; it has just been chosen the best book of 1987. Marvelous, most writers think. But, perversely, I find it all rather depressing; men of sixty still expect to hurdle, or run marathons, as well as they did thirty years before!

Interviewer: The visual image seems very important to you, as it was to D. H. Lawrence. You constantly refer to painters and painting in your fiction. When did this interest in art and art history arise in your career?

Fowles: I have no artistic ability whatever myself, but I do have a great fondness for the art of the past. I once said that if I weren't a novelist I would like to have been an artist. In a way I both envy and pity painters their general *inability* with writing and words. More practically, I think the countless word-less shortcuts the painters have to make to show *their* truths are of value to all writers. In semiological terms they have a whole vocabulary of signs totally beyond literature, obviously. A lot of very recent post-modernist art does not satisfy me. Upsetting tradition is justifiable; putting virtually nothing in its place is not.

Interviewer: Rossetti and the Pre-Raphaelites seem to have special significance for you. Rossetti appears as a mentor or Magus for Sarah in *The French Lieutenant's Woman.* Isn't he also quite close in spirit to your painter, Breasley, in *The Ebony Tower?*

Fowles: Yes, I am very fond of the Pre-Raphaelites. I was sent only the other day a copy of Holman Hunt's portrait of Rossetti as a young man, and felt a very sharp sense of almost personal identity with that; something about his slightly neurotic look. I certainly didn't link him with Breasley in *The Ebony Tower*— I had no clear model—but perhaps there was, as there so often is in fiction, some unconscious link with him.

Interviewer: Breasley is very much against abstraction and makes negative and obscene puns on Picasso's very name. He insists that great art is not mental but arises instead from nature or fullness of being. You agree with that, don't you?

Fowles: Well, yes, I am not altogether happy about some of the developments in very modern art. The great abstract artists, fine; but far too many of the lesser ones seem to me to use the abstract to hide their own lack of basic technique and of things like draughtsmanship. It does seem to me on occasion altogether too mental, too associated—especially in New York, I'm afraid—with notions of what is commercially viable or *chic* today rather than with the kind of more humanistic—and human-based—traditions from the past.

Interviewer: But is your attitude essentially "romantic"? Drawing a portrait of the artist based on your fiction and various statements you have made, one forms a Rossetti-like image of a rather isolated, anima-driven man, dependent upon the "muse," or unconscious forces, somewhat self-destructive, and dreaming always of a saner and greener world than the contemporary reality.

Fowles: Here we must differ. Everything I have learnt of other writers and most artists does constitute a portrait of the sort of figure for which you blame me—certainly the isolation, certainly being driven by largely unconscious forces, certainly having to rely on idealized images from the past. I think all the arts draw on a nostalgia or longing for a better world—at root a better metaphysical condition—than the one that is. Self-destructive, I don't know, but certainly we are all victims of some form of manic depression. That is the price of being what we are. I would never choose—even if I could!—to be a more "normal" human being; I would never choose something without that emotional cost, severe though it can become.

Interviewer: Doesn't all this remind you of Hardy? You sometimes seem to merge with Hardy's Jude—a man with a vision of the humanist's New Jerusalem glowing on the horizon, as Christminister appeared to Jude. You remember he carved into the milestone, "Thither, J. F." This isn't really a fair comparison, I suppose, since you don't have his naive faith in social evolution.

Fowles: I think every writer, certainly from this part of the world, feels a bit of Hardy in him, but I wouldn't like to be compared personally to Jude the Obscure. I really can't altogether go with Hardy's general gloom and pessimism. I certainly have doubts about social evolution, especially today, and especially as so many politicians like to use the hope or promise of it in their speeches—too often merely because it's something people want to hear. By and large I retain a kind of optimism about the human condition, a belief that we will one day—even if always a later day than naive optimism expects—correct much of what is wrong in the world, or perhaps just what makes us believe it is wrong. Do I think that things will get better in any immediate future, no; that there is some kind of slow progress, despite countless wrong turnings, yes. I am working at the moment at an attempt to dramatize the debate over Darwin's *On the Origin of Species* at the British Association meeting at Oxford in 1860—in many ways perhaps the most important event of the whole century since it was when rational science began at last to cast off the shackles of obscurantist religion, when reason began to triumph over myth. Our present scientific world, which resulted from all that, has its faults and problems, of course, and perhaps the pendulum has swung too far. But I still can't feel, despite all the wellknown intervening horrors and disasters, that the world hasn't progressed since the new reality Darwin and his followers introduced into life just over a century ago. Basically Hardy saw Darwinian theory as grist to his mill, or scientific backing for his gloom. I don't feel that. It seems to me to have represented a major clearing in the clouds over humanity.

Interviewer: Granted your philosophical differences with Hardy, there does seem to be a psychological bond between you. In your essay, "Hardy and the Hag," you recognize his rather painful last novel, *The Well-Beloved,* as a precocious (pre-Freudian and pre-Jungian) fable on the power of the muse or the anima—the erotic—in the life of the writer. A more innocent perception of this connection is the mainstay in the life and work of another writer you have admired, Alain-Fournier. Bring in Rossetti and you have a psychological brotherhood. Isn't your *Mantissa* a sort of spoof on this link between the erotic and the creative impulses—a tribute to old Erato?

Fowles: I certainly think the erotic was very important for Hardy. The avoiding any direct contact with it, or expression of it, the slipping around it, plays an enormous part in his novels. He was obviously a shy and repressed man. He liked the tryst, that first secret meeting or instinctual attraction between lovers, so much more than the fully physical side, what we should call the sex. I suppose I am the same, that is, haunted—both ravished and tormented—by the erotic; yet happiest when it is left three-quarters hidden, in secret. I spent a year of my life once writing an erotic novel—in common terms, a pornographic one. One day, when it was virtually complete, I took it and all its drafts into the garden and burnt the lot. It would no doubt have made me a great deal of money, and I was rather proud of it, for what it was. It was not prudishness that made me burn it, but much more a feeling of blasphemy, an error of bad taste. It broke that secret, bared the hidden part.

That is why I dislike what I see as the unnecessary sexual explicitness in so much American fiction; it becomes infantile, destructive of the truly erotic, in the end.

Mantissa was meant to make fun of that, in part, and also of the poor novelists, like Hardy, Fournier, D. H. Lawrence, Henry Miller and countless others, laboring under this monstrous erotic succubus they have to carry on their backs. That and the money succubus—the idiot's illusion: "I must be a great writer because I make a lot of money"—are the two main danger points for the male writer.

Interviewer: You have told visiting academics searching for "influences" to consider nature itself—as well as your long-standing interest in natural history and in conservation—as sources. The essential connection between nature and your art is explained, I think, in the most admirable of your non-fictional works, *The Tree.* I refer to that perfect essay you wrote to accompany the photographs in that volume. Would you care to clarify and elaborate?

Fowles: Thank you for liking *The Tree.* I am most happy at having written that. This relation, between man and nature, is far more important and real to me than that between man and God, even between man and other men. I also find it intensely pleasurable, endlessly rich. Men often bore, books often bore, all things human can bore; nature, never. I once had to be in a jury at the Old Bailey, London's principal criminal court. We had to listen to a series of very unpleasant cases, involving child abuse, incest, all the rest. I was left after-wards standing outside the court with my jury fee. I decided to go to the nearest bookshop and buy the title remotest from anything human that I could find. I bought the then standard work on British spiders, about which I knew nothing. Now, many years later, after endless peering down a microscope, I still know nothing scientific about spiders—that is, I can still not identify them safely. But at least I have glimpsed and spent many hours in their strangely complex and beautiful world.

For many years, and with rather more success, I have pursued wild orchids all over Europe and—through someone's kind gift of Luer's books—in imag-ination as well, all over the United States. When I was in a hospital bed just after having had a stroke recently, I was near weeping with self-rage and self-pity, reciting a mantra to myself: *tenthredinifera, tenthredinifera, tenthredini-fera . . .* that unpronounceable name belongs to one of the most beautiful *Ophrys,* or bee orchids, of Europe. I had come upon it on a Cretan mountain the previous spring; and I was saying that name like a mantra because I thought I should never climb that remote mountain again. Nature regularly brings tears into my eyes; humans very, very seldom.

Interviewer: Academic critics have questioned you again and again about literary influences, but of course there have been other influences. What people have impressed you? And what about the impact of your travels—France, Greece, America?

Fowles: Very few people, I am afraid, have influenced me, I say "I am afraid" because I think one's indifference, deep down, to most other human begins is not something to be proud of; it is a form of hopelessness. Increasingly, as I grow older, I try to justify this, and perhaps do, in part, by man's bestial treatment of nature and his overwhelmingly selfish stupidity, his letting himself proliferate to such an insane degree. There are just too many of us these days. We have a dialect expression here in the West of England—the grockles. A grockle is someone ugly, but necessary: a visitor, a tourist, a foreigner. It is not just here in Dorset, but all over the world: the grockles begin to ruin everything.

Places touch me, move me, far more. If I am lucky, *now,* in the present, visiting; but these days it seems more and more in memory they move me, what they *were* like. There is a beach on Spetsai in Greece I describe in *The Magus.* Later visitors have told me how the grockles have completely spoilt it. But I can still remember it as it once was. I do not need my own words. Words are clumsy things. In my mind I can return earlier, to the first place, my first experience, as perhaps Adam could recall lost Eden. I remember equally a site in New Mexico, that I also wrote about; and the first American woods I walked through, in Massachusetts, entrancingly new to me and strange, though it showed nothing but the commonest species.

Interviewer: Orwell wrote his late books in behalf of "democratic socialism"; you write in behalf of "freedom." Apparently you mean that the individual must free himself from conventions. We must escape from the "ebony tower" of our conventional lives. Is that the key idea?

Fowles: I have just written a conservation piece in which I suggest—not altogether humorously—that man's nearest relative is not the ape, but the sheep. I was brought up in an intensely conventional suburb not far from London by, in social terms, conventional parents. I have tried to escape ever since, and have admired the unconventional, the breakers of rules. Though often timid about that myself.

Interviewer: Many of your novels are "timescapes," as they have been called, but *Daniel Martin* stands out as a venture into contemporary realism. Like Dan, you did live in Los Angeles for a while and worked on films.

Fowles: *Daniel Martin* is certainly closer to me, or my own life, than the other books. Yes, I did briefly experience Los Angeles when William Wyler was getting ready to make *The Collector.* I enjoyed that, though I loathed Los Angeles and the vulgar tinsel of the film world. I wrote an account of it, very safely unpublishable for libel reasons.

I have a kind of love-hate relationship with the cinema. I admire it at its best, as an art, but I am increasingly hostile to the way it has invaded literature. I hate the way some silly people (often those who think themselves intellectuals) suppose we writers can know no greater glory than to have been filmed; almost as if we would never have written in the first place but for the prospect of being translated into the cinema. A year to two years ago my Chinese translator wrote and asked me if he could ask me a very important literary question, which all his Chinese readers would like answered. I agreed; there then came this very important literary question—what was Meryl Streep really like? I did not, and will not, answer, not because I in the least despised or disliked Meryl in *The French Lieutenant's Woman*—she made a very good effort at a very difficult, for an American, part—but because the Chinese were showing themselves just as foolish as the Americans and the British, totally under the tyranny of the fashionable art form, of the visual. Something in the cinema and television wants to usurp the novel totally. It will fail, I believe; in any case these visual arts will receive no help from me in their encroachment on my own art.

Interviewer: There aren't many heroes in your novels. Well, in *A Maggot* there is Lord B. who certainly qualifies, but he turns out to be a transient incarnation of qualities found only in a better world than ours. On the other hand, every novel provides a heroine. You give women most of the virtues and you imply that our time—contrary to the public myth sustained by scientific achievement—is anything but a "heroic age."

Fowles: I am certainly not a feminist in the militant sense, and I'm sure many such contemporary feminists would disown me. I have great sympathy for the general feminine principle in life. I find very little "heroic" about most men, and think that quality is far more likely to appear among women in ordinary, non-literary life. That ours is in general a heroic age seems to me ridiculous. We are near stifling and exterminating our planet. What scientific and technological advances we have made are flagrantly not paralleled by any moral or ethical ones. By and large men are never moral; they always let themselves be pressured into the amoral or the immoral. In terms of history men have failed; it is time we tried Eve.

Interviewer: You have often said you admire Golding. Is it partly because he is so well-read in scientific literature and so often attacks the myth of "objective science"? Certainly Golding would approve your book on Stonehenge for this very reason.

Fowles: I've long liked Golding's work. Though I have met him, I hardly know him personally. Without agreeing all the way, I have a general sympathy with what I take him to be doing. The piece I wrote for the volume in tribute to him on his 75th birthday ["Golding and Golding" in *William Golding: The Man and His Books* (1986)] tries to say that. I've just reviewed the last of his sea trilogy. It shows marvelous gusto in a man of his age. Thank God someone still knows what the novel is about.

Interviewer: What other contemporaries, or near contemporaries, have impressed you or directly influenced your own writing?

Fowles: None—or rather, too ephemerally for me to feel happy about talking of influence. At the moment I am for instance reading—and enjoying—a proof of Sybille Bedford's new novel, *Jigsaw.* I very much like her general attitude to life, her Europeanism, her slightly watercolorish writing technique, those seemingly haphazard, Dufy-like little dabs of description. She would very well answer my general notion of "a humanist." But I could not quite call this an influence. As I suspect happens with most writers and over most literature, she simply helps constitute a general tenor, or climate, that I like. I think baldly asking for specific names is really a much too clumsy—perhaps a masculine—way of probing a very vague, delicate and obscure process.

Interviewer: You say you feel time is running out. If you must abandon certain possibilities and projects in favor of others, what criteria come into play in making that decision?

Fowles: As we both know, this has been, through my fault, a very prolonged interview. During its midstream, early in 1988, I had a mild stroke—medically, "a transient ischaemic episode." It did not, and still does not, seem the transient episode the doctors would make it, but something much more life-altering. At one moment an eminent neurologist happened to lightly remark to me that of course I would have lost my writing ability. I was used to other people's indifference, but thought this a damned sight too much. He knew who I was, and I found his light insouciance monstrous. I was in complete error. What he had been talking of was *"righting* ability," the power to look to one side yet still to keep one's balance as one walks on—a faculty I had never before even realized I had—and which I have indeed partly lost. On bad days I go down the street like a wino, canoning from side to side.

It seems I was lucky, really. My memory was affected a little, but seems to be returning. I can still enjoy reading, I feel I can still judge books. What escapes me is composing fiction. The two main writing blocks are these. Firstly finding myself starved of alternatives. In the pre-stroke days my mind seemed automatically, and quite unconsciously, to offer ten ways of saying something. Now I am hard put to think of more than one, and that often not one I like. I never before realized I had this totally unconscious verbal dexterity; and that not having it is salutary, is reducing me to the common state of most people: "This is why I've been so lucky, this is why *they* can't write novels."

The other bar to writing is less mysterious. It is something like abulia, loss of will, indecision; but not quite. It seems more like a loss of vanity, a not really caring what I write or have written—even worse, what *anyone* writes or has written. In short, I have lost all conventional faith or belief in books, in "literature," most of that superstructure of self-regard most writers have to erect between themselves and the outside world. Only the old and very successful can throw that superstructure away; and even then, often don't.

This new slowness, the intellectual equivalent of my new physical clumsiness, this doubt of "the worth of the game," have largely kept me from serious writing during this last year. I certainly don't feel barren, bereft of ideas, just of the ability to put them into practice. Nor is it basically a question of help, human or mechanical. The individual mind is just something no other mind or a word-processor can replace.

This stroke has made me feel time is running out; in other words, much more aware of death, my own and that of the one other human being I love most—and whose ghost, in one form or another, has lain close behind all those female heroines we mentioned earlier. I can imagine my own real death, but not that of Elizabeth, my wife. The one thing I try to keep writing, as I have during nearly all my adult life, is my diary. You wonder, at times, what it is all worth, the maundering on about countless things that other people will have forgotten. Yet something drives one on; man—and woman—is profoundly self-reflexive.

Years ago in *The Aristos* I suggested death itself was like a loved wife, a vital and essential part of me. Still today I wouldn't alter any of that part of the book. I stay an atheist, a totally unreligious man, with a deep, deep conviction that there is no after-life. But I wrote it a little as one who writes things in novels: imagining them, not knowing them. Now the rough seas begin, and *Timor mortis,* though I despise it, *conturbat me.*

An Unholy Inquisition

Dianne L. Vipond / 1995

From *Twentieth Century Literature,* 42:1 (Spring 1996), 12–28. Reprinted by permission of *Twentieth Century Literature.*

DV: You call this "An Unholy Inquisition"; don't you like being closely questioned?

JF: About as much as a resistance fighter being interrogated by the Gestapo or an atheist by the Inquisition! But I don't, as some seem to think, just blindly disregard academics. Certainly not so much as that little gibe I put in the dedication to the "Behind *The Magus*" essay ("For CIRCE and all the other tomb-robbers") might suggest. The Circe there is real, the charming Kirki Kephaelea who teaches at Athens University, but by "the other tomb-robbers" I was sniffing like a fox at other academics. Most academics want facts, facts, facts, and of course I know that their pursuit is profoundly useful. It's just that my daily, present world sometimes seems very remote from theirs. Novels are like old love affairs, there is so much, not all bad, that one doesn't want to talk about, so much one can't. A great deal of all novels' beauty and excitement *for the writer* lies in the *now* in which they were or are being written. Like most I am a bit manic depressive, though the poles for me seem to lie much more between a writing self and a non-entity. One self knows profoundly it is neither important nor socially relevant at all; another, far rarer, seems sometimes possessed. I feel identity with the average tribal shaman.

DV: How do you feel about the state of the arts, especially the novel, at the end of the millennium?

JF: I should guess I'm more optimistic than most. I don't like the way pessimism—the black, absurdist view—has so often become fashionable—a supposed proof that the artist really understands the world—during this century. This isn't to dismiss its only too real and manifold cruelties and horrors, just to question whether the black view isn't being exploited because it's so much easier to maintain and defend than its opposite. Optimism, however slight, always relies on an element of the rational, of realism. I don't believe we shall ever achieve valid art through formlessness and unthinking hazard.

We need less of would-be-all-comprehending vision, and more of honest craftsmanship.

Darwin, Freud, and Nietzsche sent this century, almost as much by being misunderstood as the reverse, through a prolonged typhoon, but there seem signs that the planet is trying to right itself from the wreckage. Many of our changes of direction already seem wrong in retrospect, and we now realize better what a dangerous evil-fascinated species we are. I am torn, believing the arts *must* be allowed to evolve. Attempts to stop that are futile. At the moment I'm just reading a very good new poetic novel (Philip Marsden's *The Bronski House,* 1995) about the history of Poland during this century: its endless invasions and catastrophes, the destruction of all stable family life . . . yet somehow something seems to survive amid the horrors and holocausts. In a way it resembles that of the poor old novel, how in spite of the countless "invasions" by visual arts it still makes a nonsense of that silly question I've been hearing most of my adult life: *"Is the novel dead?"* Like Poland, it isn't!

DV: In the past, you have indicated that you have half a dozen or so unfinished novels. If I recall correctly, *Daniel Martin* once fell into such a category. Do you have any plans for revising and publishing any of these? Your readers are anxiously awaiting the next Fowles novel. Do you have any plans for a new novel?

JF: I can't pretend I sit on a hoard of unfinished books and am obsessed with being published. I should loathe the being so bound. There are two "possibilities." I have talked publicly of one, usually a sure way of aborting any project. It is a novel set in a quasi-mythical Balkans. I've been fiddling with that for nearly a decade now and my feelings towards it remain impossibly mobile and fluid. I reconcieve it ever month or so. This is a pleasant experience for a unique and only reader (myself), but a nightmare for anyone else, including publishers. I experience this book (temporarily titled *In Hellugalia*) as I might a living dream. There is another, *Tesserae,* a sort of existentialist mosaic of what it was like in the 1950s to be poor, unfocused and unpublished; but I think Kerouac and his "movement" did all that more brilliantly. I really don't have much normal literary vanity—or perhaps it is that I know my actuality miserably fails what I secretly wish for it. Almost all writers write to be known, to become a distinct flavor. I should prefer to be a sort of folk-remedy. I'm not a Buddhist, but dislike most of the typical egocentricities of artists and intellectuals, the thinking classes, both in Europe and America.

DV: What role do the female characters play in your fiction?

JF: I consider I am a sort of chameleon genderwise. I am a novelist because I am partly a woman, a little lost in mid-air between the genders,
neither one nor t'other. I certainly think that most novelists are a result of not
being clearly typed sexually. I'm just reading Margaret Drabble's excellent
new life of the English novelist Angus Wilson. He was very much such a
typical masculine-feminine writer.

DV: There seems to be a compulsion on the part of the artist to create, in
the case of a writer, the need to write, to tell, to reveal, to question, to record,
to leave a verbal trace. Does this reflect your experience? If so, how?

JF: This trace-leaving used to be an obsession with me. I am these days
much more occupied with savoring the present. I generally admire other writers who have the same mania for recapturing the fleeting now. Poets do this
best of course. The tragedy of my own life is that I am not a great poet. I
deeply envy both T. S. Eliot and Philip Larkin, in England our two technically
finest poets of this century; yet much dislike other aspects of the nature of
both. Two other British poets I more fully admire are Seamus Heaney and
the Scot Norman MacCaig. That last should be much better known than he
is.

DV: As a wordsmith of the first order, what does language mean to you?
Does it reveal? conceal? represent an attempt to impose order upon chaos?

JF: I adore language, and especially English with its incomparable richness. I think of that richness less as a doomed attempt to impose order on
chaos than as an attempt to magnify reality. I have no time for the old socialist belief that you must avoid all rare words and communicate by lowest
common denominators alone. As well say you must use inferior tools.

DV: You have mentioned the influence of Alain-Fournier's *Le Grand
Meaulnes* on *The Magus* and of Claire de Duras's *Ourika* on *The French
Lieutenant's Woman*, two of your major novels. As a student and translator
of French literature and an English writer, what do you see as the most significant differences between the two languages from an artist's perspective?

JF: I've always been glad I studied French at Oxford. It introduced me
(through the Romance languages in general) to the other great culture of
Europe and much of America. I am English, yet would guess myself closer
to the other side of Europe than most other English writers—with some obvious exceptions, of which Julian Barnes is a current example. Again I feel a

bit of a mid-air person about this . . . and happily so. This doesn't mean I speak French well at all; but I *read* it sufficiently. I had my say on this in "A Modern Writer's France" (*Imagining France,* ed. Crossley and Small, Macmillan, 1988).

DV: What aspect of writing do you find the most challenging? In the past, you have mentioned tone of voice and dialogue.

JF: Easily the hardest thing is saying what you *feel,* partly because so few of us really know what we truly feel. That is clearly connected with "tone of voice." I'm no good as a mimic, unlike quite a number of well-known writers. Perhaps that's what makes me feel dialogue, the playwright's skill, so important. I deeply envy people like Harold Pinter for his brilliant minimalist use of both spoken speech and its silences. One of the greatest arts of the novel is omission—leaving it to the reader's imagination to do the work.

DV: You refer to the other arts quite often in your novels, notably painting in *The Collector, The Ebony Tower,* more specifically the work of the Pre-Raphaelites in *The French Lieutenant's Woman,* and the Rembrandt self-portrait in *Daniel Martin.* Music seems to be more prevalent in *The Magus.* How would you characterize your use of the other arts in your novels?

JF: The visual arts, from the cinema to painting, absorb me most; music far less, though I do like some in my life. At the moment it's a new CD I have of Condon's Chicago jazz, another marvelous tape of Turko-Greek music from Istanbul, and a new record of Bach's unaccompanied cello sonatas. Almost all music interests me, but especially (almost exclusively) that performed on a solo instrument—the orchestral and choral somehow calls far less.

DV: You have written about the work of Thomas Hardy and that of D. H. Lawrence. Do you see your work, in any way, as continuing in this particular tradition of the English novel? I'm thinking of Hardy's meliorism and romance and Lawrence's social critique and depiction of male/female relationships.

JF: Hardy interests me privately because he is, so to speak, a dead neighbor, I see his "country" from my study window. I adored Lawrence when I was a student in the 1940s and have recently, although so many nowadays find him politically incorrect, discovered a deep recrudescence of sympathy for his almost metaphysical attitude to the now—the importance of conveying the immediacy and reality of the present. I am worried far less by his sometimes cockamamie views on society and man-woman relations. I feel closer to that obsessive, intensely self-absorbed line, in which I'd also put Golding, than to any other in Britain.

DV: You have written about your father's fascination with philosophy in *The Tree*. Do you attribute any of your own interest in the world of ideas as represented in your fiction and in *The Aristos* to his influence?

JF: Yes, I think so. He had been trained as a lawyer and approached all philosophy like a prosecuting counsel. But above all he made me realize that the suburban view of life was crippling and hideously insufficient.

DV: Your essay "Hardy and the Hag" refers to Gilbert Rose's psychoanalytical theory in which he posits that the love interest in most novels, i.e., the male character's pursuit of an idealized young female, masks the novelists's sense of separation from and loss of the original mother/child bond, perhaps Oedipal in the Freudian sense. You have written about your father in *The Tree,* but I don't recall any reference to your mother. Do you attribute any particular aspect of your own artistic development to your mother's influence?

JF: I found Rose's use of separation-and-loss theory useful, but to say that it has deeply influenced me is not really true. As always I am driven back to a natural history image. A common small fly of trout streams over here, the caddis *(Trichoptera),* builds a case for its chrysalis out of the grit on streambeds. I've been the same over countless theories and views of existence and literature. I have made them a part of me, but never the whole of me.

As for my mother, now several years dead, I have slowly grown into a realization of how much I owe her—I think above all for her maternal normality, in a way sheer conventionality. I have also a guilt that I never fully acknowledged this to her, indeed never had a shadow of Christian patience toward her faults, among which, poor woman, were her logorrhoea and her triviality—believing life consisted of its trivia. She hardly affected me artistically, and as a young Oxford snob I thought most of her views on art beneath notice. But psychologically I now realize, almost every day of my life, that she did make me. I am her. I am happiest that she came of Cornish—or Celtic—stock.

DV: You are obviously someone who is sensitive to words both semantically and phonetically. Is there anything to the observation that more than a few of the titles of your novels have the letters "MA" figuring prominently

in them: *The Magus, Daniel Martin, Mantissa, A Maggot,* as do several words
that seem to be central to your work: maze, mask, magic? a kind of maternal
muse, perhaps?

JF: Writers are often blind to clues like this about their work. It had never
occurred to me before. But yes, I see I am indeed M-dominated. Perhaps in
part through my attachment to feminism.

DV: You have said that you find Jung's theories most congenial to the
purposes of the literary artist, and numerous references to Freud appear in
your work. You have also noted the childlike qualities of the artist. The obser-
vations of mothers, infants, and children by the English pediatrician Donald
Winnicott have been developed into theories about the real or true self, the
"child within" of current psychoanalytical literature. Do you find these
hypotheses of any relevance to your concept of the artistic personality?

JF: Fragments of Freud and Jung have long helped me make my chrysalis-
case, especially the latter. I've always said that if I knew myself deeply disturbed I'd rather go to a Freudian; but that Jung is infinitely more valuable
for an artist. One of the Eranos yearbooks (Pantheon Books, 1955) was important for *The Magus.* I know very little of Winnicott.

DV: How do you decide upon titles for your novels? choose names for
your characters?

JF: I suspect I generally go to the subconscious, again partly to the worlds
of Freud and Jung. I remember discovering that Alison (Alysson) means
"without madness" in Classical Greek long after I had given her that name,
knowing she would be the central character of *The Magus.* It was for me a
kind of proof that whatever had made me originally pick her name was deeply
right.

DV: When you were interviewed by Michael Barber, he suggested that
Daniel Martin seemed to be Nicolas Urfe twenty-five years later; you agreed
that this was precisely what you had intended. Is Henry Breasley another
projection of this character at a later stage in life, all of them comprising
portraits of the artist as young, middle-aged, and older man?

JF: No. Breasley is in no sense meant to seem "related" or autobiographical, but much more a separate character-sketch. Years ago, as a student of
French, I was deeply impressed by the *Caractères* of La Bruyère, his whole
concept of that way of entering the world of ideas *and* commenting on social
custom. I am going to be contradictory. In another sense they are all self-
portraits.

DV: You have revised *The Aristos* and *The Magus,* which is somewhat unusual for a writer to do. They each hold a rather significant place among your work as a whole, the former, a work of nonfiction that clearly outlines your personal worldview, the latter, your "first" novel in the truest sense of the word. Your revision of these books seems to confirm this. Would you agree? Do you subscribe to the theory that a work of literature is never really finished but simply abandoned at one stage or another?

JF: I think the need for sales, for money, makes most writers eschew revised versions. But in all perfect or quasi-ideal worlds we are never truly satisfied with what we have done. It's always wanting another shot at a lottery; like a mania for exquisitely fault-free typography. Most works of literature have always been left at some stage of imperfection.

DV: The word "silence" recurs throughout your fiction. Are you using it in the same way that a musician uses silence as the backdrop to his or her composition? What role do these silences, both implicit and explicit, play in your novels? Are they invitations to the reader to participate in the text, in the heuristic process that is the act of reading?

JF: I'm a deep believer in silence—the "positive" role of the negative. Yes, certainly it can be an obvious way to oblige the reader to help form and to experience the text. Although I feel no ambition to imitate them I have long had sympathy and respect for writers like Beckett and Pinter. I feel very strongly that reading should almost always be a heuristic ("teaching by revealing self") process. I like it that in the Middle Ages literature was in the domain of the clerics or clerks. Of course that religious parallel can lead to mere preaching, didacticism, but I cherish the reminder that we writers have inherited a moral, ethical function.

DV: Most readers would agree that there is an element of eroticism in your work. In *The Uses of Literature,* Italo Calvino writes, "In the explicitly erotic writer we may . . . recognize one who uses the symbols of sex to give voice to something else, and this something else, after a series of definitions that tend to take shape in philosophical and religious terms, may in the last instance be redefined as another and ultimate Eros, fundamental, mythical, and unattainable." Do you think this applies to your work? What about to *Mantissa?*

JF: I confess to your element of eroticism. I did once (very spasmodically) collect eighteenth-century "pornography." Certainly France taught me that the usual Anglo-Saxon and American unbalance over sex (in both their obsession with and their prudishness over it) was ridiculous. I happen to like Calvino's fiction very much, indeed class him with Borges and Saul Bellow, two other writers I much admire, but don't quite know what he meant by the "other and ultimate Eros." I don't for instance have much time for texts like De Sade's *120 Days of Sodom.* I'd rather say I am *implicitly* erotic!

DV: In *The Magus,* you write about the "characteristically twentieth-century retreat from content into form, from meaning into appearance, from ethics into aesthetics." Is this a reference to the tendency toward reification that many postmodernist texts seem to exhibit? What does this statement have to say about your intentions as a writer?

JF: I suppose I hanker after a more Victorian attitude. I really don't like total obsession with form, the "look of the thing." By "content" I suppose I mean seriousness. All writers are rather like prostitutes: they know they have to sell by physical appearance, though underneath they may have far more serious intentions and meanings.

DV: On several occasions, you have quite modestly claimed only partial knowledge of French critical theory. This comes as something of a surprise from someone who studied French literature, reads French, has written a philosophical book himself, is familiar with Barthes and Robbe-Grillet, among others, and writes novels which constantly seem to test the current boundaries of the novel form. To what extent do you see the relationship between theory and the practice of writing as a dynamic, dialectical one? Has theory played any part in the tasks you have set yourself as a writer? or influenced your thinking about the contemporary novel in any way?

JF: As I have repeatedly said, I wouldn't count myself even remotely an academic. I really don't know the post-structualists and deconstructionists at all well. But I suppose my partial knowledges of Barthes, Kristeva, and so on are like bunkers on a golf course—by being there they do slightly direct where you drive. But I'd doubt if anyone plays golf just to think about bunkers. I'm not unaware of them, but don't feel they have much to do with writing. I dislike in any novel a too overt use of theory. I'd say more realism, not more fantasy, sci-fi and all the rest is what is needed in the twenty-first.

DV: During your discussion of *The Tempest* in *Islands,* you raise the question of whether art has the power "to change human nature in any but very superficial ways." Yet in your own work you consistently seem to engage in social critique in one form or another as you chronicle the second half of the twentieth century. You have described yourself as "broadly socialist." What opinions do you hold about the relationship between art and social change? literature and politics? (his)story, i.e., narrative and history?

JF: I have always felt much closer to socialism, even the old Marxism, than to its rightwing and fascistic opposite. I'd say what is wrong with most European socialism, like the Democrats in the U.S., is that it is too static, too trammelled by past—and partly unionist—theory. I'm afraid socialism has never understood the vital importance of art: how important the avant-garde is as a cultural barometer, yet how it must partly cling to tradition. Art may change human nature, but only very generally . . . very slowly also.

DV: Considerable attention has been given to low self-esteem as a cause of individual acts of violence and aggression. What does your concept of the nemo described in *The Aristos* have to say about this?

JF: Man is wedged between being both a social creature and the individual. I think the nemo, the sense that you are nothing or nobody, can drive all of us to violence and unreason.

DV: Novels have been described as elaborate lies, yet most serious writers appear to be trying to get at some sort of ineffable truth through writing. What kind of truth do you strive for?

JF: Every writer knows this dilemma. That for a novelist his trade demands the ability to lie and yet something in him or her is yearning to express a whole truth about the human condition. The one I hope for is the Socratic. Partly skeptical, often cynical, but always looking for an ethical truth. I find that the truth seldom lies too far from socialism and Marxism.

DV: In *Islands,* you have written, "The truth is that the person who always benefits and learns most from the maze, the voyage, the mysterious island, is the writer . . . the artist-artificer himself." Is this psychographic self-exploration distanced by invention and the intervention of fictional characters a form of self-creation? Is it another version of *"Madame Bovary, c'est moi"?*

JF: Yes, I'd agree with that. Above all you are in search of yourself. The trouble is that so often you lose track, through vanity. Vanity is the nightmare haunting every writer's step. Of course, most audiences don't help at all. They take a writer's self-absorption unto themselves. He or she does what they imagine they secretly want to do themselves.

DV: To what extent do you believe that complete self-knowledge is possible? Is this similar to "whole sight" to which you refer in *Daniel Martin?*

The quest for selfhood, the journey of self-discovery itself seems to be as, if not more, important than any of the conclusions that your protagonists tentatively reach at the end of your novels. Is this a gesture in favor of process over product?

JF: Yes, that is what I meant by "whole sight." This thoroughness of vision is more important than any seeming recipe for success in life . . . being a socialist or anything else. We still haven't beaten Socrates's most famous piece of advice: *Know thyself.*

DV: In *Daniel Martin,* Jenny observes that Daniel's real mistress is Loss. You have also repeatedly mentioned the impact of Alain-Fournier's *Le Grand Meaulnes* (another novel which centers around the motif of loss) on your writing of *The Magus*. In *The French Lieutenant's Woman,* Charles's quest lies in his loss of Sarah. You have written in *Islands* and in several other contexts that the "genesis of all art lies in the pursuit of the irrecoverable, what the object-relations analysts now call symbolic repair." Would you comment on this?

JF: I agree with all this. It seems so obvious it needs no commentary. Deep down, I write today because I shall die tomorrow.

DV: You quote from *Ourika,* "Ideas are the only motherland." This seems to get at something which in part may account for the international appeal of your work. You have been described as a novelist of ideas. How important are ideas and what part do they play in your fiction? Could *The Aristos* be regarded as something of an intellectual/philosophical blueprint for the concerns of your fiction?

JF: Ideas, right down to the symbolic aspect of object, that whole vast and peculiar city of being, are all vital to me. Yes, certainly *The Aristos* was an early attempt to explain both this and myself. I would still very largely hold by what I said there—if not always with how it is said!

DV: With the publication of *Daniel Martin,* you described yourself as a humanist, yet existentialism seems to be as present in that novel as in any of your earlier ones. What is the relationship between these two worldviews as you employ them? Are you using humanism in a broad rather than a narrow philosophical sense? What does humanism mean to you?

JF: For me humanism is essentially the holding of a dislike or contempt for violence. It is in one sense a philosophy of compromise. The present world is a disturbed wasps' nest, socially, politically, *and* personally. For me mankind's most obvious fault, not least in its appalling attitude to other species, is its lack of humanism.

DV: How would you describe the free will versus determinism tension in your writing?

JF: I wouldn't, and couldn't! But know it exists.

DV: Are individual freedom and self-conviction antidotes to the abuse of power? To what extent is the responsible use of power a motif in your fiction?

JF: First, I think very much so; secondly, I should hope always, if analyzed. "Power" seems always fascistic, potentially. It always kills true thought and feeling. That is why individual action and at least seeming free will are so important. The irresponsible interests me far more. As every decent journalists knows (most novelists also!) abuse and indecency yield much more (are far more spicy) than use and decency.

DV: Your non-fiction, which is often about a subject other than art, frequently reveals your own aesthetics. Why do you choose these vehicles to discuss artistic concerns in general and sometimes your own art in particular? Are these books masked volumes of literary criticism?

JF: It's just that I venture to suppose that my general views of art, even in the little novel reviewing I do, will be of some general interest. I never approach someone else's book without thinking that this will be a little square of mosaic in my general portrait. This is very vain. I am aware of that.

DV: In the foreword to your book of poems, you suggest that the "crisis" of the modern novel is its self-consciousness. Do you think metafiction is a natural stage in the evolution of the genre as a literary form?

JF: Well, I suspect there was such a crisis until fairly recently. Whether it was a "natural" stage or one leading to eventual extinction . . . who knows? But I strongly feel the novel is *not* dying. And that the greater complexity of technique caused by its added self-consciousness does or can fulfill the ultimate purpose of both explaining and teaching more.

DV: You have been called a protean novelist—always breaking molds, trying something new. Is part of your reason for employing various types of novels as vehicles for your fiction an effort to be true to the original meaning of the word "novel," new? Do you consciously set out to experiment with narrative form or does the narrative itself dictate its structure? How does your experimentation with form represent an expression of artistic freedom, a refusal to be categorized? To what extent does your preference for multiple endings indicate a refusal to conform to the dictates of tragedy or comedy? an incorporation of chance/hazard?

JF: I am a great believer in freedom, but don't like totally irrational freedom, or anarchy. I remember when I studied French that I really didn't get on with what most of my teachers assured me was true greatness, as manifested in Racine and Corneille. I found a far greater depth in Molière. Simply, I just don't like very constricting, mathematical symmetry and forms. Disbelieving set form is how I feel free.

DV: The *doppelgänger* motif is ubiquitous in your fiction. Twins, sisters, parallel characters, and often the dynamics of male-female relationships all seem to point to "the double." Your poem "The Two Selves" also deals with the idea of a dual persona. Could you comment on your use of the double?

JF: I honestly don't know, but I suppose it's a sort of longing for an impossible freedom. I have some sympathy for those suffering from that psychiatric illness, I think they call it multiple personality disorder. I often wish I were someone else, and very much so with some other forms of non-human life. This is another reason that I adore nature.

DV: Both in *Daniel Martin* and in *The Tree,* you make a distinction between "looking for" and "looking at," in both contexts with specific reference to orchids. Looking at seems to be the favored stance. Doesn't one need to look for before one can look at? Something on the order of a kind of marriage of the Western quest (looking for) with the Eastern, Zen-like contemplation or looking at. Is this the psychological work that most of your protagonists are engaged in during their quests for selfhood?

JF: Of course one begins to "look at" very often by first "looking for." "Looking for" I do vaguely attach to science, wanting to increase scientific knowledge. "Looking at," in a full sense of existential awareness of the now, is an art we have more or less lost in the West, far commoner with peasants and, I'd guess, women than with intellectuals of either gender. I do try to suggest a realization of that. I called it a sense of existingness in a recent essay. It is abominably difficult to define, but I think both D. H. Lawrence and Virginia Woolf—and indeed Golding in his last and posthumous novel *The Double Tongue*—at least sensed it.

DV: In *The Tree,* you write, "the key to my fiction . . . lies in my relationship with nature . . . in trees." You refer to the journey into the artist's unconscious that is never fully comprehensible but yields the artistic product and is experienced second-hand by the audience. You liken the choices of the artist to the choices of paths that one could take during a walk in the forest. "Behind every path and every form of expression one does finally choose lie the ghosts of all those that one did not." Is there any connection here with the concept of loss to which you have referred as a necessary condition for artistic creation? How does this relate to the sacred combe, *la bonne vaux?*

JF: The knowledge that you haven't, *can't,* explore every path is part of the sense of loss—all that you've missed seeing. Perhaps what I said to Susana Onega in Spain [*Form and Meaning in the Novels of John Fowles* 179] puts this best:

> I am, I suppose, a wanderer or a rambler. A person who strolls and deviates through life. I always think the notion of the fork in the road is very important when you are creating narrative, because you are continually coming to forks. You don't exactly know where you are going, but you have deep principles or feelings that guide you very loosely. On the actual page you often do not know when a scene is going to end, how it is going to end, or, if you end it in this or that way, how it is going to change the future of the book. This is a state of uncertainty, or in terms of the modern physics, indeterminacy. . . .

DV: In your essay, "The Nature of Nature," you suggest that your inability to write about nature in any profound way is because of your perception of it as sacrosanct; your experience of nature is not translatable into words. Are you intimating that despite your inability to write about nature *per se,* your perception and experience of nature are somehow mysteriously related to your creativity as an artist?

JF: Yes, very much so, others such as Woolf have felt this.

DV: Your attribution of *The Odyssey* (like that of Butler and Graves) to a woman writer, your praise of the *lais* of Marie de France, and of course, your generally strong, grounded female characters all suggest an egalitarian attitude toward gender. You have aligned men with external reality and women with internal imagination. Is there a hint there of an attempt to reconcile the world of ideas with the realm of the imagination? intellect and art? the Jungian anima and animus? the male and female attributes that are inherent in each individual but which society so often misshapes for its own not always honorable ends?

JF: There seems a general tendency to associate "ideas" with the male sex and intuitive imagination with the female. It's always secretly surprised me that so many of the artists we now consider great were *not* feminine. I'm afraid the well-known historical bias toward my own gender can't be balanced by supposing there are countless women who haven't yet been recognized. I don't think that there have. One much more likely explanation may be that so many male artists do have a deep feminine element in both their subconscious and their conscious. Perhaps we assess the artists of the past too clumsily by using mere animal-sexual definitions. I'd love to think that Homer had been a very feminine ancient Greek male. A homosexual?

I have sympathy with Lou Salomé's view after her relationship with Rilke. Male artists, while better than mere men, are at best no more than imperfect women.

DV: Are there any specific models for your female characters? You once mentioned that your wife Elizabeth was inspiration for some of them.

JF: I've often said that I've only written about one woman in my life. I often feel when writing that the heroine of one novel is the same woman as the heroine of another. They may be different enough in outward characteristics but they are for me a family—just one woman, basically. In my own life that woman has been my wife Elizabeth, who died in 1990. I've thought about trying to do an account of her, but so far haven't, knowing she lies so close behind many of my characters.

DV: You have claimed to have a feminine mind. Could you elaborate on this?

JF: I'll quote a previous answer from 1977:

> The women in my books are usually standing for other things. I've used a phrase in *Daniel Martin,* right feeling, which I derived from Jane Austen, that central moral position that hovers behind all her scenes. Women enshrine right feeling better; a comprehensiveness of reaction to the world. It suits me to set that in women characters only because I am a male writer. If I were a woman writer, I think I would simply reverse the situation as many women writers do, as Emily Brontë does in *Wuthering Heights.* Reason and right feeling are not the same thing.

DV: *The French Lieutenant's Woman* has been described as a feminist novel. Do you see yourself as a feminist writer? Is it possible to be a feminist writer if one's female characters are essentially symbols as opposed to fully integrated, individuated characters in their own right?

JF: I hope I am a feminist in most ordinary terms, but I certainly wouldn't call myself one compared with many excellent women writers. Part of me must remain male. I have a very good academic friend, Dr. Jan Relf of Exeter University, and she is constantly pulling me up for the careless way I talk of women. Masculinity is like the old pea-soup fog, a weather condition I remember from youth. It takes you a long time to realize not only where you are but where you ought to be. True humanism must be feminist.

DV: You have said that you rather admire the Victorian novelist Sabine Baring-Gould, though accept that he is now counted as minor, and in 1969 introduced his 1880 novel *Mehalah,* set in the Essex salt-marshes. Your emphasis on individual freedom is particularly applicable to women. Like Baring-Gould's title character, Mehalah, Sarah Woodruff is charactered as a "new woman" of the late Victorian period. One critic [Pamela Cooper] has suggested that your female characters are essentially passive, that they are objects of male desire or inspirational muse figures but not independently creative themselves. Is there any reason that you seem to take them to the brink of artistic creativity but never over the threshold?

JF: This reproach is probably justified. In part it's because woman remains very largely a mystery to me—or perhaps I should be more honest and admit that this mysteriousness has always seemed to me partly erotic. It's certainly not because I resent their artistic skills. If I ever do finish *Hellugalia,* the central character will be female.

DV: Your characters are often preoccupied with making sense of the past. You don't write historical novels *per se* but novels set during earlier periods of history that must be understood in terms of their relationship to the present, which makes them contemporary rather than historical novels. Do you see your role as a novelist in any kind of historical terms?

JF: I don't feel there's much point in any historical novel which doesn't have considerable contemporary relevance. True history is best left to the historians. I do enjoy their work, but as I enjoy traveling abroad. (See the next.)

DV: In "Notes on an Unfinished Novel," you write, "history is horizontal." Could you explain what you mean by this?

JF: I was trying to emphasize the importance of the now. The nowness of any given point in time is pure and virginal. You don't begin to understand ordinary history until you have at least some sense of this staggering perpetual yet evanescent nowness.

DV: In *Islands,* you write, "the major influence on any mature writer is always his own past work." In what ways has your own past work influenced your writing?

JF: Academics always seem to wish to explain everything in a writer by past influences. There are of course very good teaching reasons (keep the little devils quiet) for this but as I grow older I more and more deeply see myself as one being, not the several beloved of deconstructionists. The hazards and incidents of life are far too complex for me to think someone, some writer or idea, can ever have been "a major influence." Chance (what I call in a recent essay the *keraunos*)—the countless other artists and theories that I have bumped into or that have bumped into me—has made me.

DV: What kinds of changes do you see in your writing over time?

JF: There are some, a kind of hardening of fixed views, as I grow older. But I am very, very conscious that I must stay open—that is, remain capable of judging other values, both in literature and normal experience.

DV: How do you feel about your novels being taught in English classes?

JF: A great deal of pity for the poor devils. But more seriously I believe the literary process is fundamentally beneficial, both for its artists and its audiences and especially when it widens their concept of freedom, both personal and social. I like feeling a vast stream of artists is both behind and ahead of me. One can't stand on the bank. One is willy-nilly in the stream; one *is* the stream. And by "one" I mean both writers and readers.

DV: Recently, you seem to have been writing essays rather than fiction. Is there any particular reason for this?

JF: I feel squeamish about the element of lying in all fiction. Just as I wish I could have been an excellent poet, I also perhaps secretly wish I had been, like my father, a sort of philosopher.

DV: Trust the teller or the tale?

JF: Neither. Being human means automatically, given the nature of individuality and the cosmos we inhabit, that we are fallible. Everything is relative. No absolute, except our—both yours and mine—final ignorance. We may pretend we know, but we never do. Least of all how lucky we are to still dwell in the now.

Still . . . still. I exist *still* as I write this, you exist *still* as you read it. Can't you sense a mystery, a precious secret told to you alone, in that word?

A Writer Blocked

David Streitfeld / 1996

From *The Washington Post* (May 6, 1996), D1, D4. Reprinted by permission of David Streitfeld.

Lyme Regis, England

Eight years ago, John Fowles awoke to find his senses blurred and his mind askew: At age 62, he was having a stroke. In the hospital, the examining neurologist asked, "You realize that of course you've lost your writing ability?" Fowles was so upset he nearly got off his sickbed and struck the man. How could the doctor have so casually said such a thing to one of the most famous novelists in England? Many writers claim that if they couldn't write, they'd die. Fowles was being given the equivalent of a death sentence. Or so he thought until the next day, when he realized the doctor had actually said, "you've lost your righting ability." Stroke victims often find their sense of balance has been permanently distorted. They walk unsteadily, as if on a ship during a gale. This is exactly what happened to Fowles. At the time it must have seemed a bearable ailment, highly preferable to losing the capacity to compose fiction. But it turned out that that first, discarded meaning was correct as well. Fowles, once so fertile he could draft a book in a month, has not published a novel since his illness. The stroke, he says on days he's feeling particularly grim, robbed him of his imagination.

For 30 years, it had worked marvelously well. Most novelists find a particular vein and keep mining it, but Fowles began with the ambition of writing one of every kind of book, and to an amazing extent did so. His first novel, *The Collector* (1963), is a sophisticated thriller with political undertones, told in the alternating voices of a kidnapper and his victim. It was an immediate bestseller, as well as hugely influential with other suspense writers. In 1965 came *The Magus*—expansive where *The Collector* was terse, ranging across a continent and several decades instead of confining itself to an isolated house for a few weeks. Somewhat disparagingly labeled by Fowles "a novel of adolescence written by a retarded adolescent," *The Magus* is one of those rare books that become touchstones in some young readers' lives, like *Catcher in the Rye* or *Zen and the Art of Motorcycle Maintenance*. His third novel, *The French Lieutenant's Woman,* spent most of 1970 on the hardcover bestseller list, a feat unimaginable for a literary novel today. Partly a pastiche of the Victorian novel and partly a critique of it, featuring multiple endings and cameo appearances by a brooding, bearded figure who is none other than the author, the novel remains as unconventional now as it was then, and as enjoyable. Five other major works followed, most recently *A Maggot,* a historical mystery published in 1985. Since then, he has sometimes taken notes for a tale set in a country resembling the former Yugoslavia. But he doesn't do this very often. "I'm like an old milk cow that has dried up," he says, then hastily adds that this is how his publishers see him, not how he sees himself. Maybe it isn't the stroke, he speculates; maybe it's simply old age. He's turned away from the hard discipline of putting words in their proper order to practice what he calls "existingness"—letting his mind run unsculpted and free, rather like his immense, wild garden.

Most stories about novelists appear when a new book is being published. Even if he's got one foot in the grave, even if the book is awful, it's treated as a triumphant moment, a new beginning. Perhaps that's why many of them keep publishing as long as they can. It gives the illusion of fending off the inevitable. This story is different. It's about what happens when a novelist can't or won't practice the craft that has made his name and fortune and occupied him for so long. It's about the inevitable. "One of the things I've learned from nature is that things die," Fowles says. "I suppose I've done what I came to do."

Irony, a stance that prevents anything from being taken too seriously, has become so deeply ingrained in our culture that any other approach is considered positively retro. The idea that a novel should have a moral point of view seems woefully overearnest, something that went out about the same time butlers did. Fowles's rare willingness to engage issues like morality and personal freedom, even at the risk of seeming pompous, has set him apart from most of his contemporaries. The late novelist and critic John Gardner once wrote that Fowles "is the only novelist now writing in English whose works are likely to stand as literary classics."

A reputation like this generates its own momentum, even without a new novel to spur things along. This spring there is a bubble of activity surrounding Fowles. He is making a rare series of U. S. public appearances, on the West Coast. The critical journal *Twentieth Century Literature* is publishing a special issue on his work. A fine-arts press has issued two essays in a deluxe volume that retails for a cool $750. Two dozen scholars will assemble in July for an academic conference on Fowles. And a top Hollywood executive will meet with the writer in Los Angeles about plans to remake *The Magus,* considered in its first screen incarnation, in 1968, one of the worst films ever. (Woody Allen once said that if he had to live his life over, he would do it all exactly the same way, except this time he wouldn't see *The Magus.*) Fowles tries not to think too much about any of this, particularly the speaking tour. "I couldn't care less to be yattering on about literature, I don't want to meet people; but I want to see those marvelous flowers, the landscapes."

Several women—a publisher, an academic—were instrumental in persuading him to make this trip. Fowles has always been partial to women and their charms. They've beguiled him all his life, and are a large part of what makes his fiction so rich—as well as so appealing to women. A frequent motif in his novels involves the hero being taken away from the ordinary world by an extraordinary woman who shows him mysteries and forces him to grow up. Nicholas, the callow narrator of *The Magus,* is used to getting women by playing up his orphanhood, his loneliness, but he more than meets his match in Alison: "She didn't fall for the solitary heart; she had a nose for emotional blackmail. She thought it must be nice to be totally alone in the world, to have no family ties. When I was going on one day in the car about not having any close friends—using my favorite metaphor: the cage of glass between me and the rest of the world—she just laughed. 'You like it,' she said. 'You say you're isolated, boyo, but you really think you're different.' She broke my hurt silence by saying, too late, 'You are different.' " Nicholas can't grow without Alison's help. Fowles offers the same tribute to his late wife, Elizabeth, who was the model for a number of his fictional heroines. She was his muse; in a myriad of ways, the writer was devoted to her. "I can imagine my own real death, but not that of Elizabeth," he told an interviewer while recovering from the stroke. Within a year, she was dead, the victim of undiagnosed bone marrow cancer.

The couple met in 1952, on the small Greek island that he would later immortalize in *The Magus.* Even now, when he talks about her, his voice goes slightly dreamy. "All the words you can use to describe her are slightly diminishing. But she had impeccable taste, a flair for what goes and what doesn't go. Most of what I have learned about women, which I realize is only a small part of what women are, came from Elizabeth." When they met, he was teaching English in a Greek boarding school; she was married to another teacher, Roy, with whom she had a 2-year-old daughter, Anna. Roy was a Catholic convert who didn't believe in divorce; he got custody and used Anna to torment his ex-wife. He sent Elizabeth letters, written in a childlike scrawl and supposedly from Anna, saying things like, "Please forgive Daddy, I don't like it when he's unhappy." Anna survived all this to forgive her mother and eventually become extremely close to her, but Roy never relented. When Elizabeth died, he wrote Fowles a gleeful note: "Tough luck, neither of us have got her now." The new couple were unable to have children, a loss felt perhaps more deeply by Elizabeth. "Not having children is painful," the novelist says, "but perhaps it does help the writing. Perhaps you concentrate more. I always remember dear old Conan Doyle. His children were never allowed into his study when he was writing. He was an obsessive, obviously."

While a driven nature is necessary to produce the art, it often makes the artist difficult, if not obnoxious. Fowles once wrote a poem, based on a Greek folk tale, about a mason whose efforts to build a bridge always resulted in a pile of rubble. The mason is told the bridge will endure only if he buries his wife alive in the foundation. He does, and the bridge stands. "I'm afraid all writers, even the greats—T. S. Eliot, Hardy, even Shakespeare—really are selfish pigs deep down," Fowles says. "Luckily, the selfish piggery does allow us to produce the honeyed beauty and great ethical statements. But we're selfish, I'm afraid."

Like every successful artist, Fowles was constantly showered with attention and opportunities. Elizabeth once told her husband that in order to survive, she felt she had to cut off the part of herself that was most female. She had to ignore her husband's falling in love with every pretty woman who came along to interview, consult or maybe just admire him. "There was one American expert on Ezra Pound," the writer recalls. "I'm afraid I really fell for her on sight. But Elizabeth was no fool She knew at once." Understand that he was never so tempted as to act on these infatuations. "I'm not really very keen on men who play about. I regarded it as a discipline one had to keep. I'd think, 'I must not fall or I'll lose this precious gift of being able to create.' " It didn't matter. He was still letting his emotions be engaged elsewhere, however chastely and temporarily. The uneasy situation grew abruptly worse in the late '80s when Elizabeth began to suffer from pains in her back. Bedridden, she wrote poems and letters addressed to her husband, "terrible things, full of hatred. She said there were always people coming to see me— well, they weren't always coming, but she made it seem like there were—and she resented it."

Eventually, she saw a specialist about her back. After the examination, the doctor spoke first to Fowles. "I'm afraid she's only got a week to live," he said. Thinking it was a tasteless joke, Fowles laughed. When he broke the news to Elizabeth, she had the same reaction. It was a final example of the many things they had in common. A couple of days later, they were both waiting for the end when Elizabeth asked her husband to light a cigarette. She wanted the smoke blown across her face, so she could smell those sweet fumes one last time. Fowles was upset by the request—Elizabeth was a heavy smoker, just like him, and the doctors said is contributed to her illness. But when someone is dying, you do what she asks. After her death, he never smoked again. In a way, it was her final gift to him. A more difficult decision involved the fate of her scathing letters and poems. If Fowles preserved them, it meant that one day they would be analyzed by scholars or used in a biography. Elizabeth's anger at those who came to interrupt the marriage would eventually provide these folks with yet another reason to come visit. Fowles recognized the irony, but decided to keep the material anyway. If this was another writerly betrayal, he figured it was a small one.

Poor circulation in his legs and general ill health keep Fowles largely restricted to Lyme. Hospitalized for his stroke, he kept repeating, almost as a mantra, tenthredinifera, tenthredinifera, tenthredinifera. It probably just confirmed the feeling of the hospital staff that he was very ill, but tenthredinifera is a real word, the name of a rare orchid that Fowles had seen years before on the Greek island of Crete. What he meant was, "I'll never be able to travel again, I'll never be able to climb the mountain again where I saw it."

Still, if you're going to be bound to one spot, this village on the English Channel is better than most. "A town that had its heyday in the Middle Ages and has been declining over since," the writer calls it in *The French Lieutenant's Woman*. It's built in a landslide area, which has discouraged new building and kept the population constant at a few thousand. In July and August the sun-mad English briefly quadruple that number, but for most of the year Lyme is low-key and charming, blessed with practically a Mediterranean climate.

Fowles lives in a 200-year-old house that has the stiff façade of a French chateau but is endearingly casual inside. "I read quite a lot," he says. "Really, it's doing nothing, I suppose. It's quite pleasant." He still does the occasional nonfiction article—essays or introductions. At the moment, he has a review to prepare for the *Sunday Times*. All writing is done in his workroom on the second floor. From here, the deep, dull sound of the sea can be faintly heard, although the view is obscured. "You know what every American says when they come to visit? 'If I lived here, I'd cut down all the trees so you could see the sea.' " Fowles shakes his head at the barbaric notion. For him, nature is something that must never be rearranged on a mere whim.

The land behind the house slopes seaward for several acres. The writer has planted things here and takes a keen interest in their progress, but makes no attempt at cultivation or display. Where a typical city dweller, whose knowledge of the origin of plants and vegetables extends no further than the supermarket, would see only a green backdrop, Fowles observes something else entirely: "The parity of nature, the way all species are equal. We think, what a miserable little worm or what a horrible flea, but you get to a point where you realize it's all one. I suppose it's coming near to what Christians call pantheism."

His nonfiction has long circled around this notion, trying to explain what is fundamentally inexplicable, what doesn't even have a proper word to adequately define it in English: the transcendence of being, the elusive state of oneness with nature unencumbered by religion or superstition or mysticism. What strikes him most deeply about this condition is its fleetingness, what he calls in his essay "The Nature of Nature" "a perpetual miracle, so vivid and vital that ordinarily we cannot bear it. . . . There looks to be nothing; then, as with the thunderbolt, all." Illness has brought him a deeper appreciation of this sense of existingness. He can no longer fully trust his mind.

"You know when kids fire a shotgun at corrugated iron or cardboard to see how the shots scatter? Well, I had a brain scan when I had the stroke and it looked the same way, all these little white dots. I shouldn't have seen it, but by some typical hospital blunder I did. The doctor said, 'That's where your brain is giving way.' " He starts to laugh but it turns more into a wheeze, as if he is uncertain whether this is a fit subject for humor.

The house is big—he's full of plans to give it to an educational institution after his death for use as a weekend retreat—but at the moment he's here with only a housekeeper. But women still visit, for reasons as formal as painting his portrait or as casual as just saying hello. You could put it on his tombstone: The Man Who Loved Women. Three years ago, on a trip to North Carolina, he met a young woman and promptly fell in love, "one last little flame of that aspect of life." He's aware that confessions like this are fraught with all sorts of peril. "It's just so absurd, people of 60 falling in love with people of 23. It's expecting too much of God and evolution for it to work." In *The Magus,* Nicholas remarks that "it is not sex that raises its ugly head, but love." These days, Fowles's dicey health has efficiently separated the two. His interest in women may be erotic but it is not physical, which only makes the women like him more. "A friend, a university teacher, says she always felt the aggression of men inherent in almost every contact with them," he says with some satisfaction. "They don't have to be literally, physically aggressive, but she always senses it in the atmosphere. Except here."

It's early afternoon. Fowles is sorry, but he has this *Sunday Times* review that is long overdue, it can't be put off anymore, it must be written this very minute. That's fine—Lyme is a splendid place for a solitary ramble, full of shops offering cream teas and winding lanes and cliffside paths that skirt the sea. It's not terribly different than it was in 1867, the year in which *The French Lieutenant's Woman* takes place.

The novel offers a kind of guided tour of the town; occasionally you can see someone walking around, the book under his arm, doubtless murmuring little exclamations of recognition. It's an illusion reinforced by the movie, which was filmed here in 1980. That effort required some of the buildings to be clothed in period dress; at least one or two have never changed back. So the town helped inspire the book, which begat the movie, which caused the town to resemble even more closely its portrait. Few writers live in a place they have done so much to define.

One path leads along the bottom edge of Fowles's garden, and it is here that his interviewer is strolling when a voice shouts, "Hey! You there!" It's Fowles, out in the garden. But what about the review? Is it written already? "Well, no. I thought I'd just come out for a minute." And when was that? An abashed look. "About 40 minutes ago. I must get back to work, I really must." But he makes no effort to head back to the house. Instead he picks his way through the daffodils, a Judas tree, some spring-flowering myrtle, a scorpion plant—all nature growing in gloriously indiscriminate profusion, the only kingdom he still cares for.

The Endless Lessons of History
Socialist Review / 1997

From *Socialist Review* (May 1997), 16–17. Reprinted by permission of *Socialist Review.*

John Fowles, one of the most acclaimed contemporary novelists, talked to *Socialist Review* about why he remains a socialist.

What influenced you to become a socialist in the first place?

Perhaps the enclosed bit from a recent review in the *Guardian* will give some indication. It may seem absurd but the old Robin Hood "myth" has always deeply influenced me. I really have always totally lacked any sense of normal Christian ethics.

"I myself grew up as poor as a church mouse, ethically speaking. My parents didn't raise me religiously in any except a stock suburban sense; indeed my father was next door to a total atheist. I was saved by this book and its great gust of practical—or socialist—common sense, with its two stark commandments: suspect the rich, protect the poor. That good wind still carries me through life. Robin made perfect sense and so did the quasi-guerrilla exploits of his gang: their hatred of the clergy, of all uniforms and the pompously overdressed (mere appearance), the sharp irony and that marked sense of humour, mirrored in all our more serious literature, made me theirs from the very beginning."

Do you think it is possible to be political as an artist? How does politics influence your art?

It is always difficult, because all humans are split between being unique persons, fierce for themselves, and good members of society. If forced to answer I'd always say that I put artistic considerations above political ones. But I know I do have both a right and a duty to make my politics clear.

What effect has Britain and its imperialist past had on your ideas and your writing?

A considerable one. I deeply loathe the chauvinistic idea of Britain—as opposed to England, my real homeland, along with France and Greece. My whole life has stood against a red, white and blue Britain. I declared myself there in a paper of 1964, "On Being English But Not British."

Do you think that the ideas of Thatcherism and Tory values in general pushed a number of artists to the left?

I loathe Thatcher and the way she totally bent and corrupted this country. I pray the Tories will get the boot in this next election. Certainly. Thatcher has driven many of us very strongly leftwards.

Have you many expectations of a Labour government?

Yes, of course I have them, but expect to be disappointed. There's always something over idealistic in socialism, almost inviting the worst. I must confess I should have much preferred Prescott to Blair . . . the old Labour Party to the new. That Tory propaganda magazine, *The Spectator,* used that common sentiment only this week.

Why does history play such a big part in your writing? Is it easier to write about the present with references to the past?

I don't rate the now very highly and love the endless lessons of history. For me they so often, even when they're very old, speak much more directly to the present.

Have Marxist ideas had much influence on you?

Yes, because I really don't have much time for the silly suburban theory that Marx is dead, defunct. I've just been talking at the Greek Centre in London. They now have on the walls surrounding their lecture room a series of blow ups of their *andarte* (Resistance) heroes, both men and women. You'd be surprised how many were communists; and you feel you cannot betray such faces. I still feel it today, you can't lightly dismiss what drove such nobly suffering eyes. Of course, Marxism has been in part misled and misleading, but where else will you find such a lasting vein of humanism and human decency?

I've mentioned that one dark problem in the Marxist view of life. We are all two things, one social, the other unique. Marx says most of what needs saying to the first. The needs and desires of the second still go begging, and perhaps always will.

Why do you remain a socialist today?

Perhaps because I have much travelled and know France and Greece, in their different ways the two prime existentialist countries—along with ours—of Europe. This is why I cannot imagine not being a sort of socialist. I also know the enigma of America well: that "experiment" that seems always on the brink of failing. That truly hasn't "worked." They should try the cure they fear.

Fowles on a Fair Day

Melissa Denes / 1998

From *The Sunday Telegraph Magazine* (November 22, 1998), 29–32. Copyright © 1998 by The Telegraph Group Limited, London. Reprinted by permission of The Telegraph Group Limited.

John Fowles is a grand old man of letters, and a bit of a curmudgeon. He loves Lyme Regis—though he's furious that the success of *The French Lieutenant's Woman* has attracted hordes of tourists—and has bequeathed Belmont, his house there, to future generations of writers. Melissa Denes visits him

In the Sixties and Seventies John Fowles was regarded by some as our greatest contemporary novelist, attracting comparison with Tolstoy and Henry James. *"The French Lieutenant Woman,"* says Malcolm Bradbury, a friend and admirer of Fowles, "was *the* first postmodern novel. It came at the end of the Sixties, at a time when literature was very down. We'd had Kingsley Amis and the Angries, we'd had Fifties realism, and then nothing much. The extraordinary skill with which John reconstructed the Victorian novel and then set it up in dialogue with the 20th century has had a very powerful influence. I don't think A. S. Byatt's *Possession,* for instance, would have been possible without it." These days Fowles's novels are rather unfashionable: his ambitions are too grand, his themes too romantic—and he hasn't published a novel for 13 years, though he's working on one now.

It was *The French Lieutenant's Woman,* published in 1969, that made Fowles famous, and turned his adopted home of Lyme Regis, which is where the novel is set, into a tourist destination. Where once there had been peace and quiet—a couple of pubs, a chip-shop and the harbor—suddenly there were walking tours and souvenir stands, car-parks and caravan sites. Fowles admits the town's fame is largely his own fault. But it still drives him mad as year in, year out, waves of pilgrims descend on the Dorset town to gawp at the Cobb, the sea wall where Sarah Woodruff (played in the film by Meryl Streep) waited for her lover's return.

Fowles, who has no love for "grockles" (local dialect for "visitors"), recently expressed a desire to take a machinegun to all jet-skiers. After he wrote an intemperate article about the grockles for *The Daily Telegraph,* a reader wrote back to say Mr. Fowles must be "a rather irascible and unlovable person." He has come to be seen as Britain's grouchiest man of letters, a greybeard in his cliff-top eyrie, a Propsero in his cave, railing against the excesses of the times, the overcrowding of the cities, the pollution of the sea, the stupidity of the masses, the uselessness of governments past, present and future—and meanwhile turning away any poor sod who comes to his door clutching a battered copy of *The Magus.* "I do hate these letters from people who say, 'Dear John Fowles, I know you're a man who likes a pint or two, why don't we meet for a chat?' As if I'd want to go to the pub and drink beer with a complete stranger!"

"But you're here now," I say, "drinking beer with me." "Oh, but that's different," he says, patting me on the knee. "You're a pretty woman. I probably shouldn't say this—in this wretched country it's always misconstrued—but all my life I've liked young women, not nastily. To me, they have a quality of life, of living, which no other age or sex has. It's partly to do with my own sexuality, of course, but I can't stand not having them near me. All my friends joke about it."

Fowles has agreed to be interviewed because he wants to talk about his house, Belmont, a huge Regency villa with views over the Cobb which he plans to bequeath to future generations of writers. Or rather his new wife, Sarah, whom he married two months ago, has agreed on his behalf: Fowles, who is now 72, has not been well. A week ago he was in hospital, recovering from an adverse reaction to a drug. "It should be all right," his wife said on the telephone, hesitating," but he is, how shall I put it . . . ? Frail."

I was greeted at Belmont by Sarah, a slight, attractive woman in her early fifties, who stood outside the front door with her arms folded, looking slightly fierce. It's a romantic house, painted a pale apricot and with a fairy-tale turret rising to one side, its façade covered with slightly grubby stone masks by Eleanor Coade (the 18th-century entrepreneur and inventor who once lived here). Sarah leads me through a large sitting-room full of cushions and books and footstools—every other room turns out to be full of cushions and books and footstools—and into the sunny kitchen, where Janice the housekeeper is icing a cake. (Janice looks after Fowles three days a week, when Sarah is in London, where she works in advertising.)

"John!" Sarah shouts up the stairs. There are some answering crashes and bumps and then John Fowles comes slowly into the room, leaning on a walking stick, his hand outstretched and his face, if not exactly wreathed in smiles (it's hard to tell under all that beard), then certainly friendly. "Hello, Miss

Bee," he says (Melissa is Greek for "bee"), squeezing my hand and easing himself into the nearest chair, patting the one beside him. He is a solid-looking man with ruddy cheeks and watery blue-green eyes, dressed in a denim shirt tucked into navy tracksuit bottoms, a red-and-white spotted hand-kerchief tied round his neck—a typically Gallic touch. Fowles read French at Oxford in the Forties, and his literary approach, broadly speaking, has been to tackle traditional 19th-century narrative from a modern and somewhat theoretical French perspective. "Of course," he says. "I'm half-French my-self . . ." This is a surprise. Is his mother French? "No, no. I can't even say I speak it that well." Ah well. But he does read and write it. He has said before that he feels tri-national, with roots in England, Greece and France, but today he seems to be feeling rather strongly English, with just a hint of France. "I do believe that a writer who writes about England should live here. I didn't agree with all that leaving the country that went on in the Twenties and Thirties." It might be noted, at this point, that he did his fair share of leaving the country in the Fifties and Sixties.

He speaks quite slowly, in a low grumble punctuated by long pauses while he searches for the right word, and there is a slight slur from the stroke he had in 1989. At one stage he forgets his wife's name, referring to her, very affectionately, as "the lady downstairs," but otherwise he seems well. Mar-riage obviously agrees with him. Fowles's first wife, Elizabeth, died sud-denly, of cancer, in 1990 and for some time afterwards he was a bit of a recluse. Sarah, whom he has known since she was 21—she used to go walk-ing with Elizabeth—seems in many ways his opposite (expensively dressed, media-savvy, a Londoner), but these are differences he enjoys. Sarah is sharp where he is vague, quick where he is slow. For the first half of the interview she sits with us at the kitchen table, reading the local paper and throwing in the names and words he forgets. "I went recently to Greece," he says, "to make a programme . . . but I can't remember the names of those islands. North of Egypt. That's the terrible thing . . . Oh dear, you know, sometimes I forget where I am . . ."

'Oh, *John,* you do not!' she says, gathering up the paper and the coffee cups and going off to fetch him his fleece jacket to wear while he has his picture taken in the garden. Fowles brightens at her every interruption: she seems to ward off self-pity and confusion and to remind him that, actually, the past wasn't so long ago.

Fowles is delighted that his plans to turn Belmont into a writers' retreat have finally got off the ground. For years people had expressed interest in taking the house on but, on the one hand, there was too much money to be raised (it will have to be converted and endowed); and, on the other, there was the problem that John Fowles is still very much alive and in residence. "Either I had to die," says Fowles, "or I had to come up with £15 million." There have been a lot of false leads and dashed hopes along the way. The writer Catherine Cookson was "very interested," but she died this summer ("poor thing"), before anything was decided.

Fowles is still not sure where the money will come from—the Lottery, perhaps—but he has decided that Belmont will be left to a committee of academics from the University of East Anglia (chosen for its creative-writing course), his *alma mater* New College, Oxford, Chapman College (a small institution in California) and the British Council, as well as local authorities in Dorset. Fowles had hoped the house might become a college, but he has been told it is too small; it will probably be used as a centre for courses, conferences and visiting overseas writers. "I have a rather Victorian idea of it," he says. 'I'd like it to be a sort of reading centre." He is sceptical that a writer might hole up in the attic for a few months and dash off a short but brilliant novella ("With thanks to JF and Belmont")—"I don't believe masterpieces just flow like that"—but he does hope that the house will inspire young writers, who are "not well looked after."

John Robert Fowles was born in 1926 at Leigh-on-Sea in Essex (a landscape he has never grown to love), the only child of Gladys (*née* Richards) and Robert, a cigar importer. He went to Bedford School, where he was an able pupil, played cricket and became head boy. After school he did two years of National Service with the Royal Marines and then went to Oxford. Yet he says he identifies with Catherine Cookson, who was illegitimate and left school at 13 to go into domestic service, which is puzzling. The explanation seems to be that where Cookson wrote from her sense of being an outsider, Fowles is driven by his frustration at being an insider. In an autobiographical essay of 1975, he describes Leigh-on-Sea as "rows of respectable little houses inhabited by respectable little people [which] had an early depressive effect on me." Of being head boy he writes, "At the age of 18, I had dominion over 600 boys . . . Ever since I have had a violent hatred of leaders, organisers, bosses." There he was, groomed for the Establishment, and all he longed for was freedom. Cookson's predicament was her illegitimacy, Fowles's the threat of conformity.

After Oxford, Fowles taught English, first at the University of Poitiers and then in Greece. He met his first wife at a boys' school on the island of Spétsai.

She was married at the time, to a fellow teacher, but subsequently divorced. Elizabeth and Fowles were married in London in 1954, before moving to Europe, where Fowles taught in schools across France and Greece. In 1960, they returned to London.

Fowles had begun writing in Spétsai. The island and his relationship with Elizabeth inspired *The Magus*—a complex, mystical and erotically intriguing novel. But it was not until 1963, aged 37, that he published his first novel, *The Collector*—the story of a clerk and butterfly collector who kidnaps a young art student and tries to make her fall in love with him. It was an instant success. Two years later he published *The Aristos,* a "self-portrait in ideas," which mystified and disappointed many of his fans. This was followed by his two smash hits, *The Magus* (1966) and *The French Lieutenant's Woman* (1969). In the Seventies, there was a book of short stories, *The Ebony Tower* (1974), and the semi-autobiographical *Daniel Martin* (1977), which is generally thought to be his best work; in the Eighties there was *Mantissa* (1982)— the title means " a comparatively unimportant addition to a discourse"—and *A Maggot* (1985), a somewhat overblown 18th-century murder mystery about a prostitute raped by the Devil.

Fowles moved to Lyme Regis—from London, which he hates—more than 30 years ago. He says he was drawn to it for a number of reasons: the "beautiful view," the fact that the town was intensely left-wing (as he is), and the locals' reputation for being contrary. There is a Dorset word for this, he explains—"aginness," meaning they are in a state of constant opposition, which sounds exhausting but which he admires. Most of all, though, he loves Lyme, the richest palaeontological site in Britain, for its "tremendous sense of history." People find it hard enough to imagine 100 years, but here you get a sense of 20 million. I used to dig up potatoes in my garden and I'd find little oblong objects and they would turn out to be dinosaur vertebrae."

Since he moved here, Fowles has become an enthusiastic amateur geologist and palaeontologist (the house is full of his stones and bones), as well as a local historian. Apart from the five novels he has written in Lyme, he has published a book of local walks, a history of shipwrecks (1974) and an attack on formal gardening entitled *The Tree* (1979). He was also curator at the town's museum, the Philpot Museum, for several years, until he grew bored of people wanting him to trace them back to the first mayor of Lyme Regis (he would tell them their esteemed ancestor was a humble ostler).

Does he never find all this history overwhelming? "Oh *no*. I know a lot of people would, but I find it terribly exciting. I do think geologically it's a dangerous place and people should be scared of that. Last week, three boys were killed at Charmouth, caught by the tide. It's unpredictable." In 1968, Fowles and his first wife were forced to move from their first house, a farmhouse along the cliff, when they returned from a weekend away to find that a field had fallen into the sea.

Enthralled by the destructive power of nature, Fowles is keen on that of humanity, and has become a noisy and determined environmentalist, writing countless articles and letters, railing against "man the merciless wrecker." He has found much to occupy him in his old age—he reads, writes, campaigns, gardens and collects orchids. It is hard to believe he really thinks the world is the bleak and empty place he says it is. "Have you ever seen a dormouse?" he asks, suddenly looking terribly serious. "I bet you haven't. We used to have a colony of them here in the garden and you could pick them up in your hands and they were the sweetest little things you ever saw. Now they're gone and they'll never come back. If you are a naturalist, you just *cannot* be optimistic. Thing are *very* bad and I feel sorry for you and I feel sorry for anyone born into this world."

He has never had children (Anna, his first wife's daughter, remained with her father)—a source of some sadness. "But it's not bad enough to commit suicide. I am totally against that." Why? "I am an atheist but I'm also a humanist. And I suppose I have some determination to help." He says his "great guru in life" is Edward Wilson, a lecturer in evolution at Harvard who specialises in South American ants. "He is the only man alive who realises what a mess we're in." One wonders whether Fowles—like many artists— cultivates a sense of conflict. When he met his first wife she was married with a child, and while it would be facile to say that this encouraged him, he has since said that, as a writer, he found the difficulty of the relationship instructive: "The snatched feverishness of moments behind the scenes and the subsequent horror of divorce were good training ground for a novelist— doubts on her side, doubts on your side, the pain, the anger."

Fowles writes in a big room at the top of his house, with the best view over the sea. There is a large balcony, overgrown with vines, where he feeds the birds. On his desk there is a typewriter, an almost completed essay on Nabakov, a copy of *Ulysses* and a diary opened at a page marked "Blood Test *(am);* Archaeology Awards *(pm)."* Long black grooves in the wood attest to a time when Fowles let cigarettes burn down while he typed—"Filthy habit. Given it up." There is also a newspaper cutting about the trial of Charles Ng for multiple murders in America. Ng says he was inspired by *The*

Collector. Does this worry Fowles? He laughs and says wearily, "Well, I'm sick of being sued over *The Collector.* Sometimes these people get their dates wrong and say it was my fault, and they'd started before *The Collector* was published!"

A year after his wife's death, Fowles was approached by an Oxford undergraduate, Elena Lieshout, who wrote to suggest that they meet and discuss his work. Unusually, he agreed, and Lieshout, a 22-year-old American, ended up staying for nearly four years as Fowles's assistant-cum-housekeeper. At the time Fowles denied there was anything sexual about the relationship— Lieshout lived in a flat by the harbor—but when it ended, he told a journalist, "There's no one more stupid than a 60- or 70-year-old falling for a 20-year-old. She was a very pretty girl and I fell a bundle for her."

In the short time I am with him, Fowles is generous on his praise for all sorts of women. He says how much he admires both his wives, his new agent in America (Mrs. Thomas Pynchon), a classical Indian dancer called Sarabi, a 19th-century geologist called Mary Anning and his friend Jo, who works at the Philpot Museum. He has said that his first wife was the inspiration for all his female characters; and once said that his chief regret about *The Magus* was that he didn't make the main character, Conchis, a woman, as he had originally intended. In his novels, it is invariably the female characters who turn out to be stronger and wiser; men tend to get bogged down in their own egotism.

The telephone rings abruptly. Fowles looks unsure whether to answer it, then swoops on the receiver. There is a worried twitter down the line. "Mhm, mhm. I'm busy now," he says, rolling his eyes. More concerned twittering. "Yes, I've got your number. No, I won't forget." He puts the phone down with a great rattle, points a finger to his temple and makes a "pow" noise. "Old friends." He has recently begun work on a new novel but he says, rather slyly, that he can't tell me what it's about. "As a novelist you constantly have to fight clear of having your throat cut. And literature is a funny thing, like an eel: it slips about."

Before lunch, Fowles takes me on a tour of the house, pointing things out with his walking stick. His writingroom houses a great library (half of it fiction, half natural history), a huge collection of New Hall pottery and a jumbled array of fossils, bones, animal skulls, bits of dinosaur and Syrian statuary. He keeps his favorite things—"the things which amuse me"—in a wooden anteroom off the main bedroom, which he calls "the chapel." There is a large white exercise bike, a canary in a bell-jar, a Toby-jug, a family of wooden ducks, panels from a stained-glass window and , marching all around the window sashes, a herd of plastic dinosaurs Fowles has collected from cereal packets. On the floor he points to some bowls and pots "made by my ex-son-in-law." Son-in-law? "Well, a boy who used to sleep with my first wife's daughter anyway."

Before we go downstairs, he points out a recent purchase, an oil painting which depicts a dog in widow's weeds sitting in the mouth of her kennel, two puppies looking mournfully up at her. Another dog, their father, hangs lifelessly from a tree in the background. Fowles leans closer to take another look at the dead dog and chuckles. "Wonderful." It's a perfect Fowlesian moment—a modern take on a bit of old popular kitsch, rather like the premise of *The French Lieutenant's Woman.*

Before I go I ask Fowles if he will sign my copy of that novel. He hesitates, and for a moment I wonder if I have done something to offend him, and he is finally going to lose his temper. But no. "My dear," he says, a tremulous Prospero, taking the pen I hand him, holding the book and looking rather sweetly up at me, "you must tell me, what is your name?"

A Dialogue with John Fowles

Dianne L. Vipond / 1999

DV: It seems to me that the publication of *Wormholes* (1998) demonstrates that you are a serious essayist who has been writing essays over the course of your career. What is the particular appeal of this form to you?

JF: I wouldn't consider *Wormholes* very typical of my work. You must realize all writers are permanently worried about money, yet want readers to know what they think about life. I'd hardly call myself a professional essayist. Like all writing, it's the being who you are . . . what you feel. In my case I simply don't know who I really am. It would be misleading to suggest that I do. Writers have to stay mobile, undecided, so perhaps this is not altogether a bad thing.

DV: I understand that you are planning a new collection of poems. Would you say a few words about how you write poetry, for example, how some images come to have primacy over others and finally make their way onto the page in lieu of others?

JF: I wish I knew how to write and organize poems. I don't think the solution is to take the conventional poetic approach to life; I am quite sure all poems should be in some way fresh. You are inventing something new about the way you see life. That doesn't mean a good poem should necessarily shock, but something about it should surprise. I was recently reading some previously untranslated poems by the great Russian Akhmatova *(In Conjunctions: 31 Radical Shadows),* and they did that, distressed, as good poetry in any language must. They were also written under duress, which helps. Perhaps I may name some poets I have always liked: William Blake, William Shakespeare, Joachim Du Bellay, François Villon, the Greek Seferis, and Cavafy; countless others, both ancient and modern. Reading the poetry one likes should always be a pleasure, and I try to make it so. Normally I don't read what bores me; for my own work, I just hope.

DV: How do you feel about your novels being portrayed on the big screen? Do you have any film projects in progress at the moment?

JF: Like most of my generation I have always admired good films; but, alas, that is not so with optimism concerning my own work. The art of the cinema is extremely complex, and I don't like the films constructed from my work. In spite of all this, I am currently trying to get a version of a certain French novel filmed. That is *Ourika* (published in the U. S. by the Modern Language Association), which is basically about the eternal dilemma of blacks in a time of revolution. I have always felt *Ourika* is a great novel, though largely unknown; so we shall discover! A clever young West Coast academic is helping me bring it about. Her name is Lisa Colletta, from Los Angeles.

DV: Eileen Warburton is currently writing your authorized biography. You have kept a diary over the years, and it is in the process of being transcribed. Will this eventually be published as something on the order of an autobiography?

JF: Well, I have always kept a diary since I was at Oxford. It varies from day to day. I hope it may one day appear. It will be meant to give a portrait of this last century (I was born in 1926). In one way a diary is like a series of poems, and I think it should partly startle and surprise. I also feel that, as with poetry, biographies shouldn't be truly judged or considered while the writer is still alive. Silence is the great dark virtue of all would-be poets. It is very difficult and quite the hardest technique, or trick, a poet must learn. . . . Silence, the death of what you wrote, is the darkest mystery of them all. I don't know how Eileen Warburton will manage to catch the particular writer in me. Most of her previous experience concerned that slightly unreal town, Newport in Rhode Island, with its absurd "chateaux" and equally absurd millionaires and racing yachts . . . well portrayed in a book by Thornton Wilder, *Theophilus North.*

DV: You revisited the site that inspired *The Magus* after an absence of almost thirty years. Certainly, the circumstances were different from your first experience there, but did you find that the old magic of Spetsai still cast its spell over you?

JF: Yes, it did. Thanks to the Botasis family, who now own the villa I wrote about in the book, it was certainly "different." I do deeply love Greece, both modern and old. It is indeed a magical country, in which, if you're lucky, you discover both yourself, and what life is about.

DV: I understand that you have participated in the Cambridge Seminar held in July during the past few years. What is the Seminar, and what role have you played in it?

JF: The Cambridge Seminar is organized by the British Council and the U. E. A., the University of East Anglia, at Norwich. Most well-known English writers have been there, and so have many Americans. I only last summer heard of one, called Chris Godshalk from Boston, and took great pleasure in introducing her to it. It's also a kind of "test" for all would-be younger writers and is held in the old College of one of the most important critics of English Literature, Leavis, who died in 1978. Most modern writers have great respect for his opinions and attitudes to writing.

DV: You've done quite a lot of lecturing in Europe and America during the last few years. What do you see as the differences between the audiences of the two continents as far as their respective responses to writers and literature are concerned?

JF: No comment. All readers read differently.

DV: What interests you most as a reader of fiction? of non-fiction? As a writer, do you think you read differently or for things other than the lay reader does?

JF: Definitely, narrative, the ability to tell stories. I think this is why American books have had such appeal for us creepy old Europeans over the years. Almost everything about humanity interests me.

DV: During your public lectures, you have mentioned Stephen Jay Gould's work on the Burgess Shield and Edward O. Wilson's most recent book. *Consilience,* in very positive terms. It is well known that you are an omnivorous reader. Is it possible to sum up how your reading of works of science, in particular, have influenced your own writing?

JF: I admire both Gould and Edward Wilson, whom I've often declared the most worthwhile living human being. Gould is also very clever, of course. I should hate to sum up my own reading, as it varies so much. Within reason, everything affects me, not just the scientific side of matters.

DV: As I was rereading Alan Watts's *The Spirit of Zen,* I was struck by the similarity of one of your remarks when you were addressing audiences in North America earlier this year with this quotation from Suzuki. A Zen master declaims to his disciples: "Inwardly or outwardly, if you encounter any obstacles kill them right away. If you encounter the Buddha, kill him; if you encounter the Patriarch, kill him; . . . kill them all without hesitation, for this is the only way to deliverance. Do not get yourselves entangled with any object, but stand above, pass on, and be free!" You advised aspiring writers:

"Kill your parents; kill your professors; kill your lovers. . . . Be free." Would
you elaborate on the impact that Zen has had on your work and thought?

JF: I have always liked at least some of the general principles lying behind
Zen Buddhism. In some ways it may seem harsh and impractical, but I feel
all Western society is both overprolix and rich. We need Zen and its severity.
It should tell us a great deal about how we ought to live. I love most English
gardens, but Zen Buddhist ones also.

DV: James R. Aubrey has edited a volume of critical essays, *John Fowles
and Nature,* that treats the place of nature in your writing, a topic which
surprisingly has been neglected in the critical literature about your work until
now. You are passionate about preserving the environment, take a special
interest in plants and birds, and seem to spend some of your happiest moments in your enchanting garden in Lyme. How would you describe the connection between your reverence for nature and your writing?

JF: One thing we certainly ought to do is to respect nature and the environment, and be far more concerned about them than we are. In general it seems
a sadly common case of the money "drive" or motive conquering all the
better ones. I would say my sympathy for nature is very great, perhaps especially at this time of human history when we show ourselves such blind fools.

DV: One aspect of your work which has not received as much attention as
it deserves is your use of humor. It's present throughout your work but seems
particularly concentrated in *Mantissa,* a novel that is much denser and richer
than is obvious at first reading. The humor in your work is subtle, often
poised somewhere between irony and satire with socio-political barbs only
thinly camouflaged. What role does humor play for you in the creation of
fiction?

JF: It is a very vital aspect of the novel. At the moment I am re-reading
Thackeray's *Vanity Fair,* I feel partly written against Dickens. It endlessly
makes fun of the people and society of his own time. Humor is also very
difficult, good humorists have to be as sharply observant as good natural
historians.

DV: After the stroke you suffered some ten years ago, you shared your
concern with James R. Baker, who interviewed you for *The Paris Review,*
about being able to continue to write novels. Although you have mentioned
two works in progress, *Tesserae* and *In Hellugalia,* they have yet to be published. In light of the sustained effort and the resulting mental exhaustion

that so often accompany the composition of a novel, have you considered writing more short stories or novellas as a possible alternative? You certainly proved yourself a master of the genre in *The Ebony Tower,* which is definitely more complex intertextually than the typical volume of short stories.

JF: They still wait. As any writer would tell you, time is never long enough.

DV: As an artist, a writer, do you find that the lines between life and art tend to blur, or are they quite distinct for you? To what extent do you believe that life imitates art?

JF: This kind of distinction seems to me profoundly irrelevant. Life certainly doesn't imitate art in many things. My answer must seem rude, but their boundaries do not seem to me blurred at all.

DV: You taught English before you were able to devote yourself exclusively to writing and have often remarked on the inherent didactic quality of fiction. What are your thoughts on the teaching of literature?

JF: This is an academic question. It is for you (or your nearest professor) to answer!

DV: In *The Aristos* (1964), you wrote: "The noblest relationship is marriage, that is, love. . . . love is a giving without return. . . . that identifies . . . the true nature of the true marriage." You were married to your first wife, Elizabeth, for thirty-five years and have just recently married again. Is there anything you would like to add on the subjects of love and marriage from this vantage point in your life?

JF: I don't know, in view of my recent new marriage, that I would seriously define the relationship as "the noblest." I think I would simply call it the nicest and the most instructive. It teaches, and all the good things in life teach.

DV: As an addendum to your responses to questions put to you by a doctoral student at the Sorbonne, you challenged her to ask you to confess about the "harem." Although I'm not asking you to do this, I would like to know why you believe the world would be a better place if women rather than men were in more positions of power.

JF: I am very much a feminist and if I am to answer seriously, then yes. I think the world would be a happier place if women had more power and consideration. I have just read a marvelous introduction by the great French historian, Jules Michelet, to a book called *La Sorcière* (the witch). He very much defines what I believe myself about the importance of women, even though he was writing in 1862. My other peculiarity (it was Michelet's also) is that I find women attractive, and I think their good looks and kind of intelligence is infinitely valuable to our societies. In a word, we need them and what they contribute to humanity. Effectively, we men are still in the Stone Age.

Part of me is amused by the absurd Victorian mania for the Turkish "pasha" and his supposed harems. I most emphatically do not believe that the world would be happier if there were more *bayadères* and bimbos. Such a desire is effectively transporting man back to his medieval self.

DV: In "The Nature of Nature" you discuss three concepts which seem to be central to your general world view: necessity, hazard, and freedom. In addition, you focus on the importance of "the now." How are these four concepts related?

JF: A sense of the now is certainly vital for all poets. Necessity is the need (or duty) to see; hazard is the good luck to find something worth seeing. And freedom is that mysterious capacity in man to always require it yet never to really find it.

DV: An interview might be characterized as some sort of hybrid between the literary and the journalistic. What do you think is its value in coming to terms with a writer's work?

JF: My reply to your first question covers this—writers want readers to know what they think about life; I want to be both known and heard. All writers are egotists, and eternally vain.

DV: Some people believe that the explosive development of technology of all kinds poses a threat to the imagination. What's your opinion?

JF: I doubt if this would ever be possible or conceivable, outside the weirdest science fiction. I cannot believe the imagination is ever in danger. Man neither could nor would ever give it up.

DV: It has been said that one of the marks of genius is thinking in innovative ways, perceiving connections and relationships between objects and ideas that have not been recognized before. Jan Relf, the editor of *Wormholes,* once described you as "tangential and Coleridgean." If I could ask you to adopt a metacognitive stance, how would you describe your own thinking process?

JF: At the moment I am also reading Richard Holmes's excellent biography of Coleridge in which I recognize a great deal of myself. I don't think I could improve on "tangential," the constant bouncing off into other directions. Trying to describe either his or one's own thought process is the very devil.

DV: What are your plans for the future of your home in Lyme Regis, Belmont House?

JF: I hope to turn it into a college for literary students and am thinking of joining a somewhat similar organization over here (in Britain) founded by that excellent poet, Ted Hughes. I'd like tyro writers to experience this place and garden and its mysteries and charms. Hopefully this would be in the aegis of U.E.A., Exeter and my own old college, New College in Oxford.

DV: Throughout your career as a writer, you have continued to set yourself challenges in terms of literary technique. Are there any that you are working on now?

JF: I feel I'm a little too old to set myself "challenges." I got rather angry with a recent American audience in San Francisco who wanted to know what I was going to write next. They had no idea of how vague and confused the "ambitions" of most writers are, especially at my age. Even the very word "challenge" confuses the issue. Nevertheless, I would like to write one last novel about the complex nature of this century. At the moment I am calling it *Tesserae* . . . the countless bits that make up a mosaic. I don't want to say more, I'm afraid.

Index